The Freshwater Aquarium

THE FRESHWATER AQUARIUM

A practical handbook

Hans Frey

Translated by Gwynne Vevers, D. Phil., FLS

Orbis Publishing · London

Watercolours and animal drawings by Hans Frey
Plant drawings by Ernst Halwass
Colour photos by Hans-Joachim Richter

© Neumann Verlag Leipzig · Radebeul
25th edition 1983

English translation © Orbis Publishing Limited, London, 1984

Printed by Karl-Marx-Werk, Pössneck, German Democratic Republic

ISBN 0-85613-620-4

Contents

Foreword

The Chinese and Japanese began keeping and breeding a limited number of different fish species about two thousand years ago. They did this in open ponds, so that the stock, mainly goldfish and a few related species, could only be seen from above, through the surface of the water.

Modern aquarists work in a different way. They keep their fishes in tanks with a front glass pane, so that they can be viewed from the side with light coming from above. This approach to fish keeping started in about the middle of the nineteenth century and the first such aquarium in the world was opened in 1853 in the Zoological Gardens, Regent's Park, London. During the next thirty years aquaria appeared in many other places, often in association with marine biological laboratories, as at Plymouth, Naples and on the eastern seaboard of the United States.

The maintenance of aquaria, whether public or private, has seen great advances, particularly during the last fifty years. There has been happy and fortunate cooperation between professional biologists and devoted amateur aquarists. Scientific methods have been developed to control the temperature, aeration and constitution of the water. As a result I believe that the maintenance and breeding of aquarium fishes is infinitely more advanced and more successful than the keeping of mammals, birds and reptiles in captivity.

This book, written by the distinguished German aquarist Hans Frey, gives a comprehensive account of the art and science of keeping freshwater aquarium fishes. It includes a very valuable section on decorative aquatic plants for the aquarium and an extensive selection of colour illustrations.

Gwynne Vevers

A Colourful World under Glass

The attraction of aquaria

A visit to a public aquarium introduces us to an amazing, colourful and almost dreamlike world, one which moves constantly behind the clear glass of the huge tanks, the glowing, sometimes iridescent colours of the fish catching the light as they make their slow and majestic movements. Here you are in an underwater world; the other visitors, irrelevant, are perceived only dimly as shadow-like figures in the darkened hall.

Those who know little about fish will be surprised by the incredible variety of their shapes and sizes: although the majority may be the torpedo-like shape one normally associates with fish, others are long and eel-like; some are flattened, almost as though compressed from above; and a few are even disc-shaped. The colouring, too, is almost unimaginably varied—from dull brown to rainbow hues—and so are the habits of each individual species. Some, like the cichlids, swim around actively herding and protecting their young, some swim in shoals, but others are quite solitary, often appearing momentarily and then retreating to a favourite hiding place.

On a first visit it is almost impossible to comprehend the multiplicity of forms and colours presented by the underwater world, but such a visit will often fire the imagination and awaken an interest in the idea of aquarium keeping. There are many other ways of becoming interested in fish, too: there are often television programmes about fish in the wild; there are books on fish and their habits; and on a more mundane level, schools often have aquarium tanks in their biology rooms, though usually quite small ones. Last but not least, some people's enthusiasm is aroused simply because they see a tank in the living room of a friend, or in a doctor's or dentist's waiting room. The beauty and feeling of tranquillity imparted by aquarium tanks, even small ones with a few inhabitants, often makes people think wistfully of having such a display on view all the time, in their own homes.

Putting the new interest to the test

Aquaria are indeed beautiful, and even a small tank can provide much recreation and enjoyment, but aquarium keeping, like any hobby, takes care and patience, and some knowledge, if disappointment is to be avoided. First impressions are always full of promise, but often a talk with a fellow aquarist will reveal that first impressions were deceptive, and that the problems of keeping an aquarium were found to outweigh the pleasures. For instance, after a time things do not always seem quite as they should be: the water does not remain clear; the plants, which at first grew well, turn yellow and die; the fish are no longer as active as they were. This can be extremely distressing, and marks the point at which the depth of interest in the new hobby is put to the test. Some people will give up, but others will ask themselves whether everything has been done correctly, and what they can do to remedy matters. This is often the moment to compare notes with a fellow enthusiast, who may have encountered, and perhaps overcome, similar problems, but it is usually a mistake to take really drastic action, such as emptying and cleaning out the tank every two weeks and then setting it up anew each time. A well-established tank should not need the addition of fresh water every day, and if the plants are covered in algae and the fish are listless, then the cause probably lies elsewhere.

The purpose of this book is to help the aquarist to start along the right road. Although it is impossible for one book to cover all the complex processes at work in the living world in their entirety, it should help to avoid disappointment, and explain what steps to take when things go wrong. However, never neglect the advice of experienced aquarists; they, too, may have valuable hints to offer, based on their own experiences.

The rewards of aquarium keeping

In many of the more ambitious tasks we set ourselves there comes a point when the difficulties appear almost insurmountable. But when these difficulties are overcome, the reward is vast, because suddenly we are able to see the complete picture instead of just its component parts, and to comprehend much more than previously seemed possible.

This is the case with a successful aquarium. Perhaps we might originally have thought that it would provide a decorative display to please the eye. And so it does, but there is much more to it than that. We will learn from it, and continue to do so as each new step is taken, until we have built up a total picture of the world in which the fish live, their aqueous environment, the plants and rocks they need around them, and the foods they eat.

For instance, it is unlikely that the new aquarium keeper will have given much thought to the vital role played by algae in natural living processes, but anyone who has an aquarium for long will begin to find this not only important but interesting in itself. A magnifying glass or a small microscope will reveal much that is new and interesting.

The novice will probably not have considered the part played by plants in the life-cycle, the chemical processes taking place in a plant cell, or the ability of plants to convert inorganic 'biological equilibrium', or even the vital part played by carbon, oxygen and nitrogen in all living processes.

Most of us, unless we happen to be biologists, know very little about such things, but this kind of knowledge, which might seem dull and irrelevant if learned from books, will be learned from observation in the aquarium, and the knowledge is necessary if we are to understand fully the forces at work in the aquarium tank.

That is by no means all that will be learned. There will probably come a time when the fish produce a brood of tiny fry, so small they can hardly be distinguished by the naked eye, yet equipped with everything they need for living. The fry must be fed, and they will require infusorians and other micro-organisms, with which the aquarist will be totally unfamiliar. These, too, make a fascinating study with their astonishing variety of shapes and sizes.

The fish themselves have much to teach us.

A tank may contain some fish which are equipped with long, filamentous ventral fins, and which from time to time rise to the surface of the water, where they take in air from the atmosphere. Someone new to aquarium keeping may wonder why the ordinary gill respiration is not sufficient, but with a little experience he will realize that such peculiarities have evolved in response to factors in the environment.

If tank conditions are suitable for breeding, the viewer may wonder at the vigorous courtship display in some species, followed by nest-building that precedes spawning.

He might also be curious about the behaviour of some cichlids, which tend and protect their fry in a very purposeful way. After the fry have grown sufficiently to move away, they might even tend and herd a small shoal of water-fleas put into the tank for food. Obviously this is instinct at work, but what is the nature of instinct?

Question follows question, all equally fascinating, and all demanding an answer. The aquarist will seldom be bored.

From time to time it becomes necessary to renew the supply of live food for the fish, which may involve a trip to the country. If so, the aquarist will find yet another new field for study as he searches the freshwater ponds and ditches for water-fleas and other live food. These, too, he can take home and examine under a glass before feeding them to the fish. He may observe other strange phenomena, for instance the silken diving bell which a water spider constructs as a nest, or a species of water-beetle with double eyes, or the ability of the dragonfly to fly both forwards and backwards. He might learn, also, about the larvae of diving beetles which have sharp, hollow jaws for injecting a substance into their prey which liquifies the body contents.

There is much to learn, and much to wonder about, and the keeper of a tropical aquarium, sitting in front of his tank, will undoubtedly wonder most of all about those distant lands which were the original homes of his fish.

Fishes— a world survey

The fishes of temperate waters

It is well known that people in general are more interested in far-away lands than in their own, which may be one reason why enthusiasm for keeping exotic ornamental fish far surpasses that for keeping endemic species. But this is only one of the reasons: apart from the obvious attractiveness of tropical fish, with their bright colours and endless variety of shapes, they are a geat deal easier to keep, and the majority can be bred successfully in the aquarium.

Laymen often believe that endemic cold-water fish will be easier to maintain than tropical species because their habitats and environments are more familiar to us, and quite often this belief leads people to take fish from the nearest pond or stream and keep them until they die, which is usually quite soon. But, in fact, most endemic species are only safe in the hands of reasonably experienced aquarists, and the best way to acquire the necessary experience is to start by keeping the less demanding exotic ornamental fish. It is true that there are a few cold-water fish, such as stickleback and bitterling, which have no special requirements, but most of the endemic cold-water fish are much more difficult to keep.

Also, of course, the number of different species from tropical waters far outweighs those which inhabit rivers and lakes in the temperate zone, so there is a much larger selection of tropical fish that are suitable for the home aquarium. As they are usually obtained from dealers or fellow aquarists, they are easier to maintain; this is because many of them have been kept in aquarium tanks for several generations and have thus become completely acclimatized to the conditions offered by the home aquarist. Finally, with modern technical equipment and aids, it is much easier to keep an aquarium tank warm throughout the year than it is to prevent a cold-water tank from becoming too warm in the summer months.

However, it would be a mistake to think of tropical and cold-water fish as entirely separate from one another, and to ignore the endemic species altogether. Certain living conditions are the same in all parts of the world, and thus the biology and behaviour of endemic species in the wild have some relevance to the ornamental species from tropical waters. Conversely, much of what the aquarist observes in his tanks of exotic ornamental fish will be valid for those species caught in temperate waters.

The streams which flow down from the mountain districts of Europe are often called the trout region, after their principal inhabitants. Trout and their relatives can always be seen in the large display tanks of a public aquarium, and the experienced aquarist can certainly try to keep trout, provided he has large enough tanks, as they like clean, cold, flowing waters that are rich in oxygen. It has been found that the rainbow trout of North America is more suitable for captivity than the brown trout of European waters because it does not require so much oxygen and can therefore tolerate higher temperatures. This, of course, is why such large numbers of rainbow trout are kept in commercial trout farms in many parts of Europe, including Britain.

Another interesting fish found in trout streams—also for the experienced aquarist—is the little Miller's thumb *(Cottus gobio)*, a bottom-living species which in appearance and habits is somewhat similar to the tropical gobies.

The minnow *(Phoxinus phoxinus)* is usually not too difficult to keep, provided it has come from lowland waters rather than cool mountain streams. It has already been bred in captivity. Minnows make an attractive aquarium exhibit and show their finest coloration when kept in a tank with rather subdued lighting. (It has now been established that injured or dead minnows release a substance into the water which acts as a warning to other members of the species.)

There are several endemic bottom-living fish which are widely distributed in both mountain streams and lowland waters. These are mostly members of the carp family and its relatives, and include the gudgeon *(Gobio gobio)* and representatives of the loach family, the stone loach *(Noemacheilus barbatulus)*, the spined loach *(Cobitis taenia)* and the pond loach or weatherfish *(Misgurnus fossilis)* which lives in muddy waters. Gudgeons usually move about in large shoals, while the loaches tend to live separately. The endemic loaches are typical bottom-living fish, with the mouth surrounded by a number of sensory barbels which serve to detect food. In addition to the gills they possess a form of accessory respiration, taking in air at the surface and passing it along the alimentary tract to an area rich in blood vessels where the oxygen is extracted. The residual gas is passed out at the anus. This enables the loaches, and particularly the pond loach, to survive in waters that are poor in oxygen. This species is also sensitive to changes in atmospheric pressure and becomes increasingly restless at the approach of bad weather, hence the alternative name of weatherfish.

The carp family has some members which are well suited to captivity in an aquarium tank, though others are not. This family is made up of a large group of related fish, most of which inhabit lakes and ponds with reedy vegetation. The majority of endemic freshwater fish actually belong to the carp family. Most of them live in shoals of varying sizes which move along the bottom searching for food, sometimes rising to the surface to jump for a mosquito. Unfortunately from the aquarist's point of view, many members of the carp family grow quite large, and are unlikely to reach sexual maturity in the home aquarium, while some species languish and die within the restricted confines of a tank. A few small specimens, however, can be kept quite satisfactorily. Among those which will breed in the aquarium are the bitterling, which lays its eggs within the body of a freshwater mussel, the minnow, which has already been mentioned, and the Moderlieschen *(Leucaspius delineatus)*, usually known by its German popular name as it does not occur naturally in Britain.

There are several other members of the carp family which will live when young in the home aquarium. Space does not permit giving details of all of them here, but the well-known species are the common carp *(Cyprinus carpio)*, the crucian carp *(Carassius carassius)* and the tench *(Tinca tinca)* of which there is an attractive golden form. Some aquarists keep rudd *(Scardinius erythrophthalmus)*, but this is a more delicate fish which is best kept in a public aquarium with an efficient system of water circulation. The same applies to the native barbel *(Barbus barbus)*.

The cold-water fish most commonly kept are the two species of stickleback *(Gasterosteus aculeatus* and *Pungitius pungitius)*. Every budding naturalist must have kept one or both of these at some time. They are interesting, as not only do they practise a characteristic form of brood protection, but they also build a more remarkable nest than any other fish in the world.

There are several other endemic species which can be kept in the aquarium for varying periods of time. These include the common eel *(Anguilla anguilla)*, the pike *(Esox lucius)*, the perch *(Perca fluviatilis)* and the North American catfish *(Ictalurus nebulosus)*. Other European cold-water fish that are easy to keep when young and undemanding include the bleak *(Alburnus alburnus)*, orfe or ide *(Leuciscus idus)*, dace *(Leuciscus leuciscus)*, bitterling *(Rhodeus amarus sericeus)* and roach *(Rutilus rutilus)*. Naturally, these can only be kept as small specimens, and they should be returned to their natural waters when they grow too large for the restricted space of the aquarium.

Tropical fishes

Tropical aquarium fish come from many different parts of the world. These include the large land mass of Asia from the Bosporus to China and from northern India to the islands of the Indian Ocean; and further east, Australia with its relatively restricted fresh waters; Africa, increasingly important to the tropical fish trade; the giant River Amazon and its tributaries; and finally Central America, Mexico and Florida.

Wherever the fish come from, the aquarist should always try to find out all he can about the living conditions of the fish in the wild because they are so varied. For instance, the tropical waters of southern Asia present many different conditions, from the sunshine of India to the damp, humid conditions in the islands of the East Indies and Indonesia. There are dark, muddy ponds and ditches, paddy-fields with their interconnecting drainage channels, often in low-lying areas, but there are also mountain streams with clear, fast-flowing water, and shady rivers in jungle country. These are just a few of the habitats which support the rich fish population of tropical Asia.

Two main fish groups are particularly well represented in the fresh waters of Asia. These are the barbs and loaches (Cyprinodontoidea) and the labyrinth fish (Anabantoidea). The tropical barbs are closely related to many cold-water fish in Europe and North America: these include the minnow, roach, carp and chub.

The group of labyrinth fish contains a large number of brightly coloured fish, most of which are easy to breed and thus well suited to the aquarium. It is believed that the first tropical fish imported into Europe was one of these labyrinth fish, now known as the paradise fish. It caused quite a stir when brought to France from China in the 1870s, and was soon bred in Paris by a Frenchman named Carbonnier.

Labyrinth fish come from some of the

warmest parts of the world: China, India, Sri Lanka, Burma, Thailand, Malaya and Sumatra. In their home range these adaptable fish live mainly in shallow, sun-drenched waters of all kinds, such as ponds and pools, ditches and paddy-fields. Such water is very poor in oxygen and is often extremely cloudy but the labyrinth fish have evolved the means to survive in these unfavourable conditions. They have an accessory respiratory organ, known as the labyrinth (hence their name), situated in front of the gill chamber. From time to time the fish rise to the surface in order to take in atmospheric air, which passes to the labyrinth and is taken into the blood system. In this way the oxygen deficiency in the water is made up, and the fish are able to survive in waters which would be lethal to other vertebrates. Some labyrinth fish have also developed very elongated, filamentous ventral fins, which serve to sense food in the water.

However, by no means all labyrinth fish come from such unfavourable waters; some species even live in the clear streams of the mountain ranges, and they are found in enormously varied waters. One of the group, the true climbing fish (Anabas testudineus), can even leave the waters when they start to dry up and move overland to reach other waters.

Another labyrinth fish, the small fighting fish (Betta splendens), which comes from Thailand, is much valued by the local inhabitants for its bright colours and its fighting ability, and by selective breeding the Thais have increased its natural coloration. The males of the species, which swim around like aquatic butterflies, displaying their exaggerated fins, are put together in couples to fight, and vicious contests take place. Old Thai families are proud of their breeding stock, and conceal the secrets of their breeding methods.

Fighting fish have been introduced into aquarium circles in Europe and elsewhere, at first in the original wild form, and subsequently as the beautifully coloured selected forms known as veiltails. New varieties, even more spectacular, are being developed all the time.

Brightly coloured species are also found in the genera Trichogaster and Colisa with their much elongated, filamentous ventral fins. Among the most colourful are the dwarf gourami (Colisa lalia) and the honey gourami (C. chuna). Others include the wonderful pearl gourami (Trichogaster leeri) and the croaking gourami (Trichopsis pumilus), whose popular name refers to its habit of emitting croaking sounds when excited. In addition to the paradise fish (Macropodus opercularis) the genus Macropodus also has a few other beautiful species, such as the brown spike-tailed paradise fish (M. cupanus dayi).

Two other fish families were formerly believed to be closely related to the labyrinth fish, particularly as they also possess an accessory respiratory organ, although it is somewhat different in form. These are the pikehead family (Luciocephalidae), with only a single species, and the snake-head family (Ophicephalidae), with numerous species. The snake-heads are nocturnal predatory fish, which grow quite large. Their name comes from their snake-like heads, which are completely covered with scales.

Fish in the carp group (Cyprinoidea) are quite different. Some of them live in flowing waters, clear rivers and streams, often in areas of mountain and upland where the climate is rather similar to that in the temperate zone. Others inhabit pools, ponds and ditches, sometimes in areas of jungle. They all like to live in shoals, are active, sociable, colourful and quite undemanding. There are numerous species, many of which are ideal aquarium fish, and there are several special favourites among amateur aquarists, such as the zebra danio striped in blue and gold (Brachydanio rerio), the harlequin fish (Rasbora heteromorpha) with its attractive tints of pink and blue, or the appropriately named rosy barb (Barbus conchonius). In spite of efforts over several decades, some members of the attractive Rasbora species have not yet been bred successfully in the aquarium because their native water conditions cannot be imitated. They live in waters with a muddy bottom of rotting

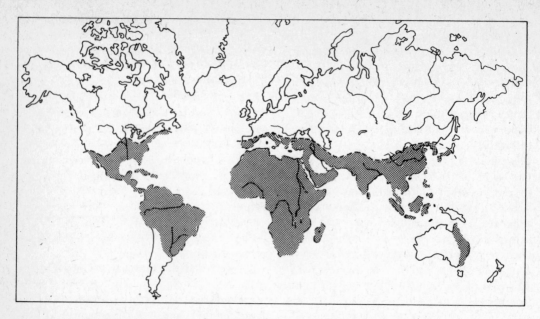

— — — —Northern limit of tropical and subtropical
        ornamental fishes

plant fragments, which are chiefly fed by tropical rain storms, so the water is very soft with
a high content of humic acids. Finally, there is
the remarkable flying barb *(Esomus),* in which
the pectoral fins are modified to form wing-
like appendages. With the help of these the
fish can glide for quite a distance over the surface of the water.

Other Asiatic fish include the stately
loaches *Botia* and *Acanthophthalmus* from
south-east Asia and Indonesia, the very attractive badis *(Badis badis),* the half-beak
(Dermogenys pusillus), which produces live
young, and a few brilliantly decorated species
of the genus *Aplocheilus,* as well as a few very
unusual transparent little fish, among which is
the glass catfish *(Kryptopterus bicirrhis).*

There are several unusual fish from South-
East Asia, such as the mudskipper *(Periophthalmus)* which lives in mangrove swamps and
other parts of the tropical shoreline. These
spend much of their time out of the water,
basking on the mud; their pectoral fins are
modified to form bony struts which serve to
lift the front part of the body when they are lying on land. To some extent these strange fish

are reminiscent of ancestral vertebrates which
millions of years ago took the first steps from
water to land.

In brackish waters where the sea mixes with
fresh water, the handsome argusfish *(Scatophagus argus)* can be seen gliding in and out
among the roots of the mangrove trees, and in
the same habitat, the archerfish *(Toxotes jacu-
latrix)* lies in wait for its prey, ready to shoot
drops of water, with lightning speed, to bring
down insects on the plants growing on the
banks. Another oddity are the pufferfish,
which inflate themselves with water and air so
that they look like little balloons. Further
upstream are southern Asia's only cichlids, a
group which is far more widely distributed in
Africa and South America. Finally, there are a
few species of the family Cyprinodontidae,
the egg-laying toothcarps, such as the medaka,
a small fish, only about 5 cm (2 in) long, with
beautiful bright eyes, which shine through the
dark waters.

Our next group of fish comes from Africa,
whose vast area provides a large number of
suitable aquarium fish. They come from all
over the continent, from the Nile valley, the

great East African lakes, the Chad region and a few coastal stretches in East Africa, and the coastal and forest areas of tropical West Africa from Senegal to Niger and Congo.

Among the wealth of fish from Africa are the well-known cichlids (Cichlidae). These are rather boisterous fish, many of which like to burrow actively in the bottom, but they are not too difficult to keep provided they are given the correct living conditions, which means that, as far as possible, the aquarist should try to reproduce an African underwater landscape in miniature. The tank should have a substrate of well-washed gravel and a few firmly embedded rocks, particularly in the background. Small caves can be constructed using suitable rocks and these, together with a tangle of tree roots, will help to create a satisfactory three-dimensional setting. The absence of plants from such a tank is more than compensated for by the colours of the fish themselves.

Some of the more remarkable African cichlids belong to the genus *Pelvicachromis*. They differ from the species in the other genera in that they do very little burrowing and they do not attack the plants. They also differ from the other cichlids in their body form, being more slender and fairly dark in coloration. During recent years some of these cichlids have been imported from the Congo region and from the great lakes of East Africa, and these have become increasingly popular among aquarists.

The African fish include a large number of mouthbrooders, fish which incubate the eggs in the mouth of one of the parents, which also provides safe shelter for the newly hatched fry. It is remarkable that the incubating fish are able to fast, for weeks at a time, while tending and caring for their offspring.

Large numbers of mouthbrooding cichlids are found in the Rift Valley lakes of East Africa, including the relatively shallow Lake Victoria, a body of water with a fringe of reeds. Here there are very large numbers of species belonging to the genus *Haplochromis*. There are also a few species of this genus in other parts of the continent.

To the aquarist, one of the best known of these cichlids is the Egyptian mouthbrooder *(Pseudocrenilabrus multicolor)*, formerly known as *Haplochromis multicolor*. This fairly small species, up to 8 cm (3 in) long, comes from East Africa, particularly the Nile region.

To the south of Lake Victoria there are the two narrow, elongated and very deep lakes, those of Malawi and Tanganyika. These lakes contain a large number of fish species, the majority being small to medium-sized. The native fishermen around Lake Malawi call them *mbuna,* and this term is sometimes also heard in aquarium circles. Most of these fish are very colourful, and interesting biologically because of their ability to change colour.

Many of these cichlids have very unusual feeding habits. Some have a specialized dentition to enable them to rasp algae from the underwater rocks along the shores of the lake; others search for small invertebrates living in the lake bottom; while some are active predators. Among the strangest of the 'food specialists' are those species which feed, as a supplement, on the scales or even the eyes of other fish.

The small cichlids of Lake Malawi are mostly mouthbrooders. The males have round eye spots on the anal fin, but the females frequently have a quite different coloration from the males. The small cichlids of Lake Tanganyika, by contrast, mostly breed in caves, laying their eggs in clefts and crevices of the rocky cliffs. The young also live there and grow up without much parental care.

The African members of the egg-laying toothcarp family (Cyprinodontidae) are numerous and varied in form, and because of their small size they are particularly suitable for keeping in an aquarium. Most of them have very beautiful colours and patterns and exhibit some interesting characteristics. The climatic conditions in their home waters have led to the evolution of a remarkable method of reproduction. They live in ponds, the backwaters of rivers and flooded areas during the rainy season when there is plenty of water about. Later on the water dries up, leaving only a crust of mud, until the next rainy season renews the water. During this relatively short period, only a few months, the fish are able to hatch, reach maturity and die. The adults all die when the waters dry up, but they leave behind their eggs, embedded in the mud.

It was some time before the full details of reproduction among these so-called seasonal fish were understood, and until that time they could not be bred in the aquarium. Even now, the breeding of species of the genera *Aphyosemion, Roloffia* and *Nothobranchius* is strictly a job for the experienced aquarist.

Not all the egg-laying toothcarps are suitable for the aquarium. Some are intolerant and aggressive, while others do not thrive or show to advantage in the mixed background of a community tank.

As we have seen, the labyrinth fish of the group Anabantoidea are very widespread in Asia, and they are also represented by a few species in the African continent. In their general appearance they are more or less similar to the climbing labyrinth fish of south-east Asia, but unlike these they do not leave the water and wander about on land. For this reason they have, in some aquarium circles, acquired the more appropriate popular name of bush fish. These African bush fish all belong to the genus *Ctenopoma,* and in their habits they rather resemble the nandids (family Nandidae) that are found in India, Africa and South America. The African representative of the Nandidae is *Polycentropsis abbreviata,* a peaceful, predatory leaf-fish which lives a rather hidden life. Unfortunately, it is only rarely seen in the aquarium.

A zoogeographical comparison of the fish of south-east Asia, Africa and South America reveals certain relationships which confirm that the present-day continents were at one time joined. Thus, the characins and related fish, so widely and abundantly represented in South America, are also found in tropical Africa. These include the brilliantly iridescent species of the genera *Alestes* and others, showing all colours of the rainbow. The related Congo tetra *Phenacogrammus interruptus* is characterized by the lobe-like prolongations in the fins of the male. Members of the genera *Neolebias* and *Nannaethiops* are attractive fish, somewhat similar in general appearance to the barbs. There are also some predatory characins in Africa, such as the pike characin *(Phago loricatus),* a relatively small species, up to 15 cm (6 in) in length, which lurks among plants and tree roots, lying in wait for passing prey.

At one time relatively few fish reached the aquarium from the fresh waters of Africa, but in recent years the capture of ornamental fish is on the increase, and it is quite likely that even more beautiful specimens from this continent will reach the aquarist's fish tanks.

The American continent, even more than Africa, has proved an almost inexhaustible source of new fish species. For most aquarists, at least those in Europe, it must be very difficult to imagine the extent of the gigantic River Amazon and the enormous amount of water it pours into the sea. Even its individual tributaries are larger than most of the rivers of Europe. The Amazon region covers areas of high mountain, plateau, lowland, bush country and tropical rain-forest. The greatest wealth of fish life is found in the waters that flow through the rain-forests.

At one time endless difficulties were encountered in finding and bringing out these treasures, and the early fish collectors had to undertake week-long journeys on river steamers, followed by hazardous motor-boat or canoe trips through the rapids, lashed by tropical downpours, endangered by disease, threatened by crocodiles, piranhas, anacondas and columns of all-consuming ants, to name but a few hazards of Amazon travel. Nowadays there are fewer difficulties to overcome, as air travel and modern equipment have made such an operation a great deal easier, but the modern aquarist should be grateful for the courage and determination of these early collectors.

The vast majority of the fish from this part of the world belong to the characin family or certain closely related ones (Characoidea), a very attractive group. Only an expert can recognize the relationships of one individual species to another, because there is such a wealth of different sizes and shapes. Some are large, others quite tiny, some slender, others disc-shaped. There are fast swimmers and those which swim almost in slow motion, and there are even a few which can take off from the surface and glide through the air with the pectoral fins beating. These characins are all very popular among aquarists, for they are active, usually undemanding, and most are very colourful. The best-known species belong to the genera *Hyphessobrycon* and *Hemigrammus,* a large group of small and very desirable fish.

Most people have at some time heard travellers' tales about piranhas. At one time these fish were regarded as one of the real dangers of the tropical rain-forests of South America. According to the tales neither man nor beast was spared; and anyone who was unlucky enough to land in a shoal of these terrifying fish was torn to pieces in a few minutes by their razor-sharp teeth. Although recent information has shown that such reports were exaggerated, the fact remains that piranhas are certainly dangerous and should be treated with special care in the aquarium.

Some of the characin species have presented aquarists with some difficult problems, particularly the characins of the upper Amazon, such as the neon tetra *(Paracheirodon innesi)* and others, which for many years were only bred on rare occasions. Nowadays it is known that the waters in the tropical rain-forests of South America are somewhat abnormal in their composition, and so the fish, particularly those from the so-called tropical black waters, have special requirements as regards water composition. Such fish only thrive and breed in water that is slightly acid and therefore with a low content of bacteria and infusorians.

South America, like Africa, also has a large number of cichlids (family Cichlidae). These live in shallow bays fringed by reeds, in the backwaters of rivers, in lagoons and lakes, either singly or in groups of several individu-

als. In shallow places cichlids can be seen swimming in among the shoals of their offspring or searching for food on the bottom. The cichlids range from dwarf forms to large fish and they comprise one of the main groups of aquarium fish. They vary in size, shape and characteristics, but they are all interesting, not least on account of their fascinating system of brood protection.

One of the most popular cichlids among aquarists in all parts of the world is the angelfish *(Pterophyllum scalare)* which has a stately way of swimming and a very unusual body form. In recent years a number of selected forms of the angelfish have been developed by aquarists, and these are now sold by aquarium fish dealers. Apart from the larger species which present certain problems because of their size, the dwarf cichlids are increasingly popular. Besides being small they are also peaceful and do not attack the aquarium plants.

In addition to the characins and cichlids, tropical South America also has a number of interesting catfish. These either have leathery skins, or the body and fins are protected with numerous spines. The body is sometimes an unusual shape and the general habits are often unusual. In general, these catfish live in waters with a muddy bottom, but they are also found in the open waters of rivers and lakes, and even in streams with strong currents. Stream-living catfish often have a sucking mouth which enables them to withstand the current by fastening on to a firm object, at the same time browsing on algae, usually from the rocks. Some catfish are predators, others feed on organic waste or an algae. Among aquarists the armoured catfish of the genus *Corydoras* are particularly popular, and several new species have been introduced in recent years. Armoured catfish are mostly kept to liven up the tank bottom and to remove the food remains that accumulate in a community tank. Young specimens are especially amusing to watch, and aquarists can derive much pleasure from them.

The egg-laying toothcarp family (Cyprinodontidae) is also represented throughout the American continent, as well as being represented in India and Africa. Among these forms the members of the genus *Rivulus* are especially remarkable, for they live a partly amphibious life, being able to move about on land almost as well as they do in the water. Mention should also be made of the members of the genera *Cynolebias* and *Pterolebias* which, like the African seasonal fish, live in waters which periodically dry up.

The livebearing toothcarps (family Poeciliidae) are found over a large area extending from South America north of the Amazon, through Central America and Mexico to the southern United States. These fish, as the popular name suggests, produce live young. There are some very beautiful forms in this family, for example, fish with much enlarged, sail-like dorsal fins or elongated, sword-like caudal fin rays. Some species are very tiny, but a few are of medium size. Some are very prolific, and thus occur in enormous numbers in their home waters. Some of these live-bearers have been introduced into other countries to combat malaria by consuming the mosquito larvae. Thus, species of *Gambusia* can be found in Spain, the southern Soviet Union, Italy and other countries where the conditions are favourable and where they have become naturalized. Certain species, such as the guppy and swordtail, have provided the basic material for the production of numerous selected forms. Because they are so prolific, these fish have been of service in scientific investigations, as the rapid succession of generations has enabled observations to be made on variation and mutation.

This survey of tropical freshwater aquarium fish can be brought to a suitable close with a mention of the sunfish (family Centrarchidae) of North America. These are rewarding, easily bred fish, which can be kept successfully in unheated aquarium tanks and, in some areas, in ordinary garden ponds. The smallest of these fish is the Everglades pygmy sunfish *(Elassoma evergladei)*, which has a beautiful pattern of blue and black stripes. It is very peaceful, and darts through the tank like a little butterfly. In a sufficiently large tank with dense vegetation it will breed without any difficulty. The other members of the family, mostly medium-sized, include the pumpkinseed *(Lepomis gibbosus)* and *Mesogonistius chaetodon*. There are other species, but they are not often seen nowadays, mainly because they are rather large and thus require spacious tanks, but they are completely undemanding, and have the advantage of not needing any supplementary heating. North America has some other very attractive fish also, mainly of the barb and egg-laying toothcarp families, but nowadays these are not often seen in the aquarium.

The Aquarium

The history of aquarium keeping

The emergence of aquarium keeping as a hobby is closely associated with the upsurge and distribution of scientific knowledge since the middle of the nineteenth century. This was the period when the natural world was, in some respects, rediscovered. For some decades before then zoologists had begun to keep animals and plants in water-filled glass containers for research purposes. This procedure must have been very primitive, because there were no really suitable containers or appropriate apparatus of any kind, but even so, there were several important advances in knowledge.

The start of true aquarium keeping dates back to the 1850s when various publications appeared on the subject. It began to be recognized that a tank of living aquatic organisms was not only of scientific interest but could also form an attractive decoration. It was at this time that the word 'aquarium' was first used, by Philip Gosse, who was closely involved in the establishment of the world's first public aquarium in the Zoological Gardens, London. Some of these early attempts were, of course, quite limited in scope, but they clearly marked the start of the aquarium hobby as we know it today. Enormous advances have, of course, been made in aquarium methods since these early days.

It was not long before the first exotic ornamental fish appeared. One of their forerunners was the goldfish with its fantastic varieties, the result of sophisticated breeding techniques stimulated by the admiration for bizarre shapes in the Far East. The goldfish thus became a 'pioneer' in aquarium keeping, although for much too long it led a miserable existence in the deplorable goldfish bowl with poor food and insufficient air.

Among the earliest imported tropical fish were two with such striking colours and forms that they soon captured the hearts of all nature lovers. These were the paradise fish, which arrived via Paris, and the fighting fish, which came via Moscow. These two species were the forerunners of some hundreds of imports, the number increasing year by year.

From the beginning of this century aquarium hobbyists started to establish clubs and societies, to found journals and to promote meetings for the exchange of information. At the same time a fruitful exchange of ideas between scientists and laymen began. Science became the godfather of the infant hobby and has remained so. From rather amateurish beginnings new ways of keeping and breeding fish have been found, and a vast array of modern techniques developed.

The link between science and the aquarium hobby is today closer than ever, and they help each other. Thousands of tiny observations made in the aquarium provide valuable information to biologists, while the aquarium hobbyist has become aware that the natural world presents a unified whole, like a web of delicate but indissolubly attached threads.

Tanks made from various materials

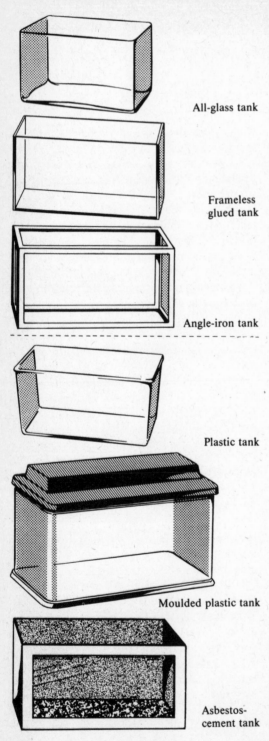

All-glass tank

Frameless glued tank

Angle-iron tank

Plastic tank

Moulded plastic tank

Asbestos-cement tank

Practical problems which concern both fish scientists and commercial fishery are involved in the general progress of biological research. An example of this is the contribution made over the years by aquarists to the study of fish diseases. Also much of the detailed knowledge of underwater life has been achieved by aquarium keeping, and likewise the study of micro-organisms in inland waters.

Ornamental tropical fish are particularly suitable for experimental work in biology, as they are small, adaptable and breed rapidly. Various other questions concerning the composition of aquarium water and the effects of hardness, pH value, light, gases and trace elements on animals, plants, fish spawn and fry have also been of both scientific and economic significance.

Last but not least, scientific benefits aside, aquarium keeping provides enjoyment and relaxation for thousands. It is an excellent method of spreading biological knowledge, and is a valuable aid in schools, helping young people to acquire a love of nature. Experienced aquarists often co-operate in the establishment and maintenance of exhibits in museums and zoological gardens, and can be of help in nature conservation.

Setting up the aquarium

This section provides some practical advice on setting up an aquarium. This will help the beginner to avoid unnecessary disappointment, because nothing is more likely to kill off initial interest than a series of mishaps. The section may also help the experienced aquarist.

Attention must first be given to the type of tank. Many beginners start with an all-glass tank. This has the advantage of being cheaper than other types, but often the disadvantage of having wavy glass walls, so that its inmates appear distorted. Furthermore, the moulded glass tank is not very stable and has a tendency to crack without warning.

But this is not to imply that all such tanks should be rejected, indeed small all-glass tanks are excellent for observing pond life and for segregating the females of livebearing toothcarps and quarrelsome male fighting fish. In such cases tanks up to 15–25 cm (6–9·8 in) in length are useful, but it is wiser not to use larger ones.

All-glass tanks must be placed on a thick underlay of felt, paper or foam plastic in order to minimize the danger of cracking. The same applies to small tanks of transparent plastic and to those with cemented glass panes, which are mentioned below.

It is sometimes recommended that all-glass tanks should be heated from below, for instance when breeding fighting fish. For this a shallow tray of metal-plate, with walls about 1 cm (0·4 in) high, is filled with very fine sand on which the tank is placed. Below the tray, ordinary tungsten lamps can be used as a source of heat.

When cleaning an all-glass tank great care should be taken to avoid scratching the glass with sand particles, as this often causes the tank to crack. Similarly, care should be taken when moving such a tank, as it is often difficult to hold, particularly with wet hands.

Finally, when using an all-glass tank any sudden change of temperature must be avoided.

Small tanks of transparent plastic, now obtainable commercially, are preferable to the all-glass ones. They are not always completely transparent, particularly after being used for some time, but they have the advantage of having absolutely smooth and undistorted walls. They can also, of course, break if not handled with care. When cleaning such a tank any scratches made by sand grains must be

Standard tanks on furniture bases

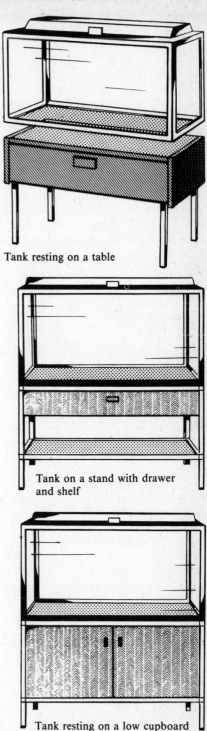

Tank resting on a table

Tank on a stand with drawer and shelf

Tank resting on a low cupboard

Height in cm	30	40	50	60	70	80	90	100/110	120/130	130/150
30	2·8	3·3	3·8	4·1	4·2	4·4	4·6	6·3	6·9	9·1
40	3·4	4·3	5·1	5·6	6·0	6·3	6·5	6·9	7·1	9·2
50	4·4	5·1	5·8	6·5	7·2	7·7	8·2	8·7	9·1	11·1
60	–	6·0	6·5	7·5	8·5	9·3	9·7	10·7	11·4	11·7
70	–	6·6	7·3	8·2	9·0	10·0	10·9	12·2	13·1	13·6
80	–	7·4	8·2	8·8	9·3	11·0	12·2	13·7	14·9	16·1

avoided, and on no account should chemical cleaning agents be used. Such tanks should not be heated from the bottom; they often have a suitable lid to which lighting, heating and other equipment can be fitted.

Hitheroto the most widely used tanks have been those with a metal frame, usually of angle-iron, but occasionally of aluminium treated to prevent damage by water. There are also tanks with a frame of tough plastic or asbestos cement.

Most angle-iron tanks have a glass bottom, but larger sizes should have a metal plate over which a glass plate is cemented. Angle-iron tanks have the advantage of being very strong and, provided the panes are of the correct thickness, they rarely break. If a glass pane should break it can in most cases be replaced relatively easily. The panes are completely smooth and are usually made of top-quality plate glass, so that the inmates can be clearly seen.

The construction of an angle-iron tank is really a job for the professional, and ready-made good-quality tanks are widely available from aquarium dealers. The details of construction, for example the strength and sizes of the glass panes, are given here only for information.

The following points are important:

a) The thickness of glass must correspond with the dimensions of the tank. The calculation of glass thickness depends primarily on the height of the tank, and the panes must be sufficiently thick to withstand the pressure of the water.

The minimum required thickness of glass is shown in the table above in mm. The left-hand column shows the tank height in cm, and the figures along the top show the tank length, also in cm. For sizes under 30×30 cm the minimum glass thickness is 2·5 mm.

b) The thickness of the bottom metal plate is shown in the table below. (For tanks less than 40 × 40 cm use 1·5 mm thick metal.) The dimensions are the length, breadth and height of the tank, from left to right.

```
50 × 25 ×  25 = 1·5 mm metal plate
50 × 30 ×  30 = 1·5 mm metal plate
50 × 40 ×  30 = 1·6 mm metal plate
50 × 50 ×  30 = 1·6 mm metal plate
50 × 40 ×  50 = 2·0 mm metal plate
80 × 30 ×  30 = 2·0 mm metal plate
80 × 30 ×  40 = 2·2 mm metal plate
80 × 40 ×  40 = 2·2 mm metal plate
80 × 40 ×  50 = 2·6 mm metal plate
80 × 40 ×  60 = 2·7 mm metal plate
60 × 30 ×  25 = 1·6 mm metal plate
60 × 30 ×  30 = 1·6 mm metal plate
60 × 40 ×  30 = 1·7 mm metal plate
60 × 40 ×  50 = 2·2 mm metal plate
60 × 50 ×  50 = 2·4 mm metal plate
100 × 40 ×  40 = 2·7 mm metal plate
100 × 30 ×  50 = 2·9 mm metal plate
100 × 40 ×  60 = 2·9 mm metal plate
120 × 50 ×  50 = 3·4 mm metal plate
120 × 50 × 100 = 4·7 mm metal plate
150 × 60 ×  80 = 4·9 mm metal plate
150 × 60 × 100 = 5·6 mm metal plate
```

When setting up an angle-iron tank care should be taken to ensure that it is absolutely waterproof and also that none of the water can come into contact with any metal parts. These must therefore be coated with a silicon-rubber sealant specially made for aquarium use, as uncoated metal may release substances that are toxic to fish. Ordinary oil paints are useless in the aquarium, but modern plastic resins have proved very reliable. Before use all parts should be thoroughly cleaned, special care being taken to remove all traces of oil or grease.

Asbestos-cement tanks are frequently used when the aquarist only wants to view his fish from in front. Glazing is very simple as only one frontal glass pane is required. All parts in contact with water should be painted with plastic resin, as new asbestos-cement tanks release alkaline substances into the water.

All-glass bonded tanks made of sheets of glass or perspex are a relatively modern innovation. Having no frame they allow viewing from all angles, and they do not release injurious substances into the water. Bonded tanks usually have a lid in which the necessary pieces of apparatus are fitted.

In the absence of a metal or plastic frame this tanks are held together exclusively by means of a silicon-rubber glue, with which the glass or plastic sheets are so firmly bonded

Aquarium tanks as furniture

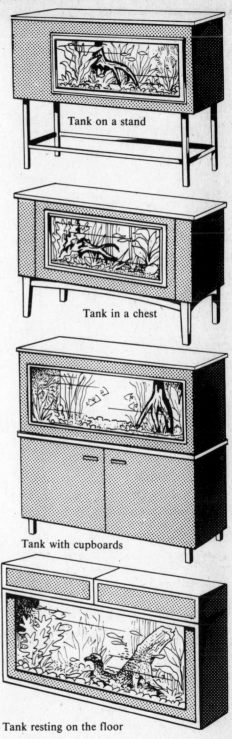

Tank on a stand

Tank in a chest

Tank with cupboards

Tank resting on the floor

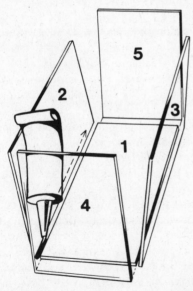

Method of gluing
a frameless tank

Bottom pane glued
inside the side panes

Aquarium installations for dividing the room

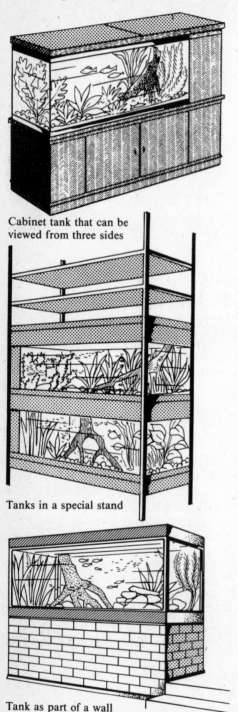

Cabinet tank that can be viewed from three sides

Tanks in a special stand

Tank as part of a wall

that they will withstand practically any water pressure likely to be found in the aquarium. Thus it is possible today to have tanks holding more than 100 litres (21 gals) of water.

The advantages of bonded all-glass tanks are considerable, the greatest being the fact that they include no substances that can corrode, nor is there any release of toxic substances into the water. Moreover, there is little or no chance of the leaks which can occur in angle-iron tanks after several years' use.

Bonded tanks can be constructed by the aquarist himself, and necessary materials and instructions are obtainable from aquarium dealers. First attempts should be restricted to the bonding of smaller tanks.

The positioning of aquarium tanks is very important. The position chosen should be one that can be kept for a considerable time, as a change of position entails a lot of work and disturbs the plants and fish, which then have to re-adapt to the changed conditions of a new site.

The aquarium should be in a light place, unless it has been decided to illuminate the tank mainly, or throughout the day, by artificial lighting. If some daylight is to be used then the following basic rules should be borne in mind.

The best position is close to an east-facing window, as the fish and plants will then receive the valuable morning sun, which in some breeds encourages the onset of spawning. A position near a west-facing window is also quite satisfactory, but a site close to a south-facing window is not ideal, as the tank may receive too much sun, which can encourage the growth of troublesome algae. In such a position the tank could, of course, be shaded by some form of blind or screen.

A north-facing window would suit a coldwater aquarium, and many tropical fish and plants do well in subdued lighting. Artificial lighting can be used to compensate for a lack of natural light, which enables the aquarist to choose a position other than one close to a window. The most suitable position in the vicinity of a window is one where the light falls on the fish rather than through them, as this enhances their colours and scale iridescence. This effect is difficult to obtain with artificial lighting, unless one fits a low-voltage spotlight.

The first job in setting up an aquarium tank is to lay down the substrate. In general, this should be sand that is neither too coarse nor too fine, and it should contain a small amount of loam. The substrate should first be washed so that only the floating particles are removed, and can then be laid over the bottom of the tank in a layer 6–8 cm (2·4–3 in) thick. It should be moist enough to allow a fall of 2–3 cm (0·8–1·1 in) to one corner at the front of the tank. The purpose of this slight depression is to receive any particles of detritus which will accumulate as the tank becomes established. The detritus, or mulm, can then be easily removed by a mulm pipette or by siphoning. Any water coming out of the damp sand can then be mopped up with a plastic sponge or a rag. On top of this basic layer should be spread a 2–3 cm (0·8–1·1 in) layer of sand that is not too fine and which has been thoroughly washed (when the washing water shows no cloudiness). This layer should be spread equally over the basic compost, and again any water that collects should be mopped up.

This type of substrate is perfectly suitable for most plants. For fish such as cichlids, which burrow very actively, the substrate should consist only of well-washed gravel. In this case it is necessary either to do without any tender plants, or to plant them in pots. Breeding tanks for certain fish species should have no sand at all, and the delicate characin and barb species also require special treatment. They are susceptible to neon disease and other disease vectors, and for them the sand can be heated. Aquarium sand bought from a dealer has usually been rendered germ-free.

A number of decorative materials can be used to furnish the tank, as it should look attractive as well as being correctly established from the biological viewpoint. Obviously the

Special types of aquarium

Two aquarium tanks with rounded corners, made from moulded plastic

Two tanks that can be seen from all sides

A tank built into the wall

type of tank furnishing should be suitable for the fish which are to live there as well as pleasing their human observers. Many fish species like to hide away from time to time, and thus need hiding-places or resting sites, possibly near the middle of their home territory. Like all other living organisms, fish are very dependent upon their surroundings, and so careful thought must be given to the type of tank furnishing used, though not at the expense of internal factors such as water composition, temperature, food etc., which are even more important.

The actual colour of the substrate affects many types of fish: on a pale background their colours tend to fade, while a dark substrate brings out brighter colours. One often has the impression that the fish feel uneasy in an aquarium tank that is too brightly lit, so it is sometimes a good idea to cover the upper layer of substrate with a darker layer. Dark gravel can sometimes be obtained, or basalt chips can be used, provided they do not have sharp edges. Basalt chips appear black in water and therefore give a rather sombre effect, but this can be softened by using the chips in combination with sand or gravel. For some purposes quartz gravel is quite acceptable, but for the normal aquarium it is too pale and should be mixed with dark sand or gravel.

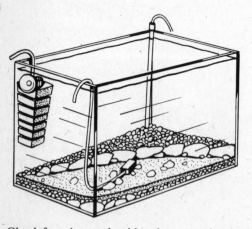

Glued frameless tank with substrate and terrace, heater and aerator stone

Sand which appears to be too pale can be toned down by using dark materials with it, such as black rocks, pieces of dark wood or peat. Peat is particularly valuable for this purpose, but before being spread over the substrate it should be steeped in water and squeezed so that it is just damp; this prevents it from imparting colour to the water. A layer of peat has a beneficial influence on many fish and plants, and does not make the water cloudy. The peat should be fairly coarse so that the fragments do not float when disturbed by burrowing species such as armoured catfish. From time to time the peat, together with any accumulated mulm, must be siphoned off and replaced, but take care not to suck up any small fish at the same time.

For most aquarium tanks rocks are an indispensable part of the furnishing, and their use depends both upon the type of tank planned and on the fish to be kept there. The best types of rock are those such as granite, basalt or syenite, which are more or less inert, that is, they do not release substances into the water, or not in appreciable quantities. For fish that do not require soft water, limestone or an easily worked sandstone can be used. The shape of the rocks depends entirely upon the type of aquarium landscape required. For instance, for a tank of shoaling fish which have come from a stream it would be acceptable to use a number of water-worn rocks and stones, or you could simulate landscape close to the banks of a river by using angular rocks, preferably laid in horizontal layers. For fish adapted to life on a darkish, muddy substrate, for example fighting fish, some barbs and catfish, it might be better to have no rocks, but instead a few pieces of the long-dead timber that has lain embedded in moorland peat. Brightly coloured rocks are usually to be avoided, and rocks with sharp edges, tufa and artificial rocks of all kinds should not be used for decoration. 'Castles' made of tufa, artificial plants, whelk shells, figures and so on have no place in a tank designed to provide a natural environment.

Roots are a particularly valuable form of

decoration. They provide unlimited opportunities for varied and natural effects, but a certain amount of care is needed. Unsuitable roots will rot, and pollute the water, particularly at places where they project above the surface and so become mouldy. When this happens some of the mould may extend on to objects below the surface.

Living or ordinary wood is unsuitable, and it is worth searching for pieces of dead root which have lain for a long time in running water. These can often be found in mountain streams. Dead roots on the banks of clear lakes can also be suitable, as can pieces dug up from peat bog, but not those embedded in mud. Suitable dead roots usually require no further treatment, apart from soaking in water for a few days, which allows them to absorb water and lose their buoyancy. If there is any doubt about how they are going to behave in water they should be left submerged for a longer period. Alternatively, they can be boiled for a few hours in a strong salt solution, after which they must lie for a long time in clean fresh water. This destroys any microorganisms and the wood becomes heavier. If it is still difficult to anchor roots or pieces of wood it may be necessary to weight them down with pieces of rock.

Reeds *(Phragmites)* that grow along the edges of lakes are also decorative, and so is bamboo. These materials can be largely prevented from rotting by dipping the ends in water-glass for a time. They are very buoyant, so the substrate must be sufficiently thick to hold them. In general, reeds and bamboo are used mainly for background decoration, but of course only where they suit the general décor of the tank.

Coconut shells are much used for cave-dwelling fish, and they are perfectly in place in a tropical aquarium. They can be used without further treatment provided a reasonably large opening has been made as an entrance for the fish. The shell can be laid on the sand, partially embedded, or even hidden among roots. Some aquarists bore a small hole at the top to allow a little light in.

Rocks collected from a river

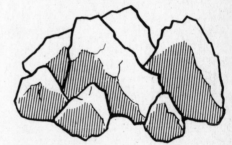

Rocks arranged vertically

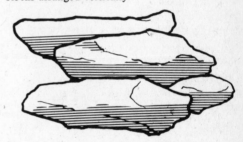

Flat rocks suitable for terrace construction

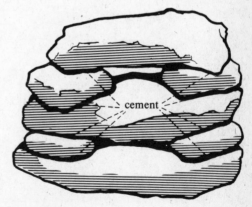

cement

Rocks with broad, flat surfaces cemented together to form a cave

Decorative scheme with small rocks, roots and reeds

(The rear wall, not shown, could have reeds behind it, outside the tank)

Decorative scheme using flat stones, roots and a coconut shell

(The rear wall, not shown, could have pieces of bark, branches and dried grasses, outside the tank)

The visual effect of a decorated tank can be enhanced if the background is closed by a rear wall. This is better outside the aquarium, but can be placed inside it. Rocks cemented together to form a rear wall are not practical, for in spite of every care there is always the chance that substances may leach out of them into the water. A tank with a moorland theme could have an inside rear wall constructed from blocks of peat held together by thin glass rods. One could then anchor to it plants that do not need to be rooted, for instance, *Riccia*, water moss or underwater fern.

Rear walls inside the tank have two main disadvantages: firstly, they reduce the water volume, and secondly, there is always the risk that fish may swim in behind them and become lost. So it is really more practical to have the rear wall outside the tank. A sheet of wood or papier mâché cut to the tank size can be decorated with bark, cork, bamboo, reeds etc., or alternatively, a rocky scene can be created by cementing rockwork to a box that is then placed behind the back of the tank. The exact layout of the rear wall decoration should conform to the character of the general tank décor.

The rear wall must not be sited too close to the back pane of the tank, otherwise insufficient light will fall on it. A rear wall gives the impression of greater depth to the underwater landscape, particularly when its decoration merges with that of the tank itself.

It is also possible to create a background by painting the outside of the rear glass pane with a waterproof paint which is preferably slightly transparent. It is best not to attempt a pictorial rendering, but to choose an abstract of greens, reds and browns. Aquarium dealers also sell colour reproductions of established aquarium tanks, which can be cut down to the size of the tank that is to be decorated.

Aquatic plants, to be discussed in detail in a later chapter, are very important as part of the

Decoration with bark, roots and dried reeds, suitable for suspending outside the rear wall of the tank

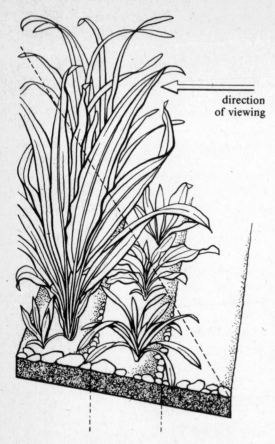

direction
of viewing

At rear: In centre: Foreground:
large,   small,   remains free
bushy   individual
plants   plants

the choice of plants depends upon the taste of the aquarist.

Plants should be arranged in groups, according to the species, each individual plant being inserted in a hole in the substrate bored with a small stick or with the finger. Some plants, such as *Cryptocoryne* species, require plenty of space for spreading, others do not thrive when they are too close to other different species. Attention must be paid to the characteristics and future growth of the plants, as it is important to leave sufficient open space in the foreground of the tank to allow the fish to swim without hindrance. Before planting, the tips of the roots should be cut off and the plant then inserted in the hole so that the roots hang vertically. On no account should any of the roots be allowed to lie on the surface of the substrate. Some plants, such as underwater ferns, are very buoyant and may need to be anchored to the bottom by glass rods or stones.

The next consideration is installing the necessary equipment, such as the thermometer, the air line with diffuser, and the heater. The air line runs along the sand, which can be used to cover it, or it can be anchored by a few stones. The contents of the tank are then covered with a sheet of strong brown paper and the water is poured in so that it hits the paper. Some aquarists put in the water before the plants, believing, perhaps rightly, that it helps them to get an idea of how the planting will look. However, with this method it is more difficult to fix the plants in the substrate, necessitating a planting stick.

Tap water can normally be used, provided it is not too heavily chlorinated. In fact, chlorine evaporates within a few hours, and so such water can be used after a reasonable period of time. In certain cases it may be necessary to use a different water, and this will be discussed later in the section on 'Chemical processes in water'.

The tank should be filled to just below the upper edge, except when shallow water is needed for breeding purposes. After filling, the plants can be adjusted, using a small stick.

biological environment in the aquarium. They are also of prime importance in creating an aesthetically pleasing underwater landscape. Choice of the right plants is not always an easy matter, as the requirements of fish and plants must conform, that is, cold-water fish should be kept with cold-water plants, warm-water fish with warm-water plants. Some fish prefer plants with a certain growth form, for instance, fine-leaved, strap-like, broad-leaved, floating, or those that grow on the bottom. The geographical origin of the plants may also be relevant, but is only really important in cases where a circumscribed fish and plant community is being established. In general,

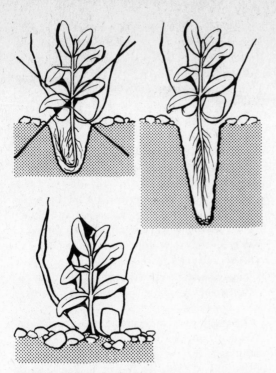

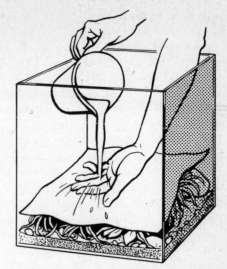

Filling the tank with water

Position of plants in the substrate

Before introducing any fish the aquarium tank must be allowed to stand for up to a week, both to give the plants time to root, and to allow the process of biological equilibrium to be initiated (this subject will be discussed later in greater detail).

After the tank has been fully set up and the control equipment switched on, its cover-glass can be put in position. For angle-iron tanks this must not rest directly on the metal rim, as this would soon lead to the formation of ugly rust marks. The cover-glass can be supported on special clips designed for the purpose and made of rustproof material; these are fixed to the upper rim of the tank. For bonded glass tanks the lid can be supported on home-made cork wedges (see illustration on p. 57). There are also plastic bands on the market which lie along the rim of the tank; these sometimes have grooves which allow the cover glass to slide in and out.

The cover-glass is intended to prevent the settlement of dust on the water surface and also to stop the fish from jumping out (many fish jump very well, and use every opportunity to do so). Great care must be taken to ensure that no condensation can reach the leads of the electrical equipment; it is a good idea to set the cover-glass somewhat obliquely to allow the condensation to run back into the tank.

Once the tank has been set up correctly, it should need only a minimum of care.

Provided the plants have had time to take root and the fish and plants are in the correct numerical balance to one another the aquarist should have no more trouble than he would have in maintaining a flower-bed. Handling must be avoided except when absolutely necessary. For this reason cleaning out the tank at frequent intervals is not recommended.

Occasionally a tank may start to leak. In some cases the leak may seal itself, but if not, the mastic around the leak should be removed and fresh mastic pressed in with a knife or a piece of wood. If the original mastic was of poor quality or if the tank has been badly glazed, it may be necessary to clear everything out and start again. Major repairs such as this should be done professionally, as this will be cheaper in the long run.

Routine maintenance of a well-established tank should only consist of removing the accumulated mulm, perhaps about once a week. This can be done using a 'mulm bell' attached to a suction tube which removes the soft particles but leaves the heavier sand in the tank. In smaller tanks one can use a type of pipette. The dirty water that is removed can be filtered and the filtrate poured back into the tank.

The side panes can be cleaned with a glass-cleaner to remove any algal growth. If the tank contains a large number of fish it is usual to replace a proportion of the water every week. This is done to prevent the build-up of metabolic products resulting from the fish faeces. It is best to remove about one-fifth of the water each time, replacing it with fresh water at the same temperature. Water lost by evaporation should be replaced by distilled water or by de-ionized water to avoid an above-normal increase in hardness; only pure water evaporates, leaving behind compounds which increase the hardness. This replacement water should be kept in a darkened container. A tank maintained in this way can function for years without the need for thorough cleansing.

Algae in the aquarium can cause considerable trouble. Algae are primitive plants, and those that grow in the aquarium are distantly related to the seaweeds found on rocky shores, and are mostly microscopic and one-celled. Some of the tiny algae form colonies of several individuals.

In general, the green algae can be regarded as beneficial. In bright light these often grow on the glass panes in the form of a green film, which can be left provided it is not excessive. The front pane should be cleaned from time to time. Green algae are good producers of oxygen. Some fish use them as a dietary supplement, and an established film of green algae will also harbour numerous tiny organisms called infusorians, which are indispensable for fish fry. With certain reservations it can be said that the biological conditions in a tank are suitable when there is some growth of green algae. Any excess of these tiny plants is due to too much light.

Filamentous algae, especially the rough species, can be harmful to fish, as they may cause injuries to the gills and to the skin. Serious infestations of these algae can be removed by winding them up on a rough stick and lifting them out of the tank. When doing this, care must be taken not to uproot the aquarium plants, round which the algae tend to grow. Filamentous algae can serve as a spawning substrate in a breeding tank, but this is not necessary as there are plenty of other ways of providing such a spawning medium.

Some filamentous algae are extremely persistent, forming colonies along the edges of leaves of higher aquatic plants. They are very difficult to eradicate, and it may be necessary to cut off any infested leaves or even to destroy the whole plant.

In poorly lit aquarium tanks a brown film may appear on the glass, the rockwork or the plants. This consists of millions of tiny diatoms of various shapes. They are sometimes known as brown algae, but wrongly; the term refers to the brown seaweeds on the sea-shore. If the film on the aquarium plants becomes too thick they will no longer be able to respire and assimilate, and they will die. In general, diatoms can only be controlled by increasing the light. They may appear during the winter

Chilodus punctatus, spotted headstander (9)

Left: *Paracheirodon innesi*, neon tetra (44)

Below left: *Nannostomus eques*, tube-mouthed pencilfish (3

Below right: *Megalamphodus sweglesi*, red phantom tetra (-

Bottom: *Copella arnoldi*, spraying characin (11)

Metynnis hypsauchen, Schreitmuller's metynnis (34)

Pygocentrus piraya, piranha (49)

Neolebias ansorgei,
African redfin (43)

Micralestes (= Phenacogrammus) interruptus,
Congo tetra (47)

Right: *Megalamphodus megalopterus,*
black phantom tetra (−)

Brachydanio albolineatus,
pearl danio (68)

Right: *Barbus 'schuberti'*, golden barb (62)

Barbus ticto (a subspecies), two-spot barb (65)

Rasbora maculata,
spotted rasbora (80)

Rasbora heteromorpha,
harlequin fish (79)

Loricaria parva (?), dwarf whiptail (271), laying eggs

Corydoras paleatus, peppered corydoras (264)

Hoplosternum thoracatum, spotted hoplosternum (269)

Kryptopterus bicirrhis, glass catfish (270)

Nothobranchius guentheri,
Guenther's
nothobranchius (–)

Nothobranchius korthausi,
Korthaus's
nothobranchius (–)

Nothobranchius rachovi,
Rachov's
nothobranchius (124)

Top: *Cynolebias alexandri*,
Alexander's cynolebias (−)

Above: *Aphyosemion striatum*,
red-striped aphyosemion (97)

45

Left: *Xiphophorus variatus*, variatus platy (152)

Top left: *Colisa lalia*, dwarf gourami (161)

Top right: *Helostoma temmincki*, kissing gourami (164)

Above: *Macropodus opercularis*, paradise fish (166)

Belonesox belizanus, pike top-minnow (136)

Studies of spawning behaviour in
Trichogaster trichopterus, Cosby form (175)

Top left:
early courtship, fish lying parallel

Top right:
courtship with fish in T-position; the female is ready
to spawn and touching the male lightly with her lips

Above left:
preparation for the coiling phase, the female swims
in to the male whose body is already bent

Above right:
the male coils round the female and, with slight quivering,
the eggs and sperm are released

Cichlasoma meeki, firemouth cichlid (193), in a shoal of fry

Apistogramma ramirezi,
Ramirez's dwarf cichlid
(185)

Apistogramma trifasciatum
three-striped
dwarf cichlid (187)

Geophagus brasiliensis, Brazil earth-eater (−)

Top left:
Julidochromis marlieri, Marlier's julie (210)

Top right:
Tropheus duboisi, Brabant cichlid,
a young specimen (239)

Above:
Lamprologus leleupi, Tanganyika golden cichlid (–)

Lamprologus brichardi,
'Princess of Burundi' (217)

Pelmatochromis thomasi,
Thomas's pelmatochromis (222)

Tetraodon fluviatilis,
green pufferfish (249)

Scatophagus argus,
argusfish (248)

Monocirrhus polyacanthus, South American leaf-fish (–)

Examples of suitably
decorated aquarium
tanks

(Photos
of planted tanks
by Ingo Hertel)

Corks cut to hold the tank lid

Tank lid clips for an angle-iron tank

months when there is little light, but usually disappear with the onset of spring.

Blue algae are the most unwelcome of all algal types. In a short time they can completely overrun an aquarium and then produce an evil-smelling mass in which no living organism can survive. It is best, therefore, to attack them as soon as they are spotted. They can be scraped off the glass and rockwork and carefully rubbed off plants with the fingers. Every speck must then be removed, together with any growing on the bottom of the tank.

Many species of blue algae, but not all, like alkaline water. They are almost always a sign that something is not right. The best method of prevention is to establish 'healthy' conditions: clear water rich in oxygen, luxuriant plant growth, a moderate fish population and carefully controlled feeding, with no uneaten food left in the tank.

There are no absolutely reliable methods for combatting blue-green algae, although substances have appeared on the market which are said to destroy some fish parasites as well as these.

Filtration of the water through peat may also help to curb excessive algal growths, and this will be discussed in more detail later on. This filtration removes hardness from the water, enriches it with humic acids and gives it a pale brown colour, all factors which are deleterious to some algae.

To a certain extent algal growths can be controlled by some of the fish themselves. Among those which browse on algae are the livebearing toothcarps of the genera *Xipho-*

phorus, Poecilia (Mollienesia) and *Poecilia (Limia)*, the species of *Otocinclus* and also *Gyrinocheilus aymonieri* and *Epalzeorhynchus siamensis*. All these consumers of algae feed on algal films, but not on filamentous algae, although it seems that *E. siamensis* may possibly do so.

Algae are not removed efficiently by snails, which leave trails of faeces on the alga-infested glass panes. In fact, it seems that because of their active metabolism snails tend to encourage algae.

Milky cloudiness of the water is usually the result of errors in management. If more food is given than the fish can eat, or when live food dies in the tank, the water becomes enriched with the products of protein degradation and this stimulates the mass multiplication of bacteria and protozoans. This goes hand in hand with oxygen deficiency, which can be extremely injurious to fish, indeed even lethal to fish fry. In some cases cloudiness can be removed by stirring in a solution of potassium permanganate, strong enough to give the water a pale pink colour. This treatment does not harm the fish. The coloration soon disappears on its own as the potassium is taken up as a nutrient by the plants. As already mentioned, peat filtration inhibits the mass proliferation of bacteria and infusorians in the aquarium, and there are also preparations on the market which quickly solve the problem. However, these are only emergency measures; proper care should always be given which will deny living conditions to bacteria and infusorians.

Green cloudiness or water bloom is caused by the presence of floating algae. It is usually not injurious when the fish can become slowly accustomed to it, but it can be cured by putting in more water-fleas *(Daphnia)* than will be immediately eaten by the fish, as the survivors quickly remove the algae. The milky cloudiness mentioned above can also be removed in this way.

Sometimes a thin skin of fat forms on the surface of the water. Apart from being unsightly, this also prevents the necessary

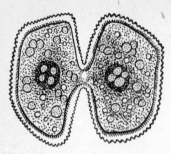

A much enlarged drawing of green alga from a film on aquarium glass

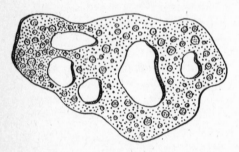

Blue-green alga, much enlarged

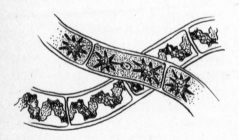

Filamentous alga, much enlarged

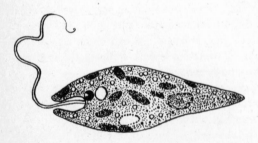

A much enlarged drawing of flagellate, of the type responsible for the formation of 'water blooms'

exchange of gases in the aquarium. It can sometimes be dispersed by aeration, but a neater method is to take a sheet of newspaper cut to the same width as the tank and draw it carefully across the water surface. The fatty layer remains attached to the paper, which is then removed. This procedure must be repeated from time to time. The fatty layer consists of bacteria which subsist on the dust and particles deposited on the water surface.

It is not usually necessary to make special preparations for the winter, because with the normal artificial lighting the natural processes in an aquarium continue uninterrupted. During the autumn any vegetation that has become too dense can be cut back, leaving only the strongest and healthiest shoots. Withered shoots should be removed and the fish population checked, leaving only the breeding stock and any others that can be fed over the winter. It is essential to avoid overcrowding.

As already mentioned, with artificial lighting the biological processes in the aquarium scarcely change according to the season. Nevertheless, it is a good idea to reduce the temperature from November to February, even in a tropical tank. Unless particularly delicate species are being kept a temperature of 22 °C (71 °F) should be sufficient. Some plants, for instance, the *Aponogeton* species, like a period at a reduced temperature. With artificial lighting, cold-water plants and fish can also be overwintered at room temperature (18 °C or 64 °F) and no supplementary heating should be required. Many cold-water plants die down in winter.

Winter is also the time when those who keep fish with special food requirements should make up new food cultures and check any old ones.

There are also a few jobs to be done during the spring. About the middle of February any deficiencies in the heating, aeration and filtration systems should be rectified, the tank glass cleaned, and regular replacement of a proportion of the water continued. This is also a good time to carry out any new plantings and to make up breeding tanks.

Types of aquarium

The major types of aquarium described in this chapter are identified according to their temperature and the characteristics of their fish and plant inhabitants.

The cold-water aquarium

A habitat aquarium for lower aquatic species enables the aquarist to observe some of the interesting and varied living organisms of his own area (the actual species concerned will be mentioned later on). For study purposes any small tank is suitable, for instance, the small moulded all-glass tanks. These are cheap and easy to obtain, and should form part of the normal biological equipment of all schools. Here it is not necessary to have a substrate, as plants such as milfoil, Canadian waterweed or hornwort are quite sufficient. Larger tanks for teaching purposes are best set up as bog or marsh aquaria. In these, the substrate should be laid in the form of a terrace, so that it rises towards one of the rear corners of the tank, leaving a sufficiently large land area. The planting will depend upon the depth of the water, so that in one tank there can be rooted underwater plants, floating plants and shore plants.

Large empty flowerpots can be built into the terrace so that smaller potted plants can be inserted; this enables the latter to be changed from time to time. A few plants can also be cultivated outside but close to the actual tank itself; some of these will die down in the autumn. Depending upon the teaching requirements the bog aquarium can then be stocked with fish, newts and aquatic invertebrates. A tank of this type provides good facilities for observing the biological processes that take place in fresh waters.

Many aquatic insects fly well and can escape from the tank, so it is necessary to fit a lid, part of which should be glass, and part fine-mesh wire gauze.

Naturally, the stocking of such a tank requires some thought. Certain species, such as the giant diving beetle and its predatory larvae, are obviously unsuitable, but these would be well worth keeping in separate tanks.

A cold-water aquarium for cold-water fish from other countries requires no special heating, but can be overwintered at room temperature. Such fish include the North American sunfish, the freshwater 'dogfish' *(Umbra)*, catfish and a few others.

The warm-water aquarium

There are, of course, several different types of warm-water aquaria, and the main differences between each are discussed below. But for all of them it is essential to have proper heating; positioning the tank near an oven or on a shelf above the central heating is only a makeshift. Heating methods are discussed in detail later in this chapter.

A community tank is usually one that is established mainly from the aesthetic viewpoint, with only secondary regard to the origins of the plants and fish. Emphasis is placed on the bright colours of the fish and on the decorative effect of the plants. It is, of course, obvious that the tank should only be stocked with fish of the same general type and size, with the same swimming habits, temperature and dietary requirements. It would never do to bring together predatory and peaceful fish, active and slow-moving ones, or very large fish with much smaller ones. Fish requiring a special diet are not suitable for a community aquarium.

It is essential that a community tank should

A marsh aquarium

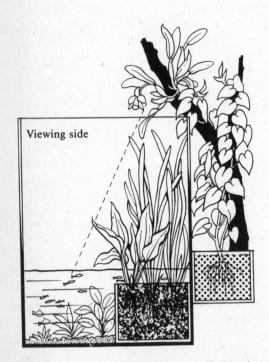

Viewing side

Tank   Marsh plants   Hydroculture

not contain a hotch-potch of all kinds of fish species. Fish which are to be kept together must be chosen with great care, as each species has its own behaviour pattern and its well-being and livelihood will be destroyed if it has to live with unsuitable neighbours.

A landscape aquarium is a term sometimes used for a tank stocked with fish and plants from a particular part of the world. It must be set up to look as natural as possible, even though it is never really possible to produce a true replica of a natural underwater landscape. Even more important than the external appearance of such a tank are the internal factors: lighting, temperature, water composition and condition, oxygen content, food and the fish community.

Nowadays there is a move away from planting according to geographical origin, since the diversity of an entire continent can scarcely be represented within the confines of an aquarium tank. For example, in an African tank, although all the fish and plants in it may come from the same country, they seldom all come from the same environment. Thus it would be more relevant to attempt to reproduce an aspect of the environment, such as a landscape representing the shore of African rain-forest. Such an aquarium could reflect the actual living conditions, provided, of course, the aquarist has the requisite knowledge.

The establishment of a miniature landscape can also take the form of a biotope, or habitat aquarium. This kind of tank does not contain the fish and plants of one particular geographical area, but rather those that require the same living conditions, and an attempt is made to reproduce the biological factors as accurately as possible. Thus such a tank could have fish from south-east Asia with those from South America provided they all have the same biological requirements.

A species aquarium is one in which only a single species is kept, alone, as a pair, or even as a shoal. This allows the aquarist to observe fish behaviour better than is possible in a community tank. A species tank is also suitable for breeding, provided it is tended with extra care and attention (see below) but its great advantage is that it allows the aquarist to concentrate on reproducing the special water conditions, temperature, diet and decoration appropriate to the species concerned without having to worry about the varied requirements of a number of different species.

The breeding aquarium

A tank for breeding fish has to be set up quite differently from one designed just for keeping ornamental fish, and it has to take special account of the peculiarities of the species concerned. Here only a few general guidelines can be given.

The principal aim is to produce healthy offspring. Unless commercial interests are involved, the aquarist should not set out to produce large batches of fish fry. For the ordinary aquarist the breeding of a fish species is the high point of the hobby. (The section 'Hints on breeding aquarium fishes' provides full information on the subject.)

The professional breeder, on the other hand, has to produce sufficient fish to satisfy the demand, which requires the fulfilment of certain basic requirements such as water composition, diet and so on. It is also essential for the professional breeder to be able to inspect his tanks and efficiently carry out routine tasks, such as changes of water, feeding and catching breeding stock and young offspring.

The positioning of breeding tanks also requires careful planning, so that there is sufficient space to carry out essential operations; this applies particularly to the need for enough headroom if the tanks are arranged one above the other. When the young are being reared the tank itself must be sufficiently spacious. Naturally, space requirements will depend upon the size of the breeding pair and the number of offspring expected. In general, the depth of water should be less than in a normal aquarium tank.

All the technical equipment must be capable of working without interruption. Even when the equipment is as near perfect as possible, the electricity supply could fail, so auxiliary equipment should be available. According to circumstances, failure of the heating and aeration can prove fatal for fish fry. Although some fish are stimulated to spawn by sunlight, this is not essential, and successful breeding nearly always takes place under artificial lighting.

Fish that are tending a brood are very nervous and may react to sudden changes in

Breeding tanks

lighting, so it is a good idea to instal a special resistance switch so that turning the lighting on and off can be carried out gradually. A separate small electric light can be fitted to provide dim light during the hours of darkness.

Practical aids

Modern technology has provided the aquarist with a series of aids, some of which are indispensable, while others are useful because they simplify the routine work.

Heating

For the warm-water aquarium some form of heating is absolutely essential. Tropical fish cannot become 'hardened'; their whole constitution is adapted to the warm temperatures of tropical waters.

In earlier times aquarium tanks were heated by oil, paraffin or gas lamps underneath the bottom plate, but these methods have been replaced by electric heating. If there is no electric supply as, for instance, in a summer house, it may be necessary to use one of the old methods of heating, but care must be taken to see that there is no risk of an explosion. At one time small lamps burning petroleum or paraffin were available in aquarium dealers, but nowadays it would be necessary to resort to a camping supplies dealer for small lamps or burners. If gas heating has to be used, there are safe burners which cannot be extinguished even in a strong draught, but

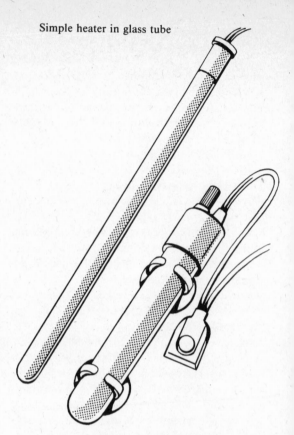

Simple heater in glass tube

Watertight, insulated control unit with two attachment suckers

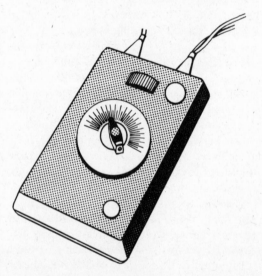

Electric thermostat with automatic setting for day and night

this type of heating must be left to a professional gas-fitter.

Nowadays electric heating is used almost exclusively. With properly fitted electric connections and tested equipment it is safe and reliable. The heating equipment is usually suspended in the tank or attached to the glass by suckers.

In general, the heaters consist of a tube of glass or porcelain. One end is shaped like the bottom of a chemical test-tube while the other end has a watertight cap through which the electric cable is led. This supplies current to a wire element wound round a ceramic former inside the tube. The heater is usually fixed in a horizontal position just above the substrate, so that the warmed water tends to rise. On no account should the heater lie on the substrate.

Heaters that cannot be regulated are not very satisfactory as it is difficult to work out the correct heating capacity for a given size of tank. It is better to use a heater connected to a thermostat. These two pieces of apparatus can either be separate or they can be in the same outer casing. The use of a thermostat provides a more reliable method of regulating the water temperature in the tank.

The actual temperature can be reliably measured with a thermometer inside the tank, attached by suckers to one of the glass panes as far away as possible from the heater. There are also floating thermometers. Some aquarists favour a contact thermometer fixed to the outside, but these could possibly be affected by the temperature of the room.

A thermostat can save a considerable amount of electricity and avoids unnecessary peaks, although some people regard its use as unnatural, believing that daily fluctuations in temperature have a beneficial effect on plants and fish.

The capacity of the heater should be such that it can always bring the aquarium water to the required temperature even when the room temperature drops. On the other hand, its rating should not be too high as there might be risk of overheating if the thermostat failed to operate.

As with all electrical equipment the cables and connections must be in first-class condition so as not to endanger other people, particularly children. With larger types of aquarium it is wise to employ an electrician.

New aquarium heating techniques are constantly being developed. For instance, there is now a heating cable that can be installed in the substrate, which is thus warmed from below. This may be beneficial for some tropical aquatic plants, which like to have 'warm feet', and also the rising warmth helps to circulate water in the substrate. Bottom heating is particularly suitable for marsh aquarium tanks.

There are also heaters on the market which use a low voltage (24 volts). They require a transformer in the circuit to reduce the voltage from the normal supply. Low voltage equipment is particularly recommended for schools for reasons of safety. Finally, there is an automatic thermostat which can be set for different night and day temperatures, but this is rather an expensive refinement.

Aeration

Aeration and filtration are important aids as they help to keep an aquarium in good condition over a long period. In general, a properly functioning, cleanly maintained filter is usually also sufficient to supply the tank with air. Now and again, however, supplementary aeration becomes necessary, particularly when breeding is being attempted or when for some reason the fish population is larger than the tank would warrant.

The task of aeration is not primarily to provide the fish and plants with oxygen from the ascending air bubbles, but much more importantly, to move the water around so that new layers are brought to the surface, where oxygen can enter. The air stream also serves to drive off excess carbon dioxide. Many fish and plants enjoy moving water and in a heated tank the aeration helps water layers of slightly different temperatures to mix together.

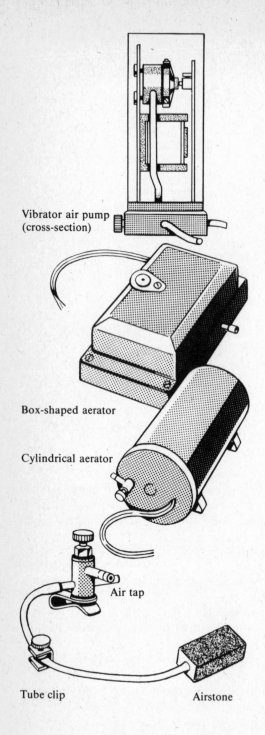

Vibrator air pump
(cross-section)

Box-shaped aerator

Cylindrical aerator

Air tap

Tube clip

Airstone

Most aeration and filtration equipment is driven by air pressure. This principle has long been known in aquarium circles, for the first rather primitive aids were air pumps worked by water or even by hand.

Nowadays various forms of electrical aerator are used. For a few small tanks an electrically driven diaphragm pump is normally quite sufficient, and various sizes are available. Using the smallest sizes it is not usually possible to drive the aeration and filtration at the same time, but for small tanks filtration alone is usually sufficient. Small diaphragm pumps should not be overworked, as this produces a disturbing noise. When buying an air pump it is best to choose one that is rated slightly on the high side. For larger aquarium establishments an electrically driven piston pump or compressor should be used. To avoid damage most air pumps should be driven at a minimum rating.

The air lines to the filter or diffuser can consist mainly of plastic tubing. Inside the tank itself the air line to the diffuser should be of glass tubing. The air supply from a diaphragm pump is controlled by a small air tap or clamp.

A diffuser, or air stone, normally of kieselguhr, is fixed at the end of the air line. This is an inexpensive item which can easily be cleaned from time to time by boiling it in water. Plastic diffusers are also marketed but tend to have a shorter life than the natural stone versions.

One good method of filtration involves circulating the water. A small, almost noiseless, special pump sucks water out of the aquarium tank and into a filter chamber. The water passes through the filter and back into the aquarium. This type of filtration produces powerful water movements and may produce too much turbulence. This can be mitigated by fitting a spray bar above the water surface. The water returning from the filter passes through fine openings in the spray bar and out on to the water surface, taking air with it. Strong aeration is often an advantage as, for instance, in breeding certain fish species.

Filtration

Filters

Filtration can play an important part in keeping an aquarium in perfect condition over a long period. The filter is powered by some form of air pump (see above) and uses a relatively large amount of air. The pump must be fairly powerful if it has to serve several filters. With really efficient filtration the tank water can be kept crystal-clear the whole time and completely without smell. In addition, filtration through certain materials, such as peat, can influence the character of the water.

There are two filtration systems, using either an internal filter or an external filter.

In an internal filter a plastic box filled with a suitable medium is suspended on the inside of the tank, near the top, or sunk into the substrate. The medium can be of synthetic fibre, such as nylon wool. In these filters water is drawn by compressed air from the tank into the filter box. The water brings with it waste particles which are deposited on the filter medium. On no account should glass wool be used as a medium as it tends to shed tiny particles of glass which damage the fish, particularly their delicate gills. Synthetic fibres do not rot and they are easy to clean. This type of mechanical filter removes insoluble, coarse and fine waste particles and to a certain extent prevents the accumulation of injurious products of decomposition. Nevertheless, from time to time it is necessary to remove a certain amount of mulm by sucking or siphoning it out. Dissolved waste derived from the metabolism of the fish is not removed by this type of filtration.

A bottom filter is merely another type of internal filter which uses the substrate as a filter medium, but in practice it is not very efficient. It has been shown that such a filter may lead to stagnation and decomposition.

With an external filter the aquarium water passes first through a layer of synthetic fibre and then over gravel or activated charcoal. This cleans the water, again mechanically, and it is then moved back into the tank by air

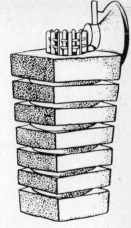

A square type of filter (can also be round)

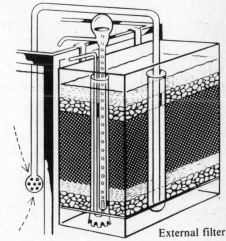

External filter

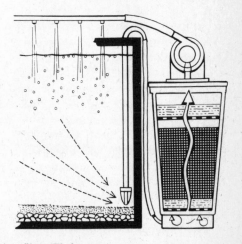

Suction filter (Eheim type)

pressure. Large particles are trapped by the synthetic fibres, which must be frequently cleaned.

In spite of the information already given, the best filter medium of all is gravel, particularly quartz gravel. This is calcium-free and so can be used in tanks that are filled with soft, slightly acid water. Naturally, other types of gravel can be used when the composition of the water is not critical. The gravel particles should each have a diameter of 2–3 mm, as anything finer tends to pack too closely. Used in conjunction with a top layer of synthetic fibres a gravel filter at first functions mechanically, removing coarser, insoluble particles of mulm. Later on it works as a biological filter once nitrifying bacteria have colonized the gravel. This type of filtration is fully efficient after two to three weeks, when the bacteria are fully active.

A biological filter of this type must be handled with care. The covering layer of synthetic fibre must be cleaned very frequently or renewed. On the other hand, the main contents of the filter should seldom be cleaned, because this would disturb the activities of the bacteria, which are busy breaking down waste matter. A biological filter must never be allowed to become dry. When drugs are used to combat fish diseases in the aquarium the filter should be disconnected but not allowed to dry out. It can be allowed to continue its activities in a water-filled bucket until the drugs have been eliminated from the aquarium by water changes. Otherwise the drugs would kill the bacteria in the filter.

Activated charcoal is no longer as highly regarded as a filter medium as it was at one time. It certainly removes coloured substances from the water, as for instance after the use of drugs, and it also removes chlorine. This can render the water clear and without smell, but troublesome products of protein degradation, such as ammonia and nitrate, are not removed, so the uses of activated charcoal are limited. Also, although the charcoal acts mechanically to remove coarse waste particles, it quickly becomes overloaded and useless.

Finally, it should be stressed that all filters of whatever type should be kept in continuous operation without interruption.

Apart from filtration a regular, partial change of water (not more than one-fifth in a tank with soft, slightly acid water) is of at least equal value, and so is a healthy growth of plants.

Filters with a different medium can also be used to change the character of the water. Peat filtration is widely used in both internal and external filters, using about 1 litre (0·22 gal) of peat per 50 litres (11 gals) of water. The best peat is one that is rich in humic acids, without any added manure or other fertilizer. It should be steeped in water, squeezed out and packed fairly firmly in the filter box.

One final point. In some cases filtration may only slightly enrich the tank water with oxygen. When a filter has been used for a long time the bacteria settled in the filter medium consume the oxygen in the water. More aeration will then be required. Aeration can be enhanced if the mixture of air and water is allowed to fall back on to the surface of the aquarium water from a horizontal spray bar, described under 'Aeration' earlier in this chapter.

Lighting

Artificial lighting has contributed a great deal to the spread of the aquarium hobby. In particular it frees the aquarist from the difficulties experienced in earlier days owing to seasonal fluctuations in light. This is no longer a problem, as the aquarium is not now dependent upon daylight coming through a window, but can be lit for at least twelve hours daily, so that the plants are able to grow luxuriantly. It is easier to maintain the aquarium, too, because the period of lighting can be easily controlled. Another advantage, of course, is that electric lighting enables the aquarium and its inmates to be observed during the evening hours. Of course the value of natural light and

occasional sunshine should not be underestimated; they are of particular value to the breeder and to the plant specialist, but even here, electric lighting is a useful back-up during dark times of the year.

The light sources used today are tungsten lamps and fluorescent tubes. By a combination of various types these lamps can be used to promote plant growth and at the same time

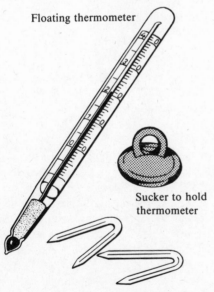

Floating thermometer

Sucker to hold thermometer

Needles to hold plants in the substrate

combat the spread of troublesome algae. Specific advice on the actual amount of light required cannot be given here, as this depends upon many different factors and requires a certain amount of experimentation on the part of the aquarist.

With artificial lighting the colours of fish do not always appear completely natural. Probably the best way to enhance the colours, in fact, would be to light them from the front, but this is scarcely practicable. For smaller tanks ordinary tungsten lamps are perfectly satisfactory, and these can be used together with fluorescent lamps to give special effects. To some extent tungsten lamps bring out the natural colours of the fish quite well, and they also encourage plant growth. However, they have one disadvantage in that they only produce about 5 per cent of their energy as light, the rest being heat, and are therefore uneconomical. They are, however, sufficient for occasional lighting, for instance in the evening for a tank that receives natural light during the day.

All light sources, whether tungsten or fluorescent, must be fitted in reflectors which should be as near as possible the same length as the tank, as in this way the aquarium is fully lit and loss of light avoided. A good handyman can quite easily make a satisfactory reflector, but they are also widely available in aquarium shops. Care must be taken not to fit reflectors too far from the water surface, as light is rapidly lost with increasing distance, but they must not be too close as the coverglass may break if it becomes too hot.

Fluorescent lights are more economical than tungsten lamps. Since they convert considerably more energy into light, a tank can be lit for a much longer period with the same expenditure of current. The initial outlay on fluorescent lights is higher because they need a choke and starter, but this is a once-only expenditure and the replacement lamps themselves are not expensive. The life of a fluorescent lamp varies considerably, between about 1,500 and 5,000 hours, and the output of light decreases with time. The light value of fluorescent lamps varies too, and specific types are available for aquaria use. The choice of lamps is important, particularly if plant growth is valued. Specialist shops can normally recommend the best type for aquarists because of many years of experience of their practical application. It is better not to use a single type, but to combine several different ones, such as 'daylight', 'warm white de luxe' and certain 'white lights'. Lights which are designed to encourage plant growth, such as Grolux (Sylvania) or Fluora (Osman) should only be used in combination with other types of fluorescent tube.

Miscellaneous

Transparent plastic bags are widely used for the transport of fish and live food, because they are light and easy to carry. When packed in cartons they are even used for transporting fish by rail or air, and they have, of course, largely replaced the metal cans once used. If the latter are used they must be well painted. Fish should never be carried in unpainted metal containers; zinc and aluminium are particularly dangerous.

Nets are useful to the aquarist who catches his own live food. For small catches one can make a simple net by stretching fine-mesh synthetic material over a small hoop. For larger operations the aquarist needs two or more nets of different mesh sizes and a handle that can be taken apart into sections. These items are available on the market.

Food trays made of wood or plastic with fine gauze bottoms are useful for transporting damp live food. Several such trays can be carried in a transport box.

For feeding, plastic or wooden rings that float on the surface of the tank are useful, as not only do they prevent dried food from spreading over the surface of the tank water, but they also get the fish used to feeding in one particular place. For feeding with *Tubifex* and whiteworms, special food rings are made,

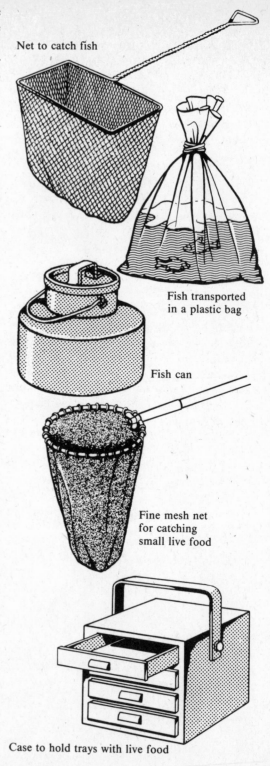

Net to catch fish

Fish transported in a plastic bag

Fish can

Fine mesh net for catching small live food

Case to hold trays with live food

which are fitted with a small sieve; the worms wriggle through the holes to reach the water.

A set of sieves with different mesh sizes is very useful too, for sorting live and dried food according to size.

Nets for catching fish are absolutely essential. The netting should be of green or colourless synthetic material with a coarse mesh, for example mosquito netting, and the frame should be oblong so that it can catch fish that retreat into a corner of the tank. In large tanks the best way to catch fish is to use either two nets or one net and a fry-catching bell or pipe. The latter is made of clear plastic or glass and is used to catch fish fry or delicate adult fishes.

Plastic or rubber tubing with a diameter of 8–15 mm (0·3–0·6 in) is used both for filling the tank and for removing water. If the tubing is too narrow it may easily become blocked by small stones or plant fragments. When used for sucking up mulm the tubing should be fitted with a mulm bell of plastic or glass. This separates the mulm from the heavier particles of substrate. A mud lifter is useful for removing mud in a small tank.

A glass-cleaner fitted with an old razor blade can be used for cleaning the aquarium glass, or an aquarium supplier will sell you a special glass-cleaner consisting of two magnets. The magnet on the outside of the glass holds the second magnet on the inside of the tank in position so that the two can be moved up and down together. The inner magnet incorporates a piece of felt or mild abrasive cloth which removes algae from the inside of the glass.

Small glass rods are useful for anchoring plants that tend to be buoyant or those that have been recently moved and are not yet properly rooted. Plants may also be anchored by wrapping around the roots artificial 'plastic lead', or heavy plastic weights, obtained from angling shops.

There are various types of aquarium thermometer on the market, but the most useful are those that can be attached by a sucker to one of the glass panes.

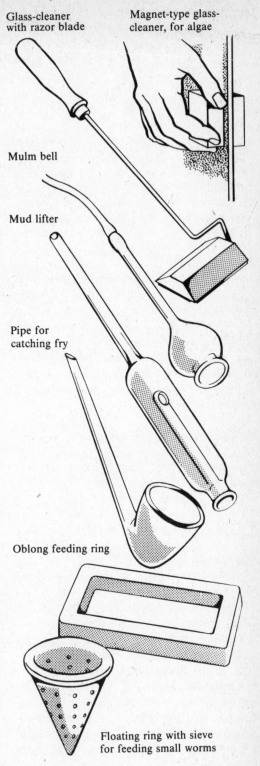

Glass-cleaner with razor blade

Magnet-type glass-cleaner, for algae

Mulm bell

Mud lifter

Pipe for catching fry

Oblong feeding ring

Floating ring with sieve for feeding small worms

Chemical processes
in water

Water provides the living environment for both fish and aquatic plants, and thus the successful maintenance of an aquarium depends first and foremost upon the quality of the water. As already mentioned, a newly installed aquarium must be allowed to stand for some days before the fish are introduced. In most cases the tank will be filled with tap water from the mains or fresh water from a natural source.

Mains water, which is delivered under pressure, usually contains excess atmospheric air, which appears in the form of numerous tiny air bubbles. This air and any chlorine that has been added to the water as a disinfectant will soon escape.

Natural water in an aquarium frequently develops large numbers of microscopic organisms, such as floating algae, infusorians and bacteria, and these cause cloudiness. However, the mass proliferation of these organisms is actually self-defeating; they soon die from lack of sufficient oxygen and nutrient, and the cloudiness disappears. Another type of cloudiness sometimes appears if insufficient care has been taken when filling the tank and particles have been washed out of the lower layer of the substrate, but this also soon disappears.

After a few days the appearance of the water changes, from a clear bluish colour to a very pale yellow. It has now become aquarium water, that is, the living processes of the water plants and the microscopic life have begun to interact and the water has reached what the aquarist calls 'biological equilibrium'. In natural waters there is a self-regulating mutual dependence in which several factors are involved. In the aquarium, however, the form of equilibrium established depends largely upon the aquarist.

The fish are introduced into the aquarium after a waiting period of four to seven days, during which time the plants will also have had a chance to take root in the substrate. The fish will start to settle down, and in most cases will not be dependent upon the composition of the water unless an attempt is being made to breed, in which case the character of the water is vitally important.

Water is a chemical compound of the elements hydrogen (H) and oxygen (O). A single molecule of water contains two atoms of hydrogen closely bound to one atom of oxygen to give the chemical formula H_2O. Such very pure water is not found in nature, but can be produced in the laboratory to give distilled water. Almost pure water can be produced with the help of certain synthetic resins.

In the wild, various substances are dissolved in the water. The process of solution can be seen when a spoonful of cooking salt (sodium chloride = NaCl) is put into a glass of water. On stirring, the salt crystals disappear, and do so even more rapidly if the water is warm. In chemical terms the salt has now broken up into microscopic units, known as ions. When a direct electric current is passed through the water, the ions, according to their electric charge, pass to the pole with the opposite charge. Thus, the electrically positive sodium ions pass to the negative electric pole and the negative chlorine ions to the positive pole. In this way, by the process of electrolysis, the elements chlorine and sodium can be obtained in pure form at the poles.

Of the many substances that can be found dissolved in water the easiest to observe is the salt in sea water, which can so readily be tasted. The fresh waters of rivers and lakes do not have this salty taste and these are the waters with which the freshwater aquarist is concerned.

Even in fresh water, however, there are certain dissolved substances, but their composition and concentration are not the same as those in the sea. In inland waters, and also in mains water, chlorides (e.g. sodium chloride) play a very minor role, and so do sulphates, which are usually only present in very small amounts. In inland fresh waters, however, the important substances are compounds of calcium (Ca), carbon (C) and oxygen (O). These compounds are calcium carbonate ($CaCO_3$) and calcium bicarbonate $Ca(HCO_3)_2$. It is mainly calcium bicarbonate that is found dissolved in fresh water, while calcium carbonate is not very soluble.

So, in addition to certain other compounds, the principal substance in solution is calcium bicarbonate. There is also dissolved oxygen, carbon dioxide and other constituents of air. The oxygen dissolved in water is used in the respiration of aquatic animals and plants. Carbonic acid (H_2CO_3), closely associated with the carbonates, also plays an important role.

Aquatic animals and plants not only respire, but also, as a result of the unique process of plant assimilation, they develop an important mutual relationship. The respiration of the aquatic animals produces carbon dioxide, which is an important plant nutrient, while the plants release oxygen. The assimilation activity of the plants also plays an important part in the decalcification of the water. This involves the splitting of dissolved calcium bicarbonate which releases carbonic acid and water, leaving behind calcium carbonate, which is mostly precipitated. In the wild the latter is seen as a chalky deposit in standing waters. The freshly precipitated calcium can also be seen as a deposit on the leaves of underwater plants, which feel quite rough. In the aquarium, however, such deposits do not normally occur.

When washing the hands with soap some waters will produce a lather with very little soap; these are soft waters. In other waters a considerable amount of soap may be required to produce a lather; these waters are hard. The hardness of a water depends upon the amounts of calcium and magnesium salts dissolved in it. Hard waters are rich in these compounds, soft waters are poor. There are two kinds of hardness, namely bicarbonate or temporary hardness, which can be removed by boiling, and permanent hardness, which cannot be removed by boiling.

Temporary hardness plus permanent hardness equals 'total hardness'. The measurement of total hardness is expressed in degress of hardness, and two systems are used. In the British/American system the hardness is expressed as parts per million of calcium carbonate ($CaCO_3$). Thus, one British/American degree = $14 \cdot 3$ parts per million of calcium carbonate. In the German system the hardness is expressed as parts per million of calcium oxide (CaO). Thus, one German degree of hardness (1 °dH) is $17 \cdot 9$ parts per million of calcium oxide. This is the system most commonly used in aquarium work.

In practice:

```
 0– 4 °dH = very soft water
 4– 8 °dH = soft water
 8–12 °dH = medium-hard water
12–18 °dH = hard water
18–30 °dH = very hard water
30 °dH and over = extremely hard water.
```

Temporary hardness has an important function in that it buffers the water. This means that the bicarbonate neutralizes the effects of excess alkali or of acid, and so keeps the pH (see below) at a level that will not endanger living organisms.

In normal waters bicarbonate hardness is responsible for most of the total hardness, and it is an important factor in the maintenance and breeding of tropical fish. It is, therefore, important to determine the proportion of bicarbonate hardness within the total hardness. For example, two waters with the same total hardness may be very different in their physiological actions, depending upon the amount of bicarbonate hardness relative to noncarbonate or permanent hardness.

Special kits are available on the aquarium market for measuring both the total hardness and the bicarbonate hardness. These produce a more accurate result than some of the older methods of measuring hardness.

In general, hard water is more fruitful than soft, which means that plant and animal life in hard water find better living conditions than in soft, possibly acid water. Anyone who has been out to collect his own live food will know that a pond in a peaty area is much poorer in small organisms than a village pond. Apart from the dissolved carbonates the productivity depends also on the presence of trace elements in extremely small amounts. For aquarium purposes there is no need to check on the presence of these substances. They are almost always present in sufficient amounts, unless the water comes from a very poor area.

A pH indicator kit

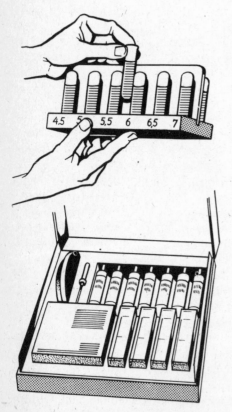

Laboratory kit for determination of total water hardness, carbonate hardness, pH value and nitrite content

Although hard waters are, in general, more productive than soft, there are exceptions. This is particularly so in the case of some fish and plants from tropical waters, which are largely supplied by rainwater. Such waters are very soft, and the organisms living in them have become adapted to these conditions, so difficulties can arise when they are kept in water that is too hard, particularly if breeding is to be attempted. Eggs and fry may then be sensitive to infections by bacteria and infusorians.

The acidity of a water can be determined quite easily. Natural waters may be acid, neutral or alkaline. These reactions can be expressed numerically by the pH value [*pondus Hydrogenii* = weight of water]. The pH is the concentration of free hydroxyl ions (OH$^-$) and free hydrogen ions (H$^+$) in a litre of water. The hydrogen ions determine the acid character of a water, the hydroxyl ions its alkalinity. Depending upon the relation between these two ions the water may be neutral (equal numbers of H$^+$ and OH$^-$ ions), acid or alkaline. In neutral water the hydrogen ion concentration is 10^{-7}.

In practice the hydrogen ion concentration figure is not used. Instead, its logarithm is used and this is the pH value, thus:

pH 7 = neutral water
pH less than 7 gives acid water
pH greater than 7 gives alkaline water.

For aquarium work the following table can be used:

pH 1–3, very strongly acid, unsuitable for fish breeding
pH 3–5, only suitable for fish breeding in exceptional cases
pH 5–6, slightly acid, only suitable for fish breeding in a few species
pH 6–6·9, very slightly acid, suitable for breeding a few 'black-water fish'
pH 7, neutral, suitable for breeding most fish species

pH 7·1–8, very slightly alkaline, suitable for breeding many fish species

pH 8–9, slightly alkaline, scarcely suitable for ornamental fish breeding

pH 9–10, alkaline, unsuitable for fish breeding, injurious to most fish

pH 10–14, strongly alkaline, very dangerous to fish.

The pH value can fluctuate. If the water is well buffered by the presence of sufficient bicarbonate, the pH value will be near the neutral point or very slightly acid or very slightly alkaline. Many fish from the temperate zone are almost always adapted to about pH 7 and do not tolerate large fluctuations. On the other hand, certain tropical fish will tolerate a reduction in pH into the acid region without any difficulty. High pH values are dangerous for all fish. In the summer an aquarium tank in strong sunlight with dense vegetation may develop pH values of 8–10 or over. If this happens the tank should immediately be shaded and a proportion of the water changed. This dangerous situation would not arise with artificial lighting.

There are various ways of determining the pH of water. A superficial reading can be obtained with indicator papers, but this method is inexact, and very accurate readings can be obtained using an electric pH meter, but this is too expensive for aquarium work. However, a pH kit, using an indicator solution, is inexpensive and reasonably accurate, and is available on the aquarium market. A few drops of indicator solution are put into a test-tube with some of the water being investigated. After shaking, the colour produced is compared with a scale of colours provided with the kit. Each colour in the scale represents a pH value.

In general, the mains water supply is not natural surface water, but often comes from rivers or from below the ground-water level. For reasons of hygiene it is sometimes treated in some way. If this merely involves adjusting the hardness, it may actually improve the water's suitability for aquarium use, but water treated with chlorine cannot be used immediately in the aquarium. Such water will probably have the characteristic smell of chlorine gas. Fortunately the chlorine soon disappears when the water is allowed to stand for a few hours, and the warmer the water the more rapidly it escapes. A tank containing only sand and plants, but no fish, will soon lose any trace of chlorine, and filtration through activated charcoal will remove the chlorine even more rapidly.

Mains water that has been used in an aquarium does not remain in its original condition; it is continually changing, and it is up to the aquarist to control the usually unfavourable changes so that the fish and plants do not suffer damage. Special attention should be paid to compounds of nitrogen which are derived from the protein in food, from food remains, from the natural excretions of the fish and from dead organic materials. The substances produced are first ammonia, and then nitrites and nitrates, which it is scarcely possible to remove from aquarium water. The aquatic plants, if they are growing well, use a proportion of these nitrogenous compounds as nutrient, but they cannot use them all. A build-up of nitrogenous waste is likely to occur when the tank has too many fish that are being overfed and the filter needs cleaning. The end product of protein degradation is mainly nitrate. Many fish can become accustomed to a high content of nitrate, but they appear to suffer a loss of vitality and readiness to breed. There is also a chance that chemical reduction may take place with the formation of very undesirable ammonia. This is relatively harmless as long as the pH value of the water is in the acid range. If, however, an acid water is replaced by large amounts of alkaline water, the situation is radically changed. Very dangerous free ammonia will be produced in increasing amounts the more alkaline the water becomes. This may account for the apparently unexplained mass mortality of aquarium fish following a too radical change of water. It is best to change not more than one-third to one-fifth of the water every week.

As nitrate is so difficult to remove from the aquarium, the aquarist must try to prevent its accumulation. The following practices should help:

1. Avoid overstocking the aquarium tank.
2. Only feed as much as will be consumed, leaving no food remains.
3. Immediately remove all dead animals and plants.
4. Remove up to $\frac{1}{5}$–$\frac{1}{3}$ of the tank water once a week and replace with fresh water at the same temperature.

Decaying food remains and dead animals and plants may lead to the formation of hydrogen sulphide, which has an unmistakable smell of rotten eggs. This dangerous fish poison is formed particularly in the substrate when it is too closely packed, or when the animals in it, such as snails and *Tubifex* worms, die.

In the aquarium all forms of decomposition are associated with oxygen deficiency, which gives rise to bacteria that consume oxygen. In such cases the fish naturally rise to the water surface in an attempt to make up for the lack of oxygen.

Similar symptoms are caused by ammonia poisoning which will also cause the fish to start snapping up air at the surface. In such cases even vigorous aeration will not be of much use, and a partial change of water must be carried out very quickly.

Preparation
of aquarium water

The available water is not always suitable for the aquarium, particularly when breeding ornamental fish. In the past it was often found that a particular fish species would readily breed in one area but, in spite of great care, not in another. This was because the composition of the water in the second area was unsuitable, and it was not until aquarists learned how to adjust the water composition that such problems were overcome.

It must be remembered that all the fish now kept in the aquarium are the result of thousands of years of evolution and adaptation, and naturally the composition of the water has played a vitally important rôle in this process. Since they come from so many different countries and environments it is self-evident that the requirements of each fish species are different. One has only to envisage the environments: clear mountain streams, large rivers, waters in the lowlands, in the coastal zone, in marshes, all with different compositions and different temperatures. To keep and breed fish successfully it is essential to find out about the living requirements of the individual species.

Although it is true that very many species can be kept and bred in ordinary mains water, either because they are very adaptable or because the composition of the water corresponds with their own requirements, some species need rather more care. At one time these were known as 'problem fish', but nowadays it is recognized that many tropical fish require soft, slightly acid water for breeding, and such water can be produced relatively easily.

If the available water is unsuitable for breeding, suitable water can be found in springs or other sources and then checked with chemical reagents. However, if the search for an appropriate natural water is unsuccessful, the aquarist must alter the available water, either chemically or by other means. He can either distil the water or, using artificial resins, partially or completely de-ionize it. Rainwater can also be used.

If rainwater is used it must not be affected by air pollution, so it is best not to collect it until there has been a good hour of heavy downpour, which will have removed most of the impurities. Rain from tarred roofs or tarred rainwater barrels must not be used. The

74

rain should be collected in a plastic or wooden bath, and the yield can be considerably increased by using a stretched plastic sheet for collecting the water.

Distilled water can be used if it has been produced in glass apparatus, but some normal water must always be added to it because it is completely sterile, and in its pure form cannot sustain fish and plants. It is also very expensive, particularly if there are several tanks with a large capacity.

Distilled water can be obtained from chemists' shops and petrol stations (where it is sold for use in car batteries); school science laboratories may also have supplies.

Water hardness can be removed using artificial resins. Before doing this the water should be tested to determine its hardness. In most waters 80 per cent of the total hardness is carbonate hardness, and it is sufficient to remove the carbonate (by partial de-ionization) as it is the part of total hardness that is physiologically significant.

Filtration through acid peat can help to reduce hardness as well as acidifying the water. Peat-filtered water is practically free of infusorians and is very close in character to tropical black water. It is a valuable aid to the ornamental fish breeder, particularly if the fish concerned are sensitive to bacteria. Peat provides the water with humins and humic acids which are beneficial to the fish and certain plants. It also acidifies the water, but only after filtration has removed the carbonate hardness. A great advantage is that the peat holds the pH on the acid side, provided other producers of hardness (e.g. calcareous substrates) are not introduced into the tank. Peat usually imparts colour to the water, which may reduce the amount of light reaching the plants, but if this happens the colour can be removed by an activated charcoal filter.

It should be kept in mind that the plants selected for an aquarium may also require certain conditions of water hardness and acidity, and these must be compatible with the needs of the fish. Plants that grow in the fishes' natural habitat are first choice.

Fish diseases

Like other animals, fish suffer from numerous ailments. Few of these can be cured, and even when they can, the treatments are complex and sometimes expensive. Thus the aquarist should always follow the basic principle that prevention is better than cure.

The following guidelines in particular should be observed:

1. Always ensure that the fish feel at ease. Robust, well-fed animals which are kept warm and whose needs are attended to are more resistant to illness.

2. Always keep fish which have recently been acquired in a separate container and observe them there before putting them in with other fish. Even if they show no obvious symptoms, they may nonetheless be carriers of disease.

3. Do not collect live food from ponds stocked with fish, and never feed live food from the container in which it has been collected. Keep the live food for a time in a separate container and use a tube to withdraw the portion to be fed. Parasites and disease germs often settle on the bottom and on the sides, and free-floating parasitic spores usually die after a few hours or days if they find no host.

4. Ensure that the aquarium tank has been properly constructed, remembering that metallic salts and some constituents of aquarium sealants can cause mass deaths.

5. Avoid sudden temperature fluctuations and do not move the fish around unnecessarily.

6. When using aeration make sure that no injurious gases, e.g. flue gas, waste gases from factories and fly spray, are pumped into the tank.

7. If the entire fish stock in a tank is ailing, take drastic measures. Throw away the substrate and plants, fill the tank with a solution of potassium permanganate and leave for several days. Disinfect all items of equipment, such as heaters, aerator, tubing and nets, then clean them with a brush and rinse.

8. If there is an outbreak of disease, ask an experienced aquarist or dealer whether a suitable preparation is available on the market.

9. Isolate sick fish immediately so that others are not infected.

General symptoms

The aquarist who is in the habit of watching his stock for long periods can usually tell at a glance whether his fish are behaving normally and are therefore healthy or whether they show any symptoms that suggest disease.

Depending upon the species every fish has its own characteristic way of moving. Fish such as characins and barbs, which are normally lively, show symptoms of ailing by a tendency to be less active. Surface-living species, such as egg-laying toothcarps, move down to the bottom of the tank or in among the plants when ailing, whereas bottom-living species, such as catfish, come to the surface. Loss of appetite can give cause for concern, so fish should be carefully watched when feeding, but this is not a completely reliable symptom, as some diseases do not affect the appetite at all.

When a fish folds its fins against the body it is very likely that all is not well. Fins held in this way, particularly the caudal fins, may indicate infection by external or internal parasites. If a fish repeatedly rubs itself against the rockwork this suggests an attack by skin or gill parasites. Rocking, rolling or vigorous jumping movements may be due to a variety of causes, but they always indicate disease of some kind. Sometimes a fish makes continuous efforts to reach the surface but repeatedly sinks back to the bottom; this suggests a disease of the swimbladder. If it remains motionless on the bottom for a long period it may possibly be suffering from constipation resulting from an over-rich or unbalanced diet. Warmth-loving fish often lie close to the bottom near the heater, and this also suggests that they are ailing.

Some fish species, such as angelfish and some of the North American sunfish, are particularly susceptible to a kind of spasm. For no apparent reason some kind of shock results in the fish darting about wildly, suffering spasms and then lying on its side on the bottom, usually with the fins widely spread. In serious cases this can be fatal, but usually the fish recovers after a time and is quite normal. This type of behaviour may also occur among fish which for months before have been quite unaffected by maintenance taking place in the tank. It may possibly be due to an accumulation of toxic and waste substances in the tank, for the symptoms often disappear after a partial change of water or if the water is properly filtered.

Toxic substances introduced into the tank by animals or plants may also damage or even kill aquarium fish, for example, the tropical water plant *Limnophila indica* releases a very powerful toxin if it is damaged in any way. Snails may also release similar substances. In the case of tropical snails this has not yet been proved, but the European freshwater snail *Radix peregra* is known to release poisons. In any case, indigenous snails should not be kept with tropical fish as they are often the intermediate hosts of fish parasites.

The leaves of the cypress *Thuja occidentalis*, and to a lesser extent pine needles, contain essential oils which are toxic to fish, so great care must be taken when using pond water which might contain such leaves, and outdoor tanks should never be sited close to such trees.

Nicotine is also dangerous. Small aquarium fish can be killed in a few minutes in a solution of 5–10 mg nicotine per litre of water. Weaker concentrations result in crippling. Experienced aquarists believe that fish can be poisoned if tobacco smoke is constantly fed into the water by the aeration pump, and the same is true of waste gas from coal (carbon monoxide), fly spray and methylated spirits. Rotting food that has lain in the tank for several days, dead fish and other aquatic animals cause oxygen deficiency during decomposition and also produce toxic hydrogen sulphide gas (H_2S). The products of protein decomposition, particularly nitrogenous compounds (ammonia, nitrites, nitrates) may be harmful in different degrees. Ammonia is a particularly lethal poison, and is the main cause of fish deaths in badly maintained tanks.

As with some internal ailments, poisoning may result in fish being unable to swim normally. They move unsteadily, turn around on their own axes, drift with tails up or float at the surface snapping for air.

Changes on the body surface often indicate illness. Ailing fish are sometimes pale, with their colours less intense, and unusual stripes and markings may appear. Dark coloration may be caused by an eye disease, and blinding in one eye sometimes results in darkening of part of the body, while the rest of the body retains its normal coloration. Protruding scales are always a sign of illness, and so is skin discoloration, often only seen at first in certain lights, but later developing as a cloudy film over the skin and fins. White nodules, up to 1 mm in diameter, scattered irregularly over the body surface and skin, are a symptom of white-spot disease *(Ichthyophthirius)*, although there are other nodule-forming diseases that are easily confused with white-spot.

Bloody markings on a fish also indicate the presence of animal or plant parasites, whereas bite wounds are usually whitish, as though covered in fungus. White, woolly films on the skin are due to aquatic fungi *(Saprolegnia)*, and these may also infect the cornea of the

eye and the area around the mouth. Such fungal attacks are usually the result of mechanical injury. Even more dangerous is an infestation by parasitic fungi that penetrate beneath the scales and attack the muscles.

Particular attention should always be given to protruding gill-covers. If the gills project beyond the edges of the gill-covers, are yellowish-white and swollen with yellow or often bloody areas, then gill parasites are present. Dark red gills suggest a risk of asphyxiation, and if this happens the gill-covers will be widely spread.

A markedly concave belly is a sure sign of well-advanced disease. This is not due to malnutrition, but usually indicates the presence of external parasites or, less often, of intestinal parasites.

A bloated body with protruding scales and eyes indicates dropsy, while an angular shape to the body or bumps on the surface suggests the presence of parasitic worms.

Two of the most dangerous fish diseases are unfortunately extremely difficult to diagnose, and then only when it is already too late. These are *Ichthyosporidium (Ichthyophonus)* disease and fish tuberculosis. Their symptoms are very similar and they can only be diagnosed with certainty by an expert. Fish infected with these diseases often show skin damage, areas suffused with blood, sores, folded and frayed fins and so on. Periods of obvious discomfort alternate with periods of completely normal behaviour. The fish stock does not become ill on an epidemic scale, but individuals die one after the other at varying intervals. These two diseases have so far proved incurable.

The principal fish diseases

Various remedies for fish diseases are available on the market. These appear under many different brand names, but will not be given in the following recommendations, which are traditional ones. The brand remedies are often just as effective as the traditional ones, and sometimes even more so, and they are frequently easier to use. Thus it is a wise policy to consult an expert first about the latest and best preparations.

Infectious skin ailments

Irritation of the skin, fins and gills caused by various pathogens can be healed quite easily if treated promptly, but if neglected it can prove fatal. It may be caused by the following animal parasites:

Trichodina (= Cyclochaeta) disease:

This ciliate parasite has a ring of fine hook-like fixation organs. It moves continuously, with a rotating motion, and gradually causes serious injury to the skin and gills. In most cases the gills are attacked first and the infection then spreads to the skin, which develops a bluish-white film. In the later stages some areas are suffused with blood. This infection can be cured, but may prove fatal if neglected.

The infection is spread by infected fish or by live food. The parasite can live for a long time, even without finding a host.

Treatment is by baths. The fish are put into a separate container, not of metal. First of all give a single fish the recommended bath, as a test. For a salt bath dissolve 10–15 g of common salt in one litre of water, and raise the temperature by about 2 °C (4 °F). Keep the fish in the bath for twenty minutes; this is known as a short bath. Alternatively, the fish can be given a short formalin bath at a slightly increased temperature: carefully mix 2–4 ml formalin with 10 litres (2·2 gals) of water.

A prolonged bath with trypaflavin, if possible in a separate container and not in the aquarium tank, is highly recommended. Make up a solution of 1 g trypaflavin in ½ litre (0·9 pint) of water and use this amount for every 100 litres (22 gals) of tank capacity. After about the fourth day, filter the water until clear. Plants, snails and particularly sensitive fish may be damaged by this treatment.

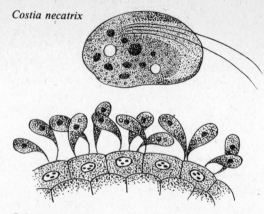

Costia necatrix

Colony of *Costia* on the skin of a fish, much enlarged

Costia disease:

This is caused by a microscopic flagellate which generally attacks the skin, less frequently the gills. There is relatively slight discoloration of the skin, otherwise the symptoms are similar to those given for *Trichodina* disease. The fish frequently rub themselves against the rockwork and make see-sawing movements, indicating discomfort. This disease is rarely seen in the aquarium. It can be cured, but in large-scale attacks may prove fatal if not treated, preferably with a prolonged trypaflavin bath.

Chilodonella disease:

A ciliate, usually heart-shaped, that attacks the skin and gills. The skin appears bluish-white. The disease first attacks fish which have been inadequately cared for, but may infect healthy specimens, particularly in overstocked tanks. The fish rub against hard surfaces and fold their fins. In the more advanced stages the skin thickens and pieces peel off. When the gills become heavily infected the fish float at the surface and gasp for air. With prompt treatment this disease can be cured, but is fatal if neglected.

Treatment is the same as for *Trichodina*. Leave the aquarium tank without fish for five to six days so that the parasites die.

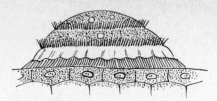

Cychlochaeta domerguei

Chilodonella cyprini

Skin trematodes (species of *Gyrodactylus*):

These trematodes are just under 1 mm in length, with two lobes at the front end and no eyes. They are viviparous.

Infected fish have a whitish film on the skin in which the movements of the tiny worms can be seen with a magnifying lens. In fairly serious attacks the fish show clear signs of distress.

The condition can be cured, using short baths of salt or formalin (see above under *Trichodina*). Tanks without fish are free of the parasites within about a week.

Gill trematodes (species of *Dactylogyrus*):

These trematodes are just under 1 mm in length, usually with four lobes at the front end and four black dot-like eyes. They are oviparous.

They almost exclusively infect the gills, and in serious cases the gill-covers are widely spread and the fish gasps for air. Sometimes only single worms are present, and this does not affect the host. Serious attacks only occur when the fish is in a weakened condition. Infections can be treated as given under *Trichodina*.

White-spot disease *(Ichthyophthirius)*:

This is a very common disease of the skin and gills which can usually, but not always, be cured quite easily.

The pathogen is the ciliate protozoan *Ichthyophthirius multifiliis,* which reaches a length of up to 1 mm, relatively large for a single cell. The parasite, which is covered by cilia, is remarkable when seen under the microscope, for it progresses with a constant rotating movement. The cell has a characteristic, usually pale, horseshoe-shaped nucleus.

Propagation is by free-swimming spores which must find a host within about fifty hours if they are to survive. On reaching the host they bore into the skin and even further. There they appear as white, gritty nodules. At a normal aquarium temperature of 24–27 °C (75–80 °F) the parasites leave the host fish after about five to seven days and sink to the bottom where each one forms a capsule around itself. Within the capsule 250–1,000 free-swimming spores are produced after only a few hours. The free-swimming parasites then search for another host.

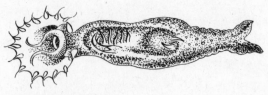

Gyrodactylus elegans

Dactylogyrus vastator

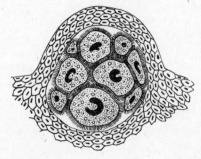

Ichthyophthirius: cyst with organisms, much enlarged

Drawing of a fish infected with white-spot, showing numerous white nodules scattered over the whole body and fins. The caudal fin is already folded

The disease spreads rapidly from fish to fish, and it does not take long for a mass infection to occur. Once they have penetrated skin the parasites cause serious irritation and inflammation and in bad cases several parasites unite to form a blister. Infected fishes rub themselves against solid objects in an attempt, usually unsuccessful, to rid themselves of the parasites. The fish twitches and folds its fins and gasps for air at the surface, and finally dies.

Treatment is by prolonged baths. These do not attack the parasites embedded in the skin, but kill the free-swimming stages as they leave the host, which gradually heals. Baths should always be carried out in a separate tank, and the aquarium itself must remain without fish for at least six days.

Trypaflavin baths are very effective. Dissolve 1 g in 100 litres (22 gals) of water. Plants, snails and some fish may be damaged, hence the necessity to carry out the treatment in a separate container, such as an all-glass tank. The yellowish-green colour of the drug is a guide to its concentration. At a temperature of 25–30 °C (77–86 °F) the treatment should be continued for seven to twenty-one days.

Alternatively, infected fish can be treated in a quinine bath. Dissolve 1 g of quinine hydrochloride (or other quinine salt) in 50 litres (11 gals) of water. In a tank containing plants this concentration will be weakened by absorption, so a supplement of 0.5 g quinine (per 100 litres) dissolved in a little water can be added every three to four days.

Neon disease *(Plistophora):*

This is an incurable disease, very difficult to diagnose in the early stages, which mainly affects neon tetras and other delicate fish species.

The pathogen is the sporozoan *Plistophora hyphessobryconis* which forms numerous spores. These live in and destroy the muscles, and also other internal organs.

The disease spreads from infected sand and plants or from infected fish, particularly their faeces. Even spawn in the ovaries of infected females may be infected.

The symptoms include white or colourless areas in the muscles, curvature of the spine, emaciation and destruction of the fins. Part of the skin coloration may be lost and in the neon tetra the luminous stripe disappears. The disease is fatal. Species of *Hyphessobrycon, Hemigrammus* and *Brachydanio* are especially susceptible. If the disease is not diagnosed in the early stages it may lead to the destruction of entire breeding stocks.

Diseased fish should be killed immediately before they infect others with their faeces. Healthy fish should be transferred to new tanks which have not yet been stocked. Preventative measures include boiling or heating the sand, especially when starting to breed neon tetras. Plants should be disinfected in a pale pink bath of potassium permanganate before putting them in the breeding tank.

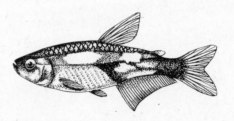

A fish with neon disease

Oodinium disease:

This is an infection of the skin and gills with symptoms very similar to those of white-spot. If not treated it can lead to large-scale mortality, and young fish are particularly susceptible. In fresh waters the pathogen is the flagellate protozoan *Oodinium pillularis*. In a serious infection the body and fins are closely covered by tiny greyish-white or yellowish-brown nodules. Damaged skin may peel off in strips, and the fish become emaciated. This disease spreads very rapidly, particularly in stocks of young specimens, in which serious losses may occur.

Treatment can be by a short bath, one to three minutes only, in a salt solution (30–50 g to 1 litre of water). The infected fish must be lowered into the bath in a net. There should be a tank of pure water alongside so that the fish can be removed from the salt bath if there are any signs of distress.

Alternative treatment involves a prolonged bath (in the dark) in a quinine hydrochloride solution (1.5 g to 100 litres of water) or in a trypaflavin solution (1 g to 100 litres of water). The bath should be used for three to four days at a temperature of 30 °C (86 °F).

Octomitus disease *(Hexamita):*

This is a disease caused by parasitic flagellate protozoans which mainly affects the liver, spleen, gall bladder and kidneys. It is transmitted in the faeces of infected fish. Severe emaciation and darkening of the skin are the usual symptoms, and the back may come to resemble a knife blade. This is a difficult disease to diagnose because it is frequently associated with fish tuberculosis and *Ichthyosporidium*. One species of *Octomitus* attacks discus fish in particular, where small sores appear on the head, back and sides. These develop into crater like depressions. The disease may prove fatal, but newly developed drugs are now effective.

Fish tuberculosis:

This is one of the most dangerous fish diseases. Early diagnosis is difficult, and the disease is incurable. It can easily be confused with *Ichthyosporidium (Ichthyophonus)*, and indeed most of the illnesses attributed to this organism may possibly be cases of fish tuberculosis, which incidentally is not dangerous to humans.

Fish tuberculosis is due to infection by rod-shaped bacteria of the genus *Mycobacterium*. It can spread as a result of an unbalanced diet, unsuitable water temperatures, overstocking and insufficient lighting, in particular a lack of ultraviolet rays.

The symptoms include loss of appetite, emaciation, a concave belly profile, loss of scales, skin damage with some discoloration, frayed fins and protruding eyes. Under a magnifying lens small nodules may be discernible on the internal organs. There is at present no cure, but optimal living conditions may prevent the disease's occurrence.

Infectious dropsy:

An incurable bacterial disease mostly found in outdoor fish ponds, more rarely in the aquarium.

The vector is a virulent strain of the bacterium *Pseudomonas punctata,* which is widespread and normally harmless. Fish infected are usually those which have been weakened by other causes, such as an unbalanced diet with subsequent fatty degeneration of the liver.

The symptoms include progressive swelling of the body, scale protrusion and exophthalmus. More rarely, abscesses may form in the skin.

All infected fish must be removed immediately; care should be taken not to introduce an acutely infected specimen, and all infected tanks should be disinfected before being

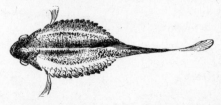

A fish with dropsy, seen from above. The body is swollen and the scales protrude

restocked. It is particularly important to avoid disturbances of the metabolism and liver degeneration.

Ichthyosporidium (Ichthyophonus) disease:

This is an extremely dangerous, incurable disease, which is usually, perhaps always, diagnosed too late. The vector is the parasitic fungus *Ichthyosporidium,* which mainly attacks certain internal organs. However, the whole body may finally be riddled with fungal hyphae. Infection passes from fish to fish and practically no aquarium fish is safe from the disease. Fish threatened are particularly those that become weakened owing to poor care or for other reasons.

This disease is easily confused with fish tuberculosis, as the symptoms are largely the same. An accurate diagnosis is only possible with a microscopic investigation.

Symptoms include emaciation, loss of the tail, scale protrusion, sores, blood-suffused areas, rolling movements and black spots on the skin. In the later stages the fish often lies on the bottom, moves forwards by jerks and finds difficulty in keeping the normal swimming posture. The rear end of the body is raised and the fish finally rolls over, rises to the surface and dies. Mass mortality does not occur, but infected fish die at intervals.

Overstocking of the aquarium should be avoided and great care taken to provide really good living conditions. Dead fish should be removed immediately. In the case of a serious outbreak the fish and plants should be destroyed and the aquarium disinfected.

A fish with *Ichthyosporidium* disease. The typical symptoms include ulcers, folded fins, fraying of caudal fin, swollen gills, black areas on the skin, and a concave belly

Fungal attacks:

Fungi of the genera *Saprolegnia* and *Achlya* form dense woolly moulds on dead organic matter and also on dead pieces of skin of living fish. As a result of external injuries the fungi settle on all parts of the body, particularly on the edges of the fins, on the eyes and around open, half-healed wounds.

These fungi, therefore, only attack damaged fish. With a fungal attack it is therefore important first to identify the primary ailment.

A short bath in potassium permanganate (1 g in 100 litres of water, for ten to thirty minutes) has been suggested as a suitable treatment for fungus; the temperature can be raised. Sometimes gentle painting with a dilute tincture of iodine may help.

Eye ailments:

Even if they heal, mechanical injuries to the eye may cause cloudiness of the cornea. Bites that destroy an eye may lead to the death of a fish. Cichlids and labyrinth fish are particularly likely to cause eye damage when fighting. A damaged cornea can become infected with fungus *(Saprolegnia),* which may subsequently destroy the eye.

The fungus can be treated by painting on a two per cent solution of caustic soda, a procedure which has to be repeated several times. After each treatment the fish must be immediately put into a one per cent solution of common salt to neutralize the action of the caustic before it attacks the eye itself.

Exophthalmus (protruding eyes) may indeed be a symptom of dropsy, but it is also an ailment in its own right and the cause is often difficult to establish. It may occur, for exam-

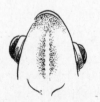

The head of fish, seen from above, with protruding eyes (exophthalmus)

ple, in old specimens of *Pterophyllum* and also other cichlids when they are kept too long in old water. The cause is then an accumulation of decomposition products in the water.

Bacterial fin-rot:

Destruction of the fins, often complete, and particularly the caudal fin, may be due to bacterial action. Treatment is not usually very successful, but there are preparations on the market which may help to prevent this ailment.

Gastro-intestinal ailments:

Newly acquired fish may occasionally refuse to feed. This may happen particularly in recently imported stock weakened in transport or because the correct dietary requirements are not known. At first there is no sign of disease. The position is quite different when well-acclimatized fish suddenly refuse food. This may be due to parasites or other ailments, and in such a case it is best to offer smaller portions of a varied diet. Sometimes the condition is cleared up by putting the patient in with fish that have a good appetite.

A diet containing no roughage may easily lead to constipation with associated intestinal inflammation. In such a case feeding with hard-shelled live food, e.g. *Cyclops* or mosquito larvae, may cure the ailment because their chitin exoskeletons stimulate digestion.

Water slaters, gammarids and midge larvae may carry intestinal parasites. This may, in part, account for the occasional losses reported after feeding with midge larvae. In addition, many of the midge larvae sold in the aquarium trade come from grossly polluted waters, and the same applies to *Tubifex* worms. After a long period of feeding with such material it is not surprising that the fish die, because poisonous substances are stored in the bodies of these food animals. The intestinal parasites carried by gammarids and others are very difficult to get rid of. Furthermore, some of the parasites mentioned above,

e.g. *Plistophora, Oodinium* etc., may settle in the intestine.

Ailments due to environmental causes:

In aquarium fish there are several ailments which are not due to attacks by parasites or disease germs. These are due to inadequate care or to the introduction of poisonous substances.

1. True or apparent oxygen deficiency:
Oxygen deficiency may occur when bacteria use up the available oxygen in the process of decomposing waste such as food remains, dead animals and plants. It may also occur when an aquarium is too densely planted (the plants then use oxygen during the night), if the aquarium is overpopulated, leaving insufficient dissolved oxygen for the fish, or when the water is overheated. Naturally, signs of oxygen deficiency may also occur when the gills have been attacked by parasites or by corrosive substances. In all these cases the fish hang at the water surface and snap for air. They are nervous and often attempt to jump out of the water. The movements of the gill-covers are abnormally rapid. At death the gill-covers are widely spread and the mouth is open.

However, very similar symptoms occur when the water has an excess of carbonic acid or if there is poisoning by ammonia. In the first case the fish cannot get rid of the carbon dioxide produced by their own respiration and so cannot take up oxygen. Thus, gasping for air at the surface is not always a sign of oxygen deficiency, and turning on the aeration will only help in some cases.

In every case, however, the fault lies in poor maintenance and care, and this must be corrected.

2. Diseases caused by unsuitable pH values:
Water that is too acid may cause the so-called acid sickness which leads to serious damage. When the pH drops below the critical point (in most fish around pH 6·5, exceptionally at

6·0–6·5) the water usually has a low hardness. The skin may become cloudy and inflamed and damage to the gills leads to respiratory distress.

The symptoms of alkali sickness can be similar. Here too there may be damage to the skin and gills, and the fins become frayed. The pH rises to a dangerous level. This is sometimes due to poorly buffered water when the vegetation is too luxuriant and the plants remove all the carbonic acid. Efforts should be made to bring back normal conditions step by step, by water changes, a reduction in light and reducing the amount of vegetation.

3. Poisoning:
The causes of poisoning include badly painted angle-iron tanks, poisonous mastic and rubber tubing (especially the pale red type), insufficiently washed cement, rockwork with metallic inclusions and the introduction of substances from outside, such as insect spray and tobacco fumes.

The symptoms include rolling and jerky movements, shyness, protruding scales and gill-covers, signs of respiratory distress, and folding of the fins, particularly the caudal fin.

Poisoning which has been affecting the fish for a long time is often no longer curable. Otherwise the symptoms disappear when the cause of poisoning has been removed.

Feeding

All living organisms require the regular intake of food and elimination of waste products derived from it. In this way new body cells are formed and dead ones removed. Substances in the body may be modified to serve in the processes of movement, reproduction and so on. Any losses involved in these functions have to be made good by new intake of food, and proteins, fats and carbohydrates are all important constructional components which animals obtain either directly from plants or from herbivorous food animals.

Every animal has its own particular way of feeding, which is determined by its body structure and general characteristics. In the wild it will seek out suitable food, but in captivity it has to rely exclusively on the insight, not to say the discretion, of its keeper. It is, therefore, essential that the aquarist should study the feeding habits of his fish so that he can feed them properly; for instance it is pointless to try to feed predatory fish on dried food, because they will either ignore it or if they take it they may become ill. It is just as bad to feed fish the same food all the time, because this is contrary to nature. Every food contains its own well-defined nutrients, and it is only by feeding a varied diet that all the requirements of the fish can be statisfied.

The following are basic rules for feeding:
1. Feed what the fish require, not what you want to give them.
2. Feed a varied diet, bearing in mind the changing seasons and what they have to offer.
3. Do not feed too much or too little, and preferably feed several times a day, observing whether the fish feed readily or listlessly.

Live food

Water-fleas (*Daphnia magna, D. pulex* and others):

These are crustaceans belonging to the group *Cladocera;* they provide an important part of fish diet and they are available in local waters at almost all times of the year. Their nutritional content may vary according to the season and locality. In general, they should be fed together with other types of live food.

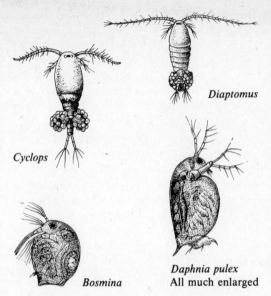

Cyclops

Diaptomus

Bosmina

Daphnia pulex
All much enlarged

The body of a water-flea is encased in two transparent shells, which enable the internal organs to be seen under the microscope. One can observe the heart pumping the blood and also the gut and the eggs or young in the brood pouch. In the adults the eyes are fused in the midline. One of the pairs of antennae is strongly developed and furnished with hair-like bristles at the end. These antennae are used in locomotion. Their downward beat moves the body forwards. As the antennae rise, the animal sinks a little, and this accounts for the hopping method of progression and for the popular name of water-fleas. The other four to six pairs of legs are inside the shell and are used in feeding. They form a filtration apparatus which collects tiny algae, infusorians and all kinds of organic particles.

The reproduction pattern of water-fleas is particularly interesting. Aquarists who go out to collect their own live food could not fail to notice that these tiny crustaceans sometimes occur in enormous numbers and then quite suddenly all disappear. Mass proliferation may go on in a pond until it freezes in winter or dries out in summer, and this is closely associated with their method of reproduction. In autumn, or in unfavourable conditions, the females produce hard-shelled winter eggs which

are able to withstand both cold and desiccation. In spring, when the snow melts or there is some warm rain, these eggs hatch into a new brood that consists exclusively of females, which in turn go on to produce more females.

Examination under the microscope will show the dorsal brood pouch which contains either eggs or restless young, which leave the female after a few days and are soon producing their own young. The eggs develop parthenogenetically, that is, without the presence of males, and the females go on producing more and more generations. This explains the phenomenon of mass proliferation, but the latter is also the cause of their disappearance, which occurs when the food supply is exhausted and oxygen is deficient. Just before this happens, males appear in the population so that fertilized winter eggs can now be produced. These lie like black, shiny scales in the brood pouch, and after the death of the mother they can often be found in large numbers in shallow water near the banks.

There are several water-flea species of which three may be mentioned:

Daphnia pulex, up to 4 mm long
Daphnia magna, up to 6 mm long
Daphnia longispina, about 2 mm long.

Water-fleas occur from April to the end of October (often even longer) in lakes, ponds and ditches, and particularly in village ponds with swimming waterfowl. In summer they sometimes occur in such numbers that the water is coloured red or grey-green. When collecting them watch the direction of the wind, as they are either driven towards the bank by the wind or they gather in the lee of an overhanging bank.

Water-fleas should not be fed to fish in large amounts at a time. In warm-water aquarium tanks and during hot summers they should preferably be fed in small portions several times a day, as they quickly die in the tank, and also they use a lot of oxygen. Water-fleas are taken avidly by all aquarium fish with the exception of some of the larger species.

Even in summer, water-fleas can be stored for a few days in large enamel or plastic pails (never in metal containers) in a cool, sunless place; the water should previously have been well aerated. It is important that they should not be weakened during transport, so remember not to collect more than can be accommodated. The temperature of the water in the transport container must be the same as that in the storage container, as big differences in temperature may kill the water-fleas immediately. They may also die if they are moved straight from the cool storage container into a warm-water tank, and those that are not eaten immediately will pollute the water.

Cyclops:

To the aquarist the term Cyclops refers to a number of tiny copepod crustaceans mostly belonging to the genera *Cyclops* and *Diaptomus*. In *Cyclops* the female carries a pair of egg sacs at the rear, in *Diaptomus* only a single egg sac. Copepods have separate sexes, so one finds both males and females. The eggs hatch into larvae (nauplii) which are an excellent food for young fish in the first stages of life. The nauplii of *Diaptomus* are much valued for rearing young Indian glassfish *(Chanda ranga)* which prefer them to all other live foods.

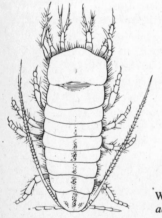

Water slater *(Asellus aquaticus)*, enlarged

Cyclops and *Diaptomus* occur in large numbers, particularly in spring and autumn, sometimes in winter under the ice. They are often found in the same waters as water-fleas, but *Diaptomus* also occurs in cool, shady forest pools.

Cyclops and its relatives should not be fed in excessive amounts as half-grown and adult specimens may attack delicate fish fry.

They can be stored in the same way as water-fleas, but are generally hardier.

Gammarids *(Gammarus pulex)* and water slaters *(Asellus aquaticus):*

These are among the more highly developed crustaceans. The water slater, which is 1–2 cm (0·4–0·8 in) long, moves by creeping slowly among water plants and decaying plant debris, but it can swim well when threatened. It survives periods of drought by hiding deep in the mud. The female carries the eggs and newly hatched young around with her in a brood sac on the underside of the body. Water slaters can be easily collected by lifting a bundle of filamentous algae or water moss out of a pond and placing it in a jar of clean water; this technique usually yields a good number.

Freshwater gammarids, which are closely related to marine sandhoppers, are much laterally compressed, and up to 1 cm (0·4 in) long. They are found mainly under stones and pieces of wood in ditches and other flowing waters. They move by creeping but can also swim rapidly by beating the tail. They feed mainly on dead plant fragments but can also take animal food. The female protects the eggs and young for quite a time.

Both these crustaceans can be found throughout the year, even under the ice. They are avidly eaten by all larger aquarium fish, but may carry fish parasites.

Gnat and mosquito larvae:

There are several species, and their larvae form a valued and nutritious fish food. Some

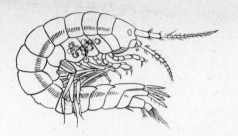

Freshwater shrimp *(Gammarus pulex)*, enlarged

ornamental fish species may only breed successfully if fed on gnat larvae.

They breed mainly in ditches, ponds, flooded areas and garden rain-butts. The adult gnats and mosquitoes bite, so care should be taken not to let them develop beyond the pupal state.

Phantom or glass larvae:

These are white, transparent larvae of flies of the genus *Corethra*. They float horizontally in the water, and move by a series of somersaults. The body has two pairs of silvery-black air-filled sacs which enable the larva to float. It can adjust its position in the water by taking in or releasing air. Unlike gnat larvae, it does not breathe at the surface, but extracts dissolved oxygen directly at the surface. The adults do not bite, and the males can be distinguished by their feathery antennae.

Phantom larvae are found in clear ponds and lakes, often in large numbers during the colder part of the year, from autumn to spring, and sometimes even under the ice. They are predatory, catching small crustaceans with their beak-like mouthparts, so they should not be fed to fish fry or very small fish species. They are appreciated by larger species.

These larvae can be kept for quite a time in large cool plastic containers.

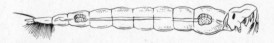

Phantom larva of *Corethra*, enlarged

Red midge larvae:

These belong mostly to the genus *Chironomus*, and the adults do not bite. The much feared biting midges belong to *Ceratopogon* and related genera.

The larvae occur throughout the year, and particularly in winter, in muddy ditches and ponds. They form a nutritious food, but the fish should never be fed exclusively on them or they become ill. Nor should too many be fed at any one time, as the surviving larvae creep into the substrate. They can be kept for a time in shallow water that is changed daily, or in slowly running water.

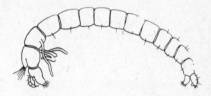

Red midge larva *(Chironomus)*, enlarged

Earthworms (*Lumbricus* species):

These can be found throughout the year in damp soil and often under leaf-mould. They form a very nutritious food if given, according to length, to large and medium-sized fish, particularly cichlids. They should not, however, be fed in too large numbers, as this may lead to digestive upsets and infertility. So far as possible it is best not to feed with large sexually mature worms, as symptoms of poisoning have been observed in this case. Worms intended for feeding can be kept in a glass jar, covered with gauze, until their guts are empty.

Earthworms can be kept in shallow boxes (about 50 × 50 cm or 20 × 20 in) filled with soil, and fed on leaves, carrot and potato. They live for a long time and may even breed. The soil should be only moderately damp.

Whiteworms or enchytraeids:

These are small relatives (about 2 cm or 0·8 in long) of earthworms, and they can be kept in shallow wooden boxes filled with damp soil. The lids should be close-fitting, and the soil must not contain any artificial fertilizer, nor should it come from a compost heap. The most suitable soil would be from woodland or meadow. The soil thrown up by moles is usually quite free of undesirable elements. A lighter texture can be obtained by mixing the soil half and half with peat.

Whiteworms can be fed with cooked potato or with white bread that has been soaked and squeezed. It is usually recommended that the feeding plate should be covered by a sheet of glass, so that the worms can collect under it, making it easier to harvest them. Each breeding cycle will take three to six weeks, and during this time the culture should not be disturbed. It is best, therefore, to have two or three separate cultures so that one can be rested while the others are harvested.

Spiders and woodlice that settle in the boxes can be left there because they will consume the undesirable mites.

The cultures cannot be left to produce indefinitely, as breeding will tend to tail off after a time. Some of the soil should then be renewed. This can be done by placing the box in the sun. The worms will then move out from the encrusted top layer and down to the bottom of the box. The upper crust is then easily lifted off and replaced with new soil and a fresh supply of food. A new period of worm proliferation will ensue.

Care must be taken in feeding with whiteworms. An excess can easily lead to fatty degeneration, infertility and loss of colour in the fish. These small worms can, however, be recommended as an occasional supplement to the winter diet.

Tubifex:

These are very thin, red worms, 1–6 cm (0·4–2·4 in) long, which occur in ponds, lakes, rivers and ditches. They live with their heads embedded in the mud, while the tail ends waggle free. In polluted waters *Tubifex* worms may occur in such enormous numbers that the bottom takes on a red coloration. They can be found at all times of the year, even in winter, when they are usually the only type of live food available on the market.

Tubifex worms are certainly a popular food for aquarium fish, but they should be carefully washed in running water before use. They are best fed from a small sieve floating at the surface, so that they can wriggle through the holes a few at a time and can be snapped up by the fish. This prevents uneaten worms from sinking and creeping into the substrate, where they may cause unpleasant cloudiness of the water or create pollution when they die.

Live food for fish fry

After a period which varies according to the species, most fish eggs hatch into fish fry, a kind of larva. At first the fry have a yolk sac which for the first few days serves them as a source of nourishment. In this stage the fry usually hang from plants or the aquarium glass or, in brood-protecting species, they are guarded in a nest or pit. It is only when they have become free-swimming that they require food. There are some fishes species in which the fry feed exclusively on live food, while others will also take powdered dried food or whiteworms and boiled egg yolk pressed through a cloth. It should be noted, therefore, that live food is in some cases indispensable. Where it is lacking, the fry of some species will remain stunted and become susceptible to disease.

Infusorians (various protozoan species):

Aquarists tend to lump together all those protozoan species which the zoologist classifies as flagellates, rhizopods and ciliates. In each protozoan the body consists of a single cell, which may have quite a complicated structure. The individual living functions are then carried out by the parts of one cell. In some cases a number of protozoans form a colony in which there is a certain division of labour among the component cells.

The number of protozoan species is extremely large, and they occur in all parts of the world. During periods of drought they are able to form a tiny capsule which can be distributed by the wind. Reproduction is usually by division of a single cell into two, also by the production of 'buds' or by the union of two individual cells which later produce numerous new individuals.

Some protozoans can undergo extremely rapid proliferation with the production of millions of individuals which cause the phenomenon known as water blooms. Certain protozoans, for example the green flagellate *Euglena viridis,* contain chlorophyll, like plants, and indeed they are regarded as standing on the boundary between animals and plants. Almost all protozoans are predatory. They either feed on bacteria, of which they require enormous numbers, or on other protozoans which they overpower with the help of delicately constructed mouthparts. Other species even attack higher animals and their eggs, and may cause lethal damage. As an example of interest to aquarists, infusorians of the genus *Coleps,* with mouthparts resembling a circular saw, bore into the coverings of fish eggs and there is also, of course, the notorious fish parasite *Ichthyophthirius multifiliis.*

A large number of protozoans can be seen in an aquarium, provided it is well-established and does not contain any young fish. Amoeba can be found on the glass, on the bottom and at the water surface. The algal film swarms with *Paramecium* and *Stentor,* the complex-structured *Stylonichia* and others. On the water plants there will be dense colonies of *Vorticella,* a stalked protozoan.

Infusorians occur in all types of water, usually from spring to autumn. They can be collected in a very fine-mesh nylon net.

The catch should be carefully graded by size with the help of very fine sieves. Feeding with infusorians that are too large can lead to unsuccessful fish breeding. Young fish should always be given a size that they are capable of

Infusorians from an aquarium tank

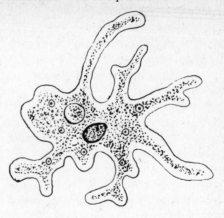

Amoeba

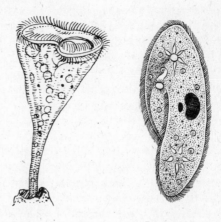

Stentor   *Paramecium*

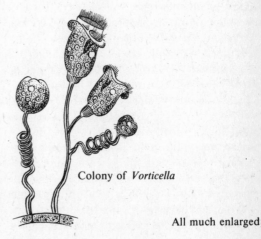

Colony of *Vorticella*

All much enlarged

89

eating. It should also be remembered that many young fish do not go hunting for food, but have to be surrounded by it. Feeding in the dark with the light from a pocket torch is often a good idea, as the infusorians and young are attracted by the beam of light and so congregate there.

The fry of some tropical fish species are particularly sensitive to bacteria and infusorians. This applies especially to the 'black-water fish' which are bred in soft and slightly acid water. It appears that in ordinary aquarium water the thin egg covering is an insufficient protection against bacteria and infusorians that attack fish spawn. The eggs can, to a certain extent, be protected by slightly increasing the acidity to a pH just below 7. This is because the micro-organisms concerned cannot thrive in an acid environment.

With fish species that are sensitive to infusorians it is essential to keep the breeding tank completely free of these micro-organisms. Further details on how to tackle this problem will be given in the section 'Hints on the breeding of aquarium fishes'. Here it should only be mentioned that the greatest care should be taken when feeding with infusorians. It is not always possible to collect them in natural waters at the time they are required for feeding to fish fry. It is therefore a great advantage for the aquarist to breed or culture his own supply. Here a microscope is indispensable, but a hand microscope is quite sufficient.

For fish that are not very sensitive, such as the anabantids, the simplest method is to encourage the proliferation of infusorians in the breeding tank itself. Place a piece of banana skin, a few drops of milk, some egg yolk or meat juice (but not too much) into the tank. After a day or two the number of infusorians will have increased considerably.

A second very useful method is to prepare an aqueous infusion of hay or other dry plant matter in a 2–3 litre glass container. Let the culture stand for a few days in a light but not sunny place. A fatty layer forms at the water surface, and beneath this there will be swarms of infusorians. Their presence can be checked with the hand microscope. The upper water layer must then be carefully scooped off with a spoon, washed through a fine-mesh cloth and fed to the fish. Water removed from the culture can be replaced with fresh water at the same temperature. The latter point is very important, as infusorians, like other live foods, do not tolerate sudden temperature changes.

The foregoing two methods have the disadvantage that the proliferation of infusorians relies on chance. Such a mixed culture cannot, therefore, be used when breeding fish species that are sensitive to infusorians. So it is better to establish a controlled culture of *Paramecium caudatum*, a ciliate protozoan known colloquially as the slipper animalcule. During their first days these are avidly consumed by most fish fry and they are completely non-injurious. Chop a turnip into 1 cm (0·4 in) cubes and dry these in the sun or in a cool oven. In this state the turnip can be kept for a long time. Place a cube in a 1-litre glass container and fill up with mains water that has stood overnight. The turnip cube will decompose and form a layer on the bottom of the container. Place a drop of an already existing hay infusion into the water in the culture glass. Quite soon a rich crop of *Paramecium* can be seen just below the surface film in the culture glass, while other, usually unwanted, infusorians die from lack of oxygen. The *Paramecium* form a slight cloudiness and when viewed against the light can be discerned with the naked eye. A little of the culture is filtered so that the *Paramecium* remain behind on the filter paper, and they can then be fed to the fish fry. Here again it is important that the temperature of the culture should be the same as that of the aquarium water.

Some aquarium dealers stock a kit for culturing *Paramecium*, and also dried preparations which, so to speak, come to life when immersed in water.

Small live food:

There are several different kinds of tiny animals that are useful to the aquarist. These or-

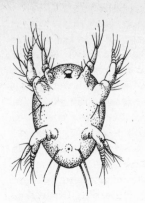

Nauplius larva
of *Cyclops* (× 200)

A rotifer,
much enlarged

ganisms form the most important rearing food for fish fry. As soon as they have become free-swimming, many young start to take these tiny animals, while others do so after feeding on infusorians, usually for three to five days.

Small live food usually consists of the larvae (nauplii) and young stages of various crustaceans, such as newly-born *Daphnia,* nauplii of *Diaptomus* and *Cyclops,* and last but not least the various species of rotifer. The nauplii of cultured brine shrimps *(Artemia)* can also be included as small live food.

As already mentioned, *Cyclops* nauplii should be fed with care. In every case only so many should be fed as can be consumed immediately, as they often grow faster than the fish fry, which they then attack. The very small *Bosmina* mostly lives in the open waters of lakes and ponds, often together with the copepod *Diaptomus* and its nauplii. Rotifers are an excellent food. These are tiny, many-celled animals with a complicated structure. They are very transparent so that all the internal organs can be clearly seen under the microscope. There are about 600 different species of very varying form. They all have a wheel-shaped organ equipped with numerous motile cilia. The movements of the cilia are co-ordinated in such a way that they produce a current of water which conveys suspended food particles to the mouth.

Small live food can be collected with a fine-mesh net and then sorted according to size before being fed to the fish fry. Most of the species are difficult to keep.

Brine shrimps *(Artemia salina)*:

These are relatively small crustaceans distributed throughout the world in brackish waters, but not in the sea. *Artemia salina,* the best-known species, is commercially important in the United States, particularly in the Great Salt Lake of Utah and in California. Identification of the different species of *Artemia* is often difficult because size and coloration may vary according to the salinity. The thick-shelled eggs are collected in large quantities and thoroughly cleaned before being put on the market. When suitably stored they can be kept dry for two to three years, but within a few hours at any time of the year they will hatch to produce a germ-free, highly nutritious live food reserve for fish fry and small fish.

The eggs are sold in the dry state in small tubular cartons. They hatch when placed in a solution of iodine-free common salt (10 g per 1 litre of water). At a temperature of 23–25 °C (73–77 °F) hatching usually takes place in twenty-four to twenty-eight hours.

There are various methods of doing this. The simplest and at the same time the least productive procedure is to pour a suitable amount of the salt solution into a shallow glass dish and to scatter a small portion of eggs on the surface, preferably in a food ring and without aeration. This only produces a small number of nauplii.

A better method is to put the eggs and salt solution in a glass jar and use powerful aeration so that the eggs are kept moving. After about thirty hours the aeration is turned off and the empty egg shells will usually collect at the surface, while the newly hatched reddish nauplius larvae will be near the bottom. They can then be sucked up through a length of fine tubing and collected on a fine-mesh sieve. The disadvantage of this method is that the solution tends to evaporate rather quickly.

The best method is to culture in clear glass flasks or even a clear wine bottle. These should be filled just over half full with the salt solution. They should have a rubber bung bored to give two holes, one for the air inlet and one for the air outlet. The inlet tube should reach to the bottom of the flask, while the other end is connected to the air pump. The air supply must be powerful enough to keep the eggs moving.

After about thirty-six hours the aeration can be turned off and the first batch of nauplii collected. In about four or five minutes the reddish larvae will have congregated near the bottom. Air is then blown through the short outlet tube, and this pushes the liquid, together with the larvae, up the long inlet tube and out of the flask, where the nauplii can be collected on a fine sieve. After rinsing in fresh water the larvae can be fed to the fish. The salty water is returned to the flask, which is then closed and aerated for a further period of twelve hours. By then most of the eggs will have hatched, although a third harvesting can be attempted. After that a new culture must be established with a fresh salt solution.

Artemia larvae only survive for about six hours in fresh water, so it is a mistake to put too many at a time into the tank. The larvae are relatively large, so the fry of some species will not be able to eat them immediately, but will usually take them after six days. The fry of cichlids, livebearing and usually also egglaying toothcarps eat them as soon as they are free-swimming.

Microworms:

These are very small nematode worms of the genus *Anguillula*. They move actively in water but normally live in soil. They form a good food for young fish from two to three weeks old. However, they are not taken by all young fish, possibly because their active movements are frightening.

These worms can be bred in glass containers in which the bottom is arched upwards. Oatflakes with a little milk are placed in the outer channel so that a kind of gruel is formed. The central domed part of the bottom rises up above the food mixture. When the latter starts to smell sour it is inoculated with a microworm culture, obtainable from aquarium dealers. The container is then well covered and placed in a warm spot. The worms multiply rapidly and soon start to creep up the walls of the glass container, from which they can be easily collected with a soft watercolour brush. The tiny worms are then shaken off into a small dish of water, where they are thoroughly rinsed before being used as a food. Any worms which sink to the tank bottom and are not eaten should be removed, as they easily cause cloudiness and may encourage the multiplication of infusorians. Some aquarists try to keep the worms afloat for a time by introducing them into the stream of bubbles from the aerator.

Grindal worms *(Enchytraeus buchholtzi):*

These are smaller relatives of the common whiteworm *Enchytraeus albidus,* and they form a good food for young fish from the third or fourth week. They can be cultured in the same way as the common whiteworm, but require a higher temperature (18−24 °C or 64−75 °F) as they come originally from the tropics; the temperature must be checked regularly with a thermometer.

The adult worms are very thin and about 10 mm (0·4 in) long, but a culture will usually yield large numbers of the young stages which are 3−6 mm (0·12−0·24 in) long.

Dried food

During recent years there has been a considerable increase in the use of commercially prepared dried food for feeding to tropical fish. This is partly due to the fact that in the industrialized countries the collection of live food becomes increasingly difficult as the years go by, and partly because the quality of the different dried foods has so greatly improved. At one time it was regarded as a substitute, to be given only when live food was not available, but nowadays good-quality dried foods contain everything that is necessary to keep fish in good condition.

It is now possible to feed aquarium fish over long periods with such foods without damaging them, so that they show a good rate of growth, increased readiness to breed and improved health and vitality.

Modern dried foods consist of a varied mixture of natural raw materials, and they are available in powdered form, as flakes, paste or tablets. In general, aquarists prefer mixed diets which are suitable for most fish species, but there are also special foods on the market for, for example, young fish or vegetarian species.

Dried food is taken by all fish that feed in the wild on small invertebrates, algae and detritus, but not by those, such as many small cichlids, which prefer a moving prey. Naturally this also applies to all truly predatory fish.

In spite of the wholesomeness of good dried food, the fish should not be restricted to this, but should be given a varied diet, including the chance to hunt live food.

With dried food, as indeed with other foods, it is particularly important not to offer too much at a time, in order to avoid overfeeding and the danger of fatty degeneration. Remember also that food remnants in the tank cause water pollution.

It is often unwise to buy the cheapest foods available. Diet is so important to the health and welfare of fish that it is worth spending that little extra, and also seeking the advice of a reputable supplier.

Whatever variety of food you give to the fish, it must be offered in the appropriate way. Some fish are habitual surface-feeders and will not eat food that has sunk to the bottom; likewise, bottom-feeders may starve if their food always floats. The food items should resemble those eaten by that species in the wild, since the mouthparts are adapted to handle only certain sizes and shapes of food, and also the instinctive feeding behaviour is triggered only by these items.

Frozen and freeze-dried food:

The introduction of domestic deep-freezers has enabled aquarium dealers to store and sell deep-frozen live foods of various kinds. Food animals treated in this way retain all the nutrients found in fresh live food. They also have the advantage that they never contain disease germs, which are always a hazard in wild-caught live food. It should, of course, be remembered that frozen food that has been thawed cannot be re-frozen, so it should be frozen in small packets that when thawed can be used fairly quickly. Thawed frozen foods decompose very rapidly.

Another type of food preservation involves the process of freeze-drying. Food animals are frozen at a low temperature and the water is then removed from them. This involves a reduction in volume but not in nutritional value. Freeze-dried food is willingly taken by many fish species and it stores well.

Dried water-fleas:

These are only to be used as a makeshift. They can be dried on gauze racks in the sun or in a very cool oven, but air must be allowed to reach them from below as well as from above. When properly dried this food should only have a very faint smell.

In addition to water-fleas, other food animals, such as gnat larvae and whiteworms, also can be dried.

For fish which require a vegetarian diet it is possible to dry and pulverize lettuce leaves. This powder is also useful when establishing a culture of infusorians.

In winter, freshly skinned mealworms form a good supplementary food for many fish species.

Finally, fish should never be fed on bread, cake, cooked potato or the so-called ants' eggs (which are really ant pupae).

Keeping invertebrates in the cold-water aquarium

Serious naturalists are unlikely to ignore the numerous creatures which live in their local waters, and many of them will have been found by aquarists during trips to the country for collecting live food. They can be taken back home and studied at leisure with very little trouble, and are extremely interesting; the varied feeding mechanisms of many aquatic insects and their larvae make a fascinating study in themselves. The struggle for existence in fresh waters is as acute as anywhere in the living world. Only a few aquatic animals are completely vegetarian, feeding directly on organic food from plants; most rely for their livelihood on other animals which have fed on plants. In addition, the cold-water community contains a large proportion of detritivores – detritus-feeders that sift through the silt and mud to obtain their organic nutrients.

Freshwater life is also an excellent subject for schools, where it is often studied under the title of 'pond life'. Little special equipment is required for this study; a fine-mesh net, a glass jar and a magnifying lens are usually sufficient.

The following section on freshwater invertebrates deals only with a small selection of the wealth of animal life to be found in this habitat. A few of these species have already been mentioned in the section on food for aquarium fish. Many of the invertebrates dealt with here are, of course, injurious to aquarium fish, and must be kept in separate tanks; certainly none of these endemic species should be introduced into a tank of tropical ornamental fish.

Freshwater polyps

These include various species of hydras, such as the grey hydra *(Pelmatohydra vulgaris attenuata)*, the green hydra *(Chlorohydra viridissima)* and the brown hydra *(Pelmatohydra oligactis)*. These occur throughout the year in all types of water, but particularly in weedy ponds and ditches.

In spite of their simple structure, they have a number of special features of interest and are fascinating to observe.

The hydras, or freshwater polyps, belong to the Coelenterata, a group of invertebrates that also includes the corals and jellyfishes or medusae. The body consists of a simple tube with an opening at one end which is surrounded by a variable number of tentacles. The opening serves both as a mouth and as an anus. The body walls consist of two layers of cells, the outer with muscles, nerves and sensory cells, while the inner layer has a digestive function. The tentacles carry large numbers of sting-cells with the help of which the animal captures and paralyses its prey, which is then conveyed to the mouth by the tentacles.

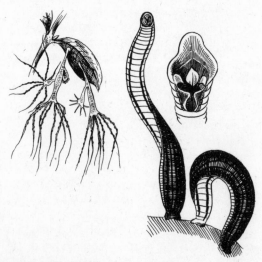

Freshwater polyp
(Hydra), enlarged

Medicinal leech

94

When disturbed a hydra with expanded tentacles will very rapidly contract into a small clump of tissue. A few hydras can easily be kept in a small glass tank with water plants. They are able to move about quite actively by movements resembling those of a looper caterpillar.

Hydras are dangerous in a fish tank, particularly in a breeding aquarium, and unless special precautions are taken they are easily introduced with live food. They breed rapidly, either asexually by producing buds from the body which grow into small hydras, or sexually with the production of eggs and sperm. As their numbers increase they may compete with fish for the available food, and they will also catch and eat free-swimming fish fry.

Here are two methods of controlling hydras in the aquarium:

1. Use $0 \cdot 6$–$2 \cdot 0$ g ammonium nitrate for every 10 litres ($2 \cdot 2$ gals) of tank water. The disadvantage of this method is that with a rising pH (over $7 \cdot 0$) the ammonium nitrate is converted into poisonous ammonia. In fact, the concentration to be used depends upon the pH value of the water. At pH $7 \cdot 5$–$8 \cdot 1$ use $0 \cdot 6$ g, at pH $6 \cdot 5$–$7 \cdot 5$ use 1 g, and at a pH below $6 \cdot 5$ the dose can be 2 g per 10 litres.

During treatment the water temperature should be raised by about 5 °C (9 °F), and the hydras should not be fed. At first the tentacles will be withdrawn, and quite soon the hydras will die. With a serious infestation the treatment can be repeated after two days. The plants can remain in the tank where they will utilize the ammonium nitrate, but it is better to remove the fish before treatment starts. After the hydras have died off the water should be changed and the fish re-introduced.

2. This method involves the use of metallic copper. First, remove the fish from the tank. Then suspend a coil of bare copper wire at each end of the tank. The hydras will lose their tentacles and after a while will fall to the bottom. This treatment should be repeated from time to time until no more hydras can be seen; the copper can then be removed. The water must be changed completely before the fish are re-introduced.

After a period of fasting some tropical fish, including the selected forms of *Trichogaster trichopterus*, will feed on hydras. This biological method of control is preferable to the other methods.

Moss animals (Bryozoa)

These are completely harmless, usually much-branched, small animals which in the aquarium often settle on the glass and plants or on the tank equipment. The tiny tentacles of numerous individual animals protrude from a form of exoskeleton, and these can be seen with the naked eye when the light is behind them, or with a magnifying lens. When disturbed the tentacles are very rapidly withdrawn. Moss animals feed on protozoans and on organic particles in the water. There is no need to control them.

Leeches (Hirudinea)

Leeches, found in waters of all types, from spring to autumn, are quite suitable for a small cold-water aquarium, preferably one with a small area of damp land, in which some species lay their eggs.

Leeches are hermaphrodite and the eggs are usually self-fertilized. Some species practise brood protection. They feed either by sucking blood or swallowing their prey with a jaw-less pharynx.

Various species of leech are occasionally introduced into the aquarium with live food. If this happens they must be removed immediately, although they do not generally cause much damage. The medicinal leech *(Hirudo medicinalis)* is not very common in the wild, but it is bred for medical use.

Planarians

These are non-parasitic flatworms which can be a nuisance in the aquarium and are not always easy to get rid of. They occur in waters of all types and are introduced into the aquarium with live food or with water plants from other tanks. Great care must therefore be taken when collecting food from the wild; it should be well washed and checked to ensure planarians are not included. Tropical planarians are also brought in with fish imports.

Planarians are nocturnal, flattened worms with a clearly defined head end. The whole of the body surface is covered with very large numbers of microscopic cilia, the movements of which enable the animal to glide along the bottom. The mouth is on the underside of the head, and it leads to a protrusible pharynx. Planarians feed on small invertebrates, fish spawn and organic waste of animal origin. They reproduce rapidly. In the early morning they can sometimes be seen in large numbers on the aquarium glass.

Planarians have to be eliminated, particularly from breeding tanks. The best method is to catch them by means of a bait. Suspend a little chopped meat in a small gauze bag just above the plants or in among the plants. Planarians have a good sense of smell and quite soon they will have collected round the bag, which can then be carefully lifted out. It is a good idea to hold a fine-mesh net below the bag as it is being removed from the tank so that none of the living flatworms drop back. The bag should then be put into boiling water. This treatment can be repeated on several evenings and then again eight days later to catch any more worms and their newly hatched young. If this method does not help it will be necessary to clean the tank out very thoroughly, boil or discard the substrate, and bathe the plants and equipment for ten minutes in dilute vinegar.

Some aquarium fish, such as members of the genus *Macropodus*, are efficient consumers of planarians.

Fish louse
(*Argulus foliaceus*),
enlarged

Planarian (× 8)

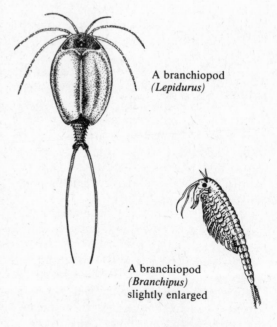

A branchiopod
(*Lepidurus*)

A branchiopod
(*Branchipus*)
slightly enlarged

Mitten crab (*Eriocheir sinensis*), half natural size

Crustaceans

Branchiopods:

This group of entomostracan crustaceans includes *Chirocephalus grubei, Branchippus schaefferi, Triops cancriformis* and *Lepidurus apus*. The related brine-shrimp has already been described in the section on live food for aquarium fish.

These small crustaceans are found either in early spring or in summer in waters which sometimes dry out and which may freeze in winter. They are active, often dark brown, and have become very rare. Branchiopods which appear in early spring can be kept at low temperatures with good aeration. They are usually harmless, but care should be taken with *Triops* and *Lepidurus*.

Fish louse *(Argulus foliaceus):*

These are small flattened parasitic crustaceans with a round dorsal shield which occur throughout the year in fish ponds. They feed on the body fluids of host fish, piercing the skin with a sucking proboscis. The continuous movements of the legs cause inflammation of the skin which usually becomes secondarily infected with fungus. Infestations may be highly injurious, particularly among young fish, and can be fatal.

Fish lice can be removed from the fish's body with forceps, and sometimes they fall off when the infected fish is taken from the water. Vaseline should be applied to the site of the wound.

Water slaters *(Isopoda)* and gammarids *(Amphipoda):*

These have already been described in the section on fish foods.

Decapod crustaceans:

These include various crayfish, such as *Astacus astacus, A. leptodactylus* and *Cambarus affinis*. They occur in streams, rivers, lakes and ponds with a soft bottom, but with sufficient hiding-places under rocks and roots, and particularly overhanging banks.

Decapods have a stiff carapace, two powerful pincers and a moveable abdomen. Like all crustaceans they have to moult from time to time as the rigid carapace is unable to grow. After moulting they are soft and helpless for some days. In autumn the females lay hundreds of eggs, which are attached to the underside of the tail. These hatch in the spring and the young climb on to the swimmerets of the female, which carries them around for a time.

Crayfish can live for years in a sufficiently spacious aquarium with a soft sandy substrate and rocks and old roots to provide shelter. The water should be filtered and vigorously aerated. Crayfish can be fed on fish or frog flesh, insect larvae, tadpoles, earthworms, some plant matter or even dried foods.

Mitten crab *(Eriocheir sinensis):*

This crab is now distributed over wide areas of central Europe. It was probably introduced in the form of free-swimming larvae in the water tanks of cargo ships from China.

The carapace is up to 10 cm (4 in) across and the pincers are covered with a dense hairy felt. The crabs dig into dams and river banks and attack fish caught in traps, causing serious damage. They migrate to the estuaries for breeding.

Mitten crabs can be kept in a large, spacious tank with an area of dry land. The tank must be covered with a good lid, as they like to climb. They are also very powerful, so the lid should be fastened. They are omnivorous and rather intolerant of other members of their own species.

Insects

Most of the invertebrates of fresh waters are insects. Many beetles and bugs are aquatic,

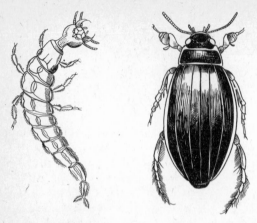

Great diving beetle *(Dytiscus marginalis)* with larva, slightly enlarged

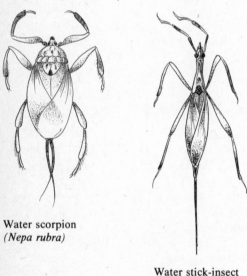

Water scorpion
(Nepa rubra)

Water stick-insect
(Ranatra linearis)

Saucer bug
(Naucoris cimicoides),
slightly enlarged

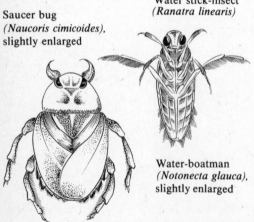

Water-boatman
(Notonecta glauca),
slightly enlarged

both as larvae and adults. Other insects only live in the water as larvae.

Beetles (Coleoptera):

These occur in waters of all types, especially in ponds, lakes and ditches. Water beetles are particularly well adapted for an aquatic life both as larvae and adults. They can take in atmospheric air at the surface by means of special organs, and as a result can survive in polluted waters. Most water beetles, and especially their larvae, are predators which attack anything that they can overcome. The larvae pupate outside the water in soil. The following are the principal aquatic representatives of the order:

The great diving beetle *(Dytiscus marginalis)* is one of the most active predators, particularly as larvae, which are good swimmers. These have fang-like, pierced upper jaws with which they inject the prey with a poisonous juice. This digests its contents into a liquid form that is sucked up.

Other members of the family are *Cybister laterimarginalis, Colymbetes fuscus* and *Acilius sulcatus,* whose larvae are distinguished by their paddle-like limbs.

The great silver beetle *Hydrous piceus* moves clumsily and is a poor swimmer. It reaches a length of 7 cm (2·75 in) and is pitch black with thick club-like antennae. The adult beetles feed on plants, but the larvae are predatory, feeding mainly on snails, which they do not, however, digest externally. The eggs are spun into a cocoon which is so anchored among surface plants that its respiratory tube protrudes above the water surface. This is a rare beetle which is protected in some areas.

The smaller *Hydrophilus caraboides* is another species with similar habits.

The whirligig beetles *(Gyrinus natator)* are smaller beetles which gyrate at the water surface at great speed but can also dive. The eyes, which are divided into two halves, can see above and below water. The larvae are predatory, and like those of the great diving beetle, they have pierced jaws.

Water bugs:

The group includes the common water-boatman *Notonecta glauca*, the pond-skater *Gerris* and water-measurers of the genus *Hydrometra*, the water scorpion *Nepa cinerea*, the water stick-insect *Ranatra linearis* and other species. They occur in standing and slow-flowing waters.

Some of the water bugs are active and skilful swimmers which, with the help of a pair of elongated, paddle-like limbs, swim either on their backs or in the normal position. Other species run along the water surface, utilizing surface tension, or creep along the bottom or among plants. They are all predatory and have a powerful, piercing proboscis. They have no larval stage, but a juvenile phase in which they are unable to fly. Some of the water bugs fly well and so the tank should have a good lid if they are to be kept in captivity. Like the water beetles, they are adapted to take in atmospheric air.

Care should be taken that water bugs are not introduced into the breeding tank with food, as they are very likely to attack young fish.

Caddisworms:

These, the larvae of caddisflies (Trichoptera), are interesting to keep in a cold-water tank. They construct a tube of sand grains, plant fragments or tiny snail shells around their body. When disturbed they can withdraw the body into this tube, which thus acts as a protection for the soft abdomen.

Dragonfly larvae:

The larvae of various dragonfly species are active predators. They have a jawed mask below the head which can be shot out to catch prey. In a cold-water aquarium their development can be observed right up to the emergence of the adult insect. Larvae of the larger species are powerful predators and will tackle fish bigger than themselves with success.

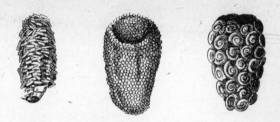

Houses of caddis-fly larva (caddis-worm), the one on the left with its larva, enlarged

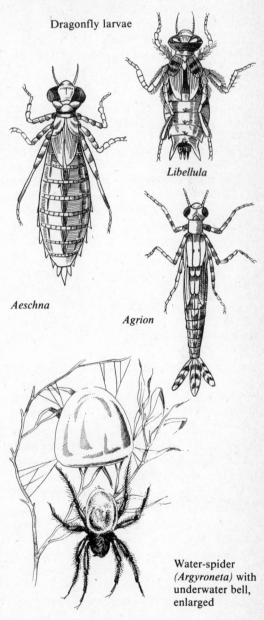

Dragonfly larvae

Libellula

Aeschna

Agrion

Water-spider (*Argyroneta*) with underwater bell, enlarged

99

Spiders and mites (Arachnoidea)

Water-spiders *(Argyroneta aquatica)*:

These occur in standing waters, often in ponds with dense vegetation. They build a silken nest similar to a diving bell in among the plants. Rising to the surface, they collect air around the hairy abdomen and then dive down to release it into the nest. They feed on small aquatic invertebrates.

Water-spiders should not be confused with other spider species which jump rapidly across the water surface.

Water-mites (Hydracarina):

These are often introduced with food, but they are not eaten by the fish. There are various yellowish to red species which swim very actively. The body has a diameter of 1 mm or less. In a tropical tank they usually die after a time. They are dangerous in a breeding tank as they attack fish spawn.

Molluscs (Mollusca)

Gastropod snails (Gastropoda):

Several species of endemic water snails are quite suitable for a cold-water tank, but they should not be introduced into a tropical aquarium as they frequently carry fish diseases. On the other hand, some snails from tropical standing waters can acclimatize quite well to the changed conditions of a cold-water tank. Certain snails are voracious consumers of plants, others do not attack them provided they are properly fed in other ways. Suitable foods for snails are blanched lettuce leaves and any kind of dried food.

The viviparous or river snail *(Viviparus viviparus)* is the most interesting, but at the same time most delicate of endemic aquatic snails. The species occurs throughout the year in ditches, backwaters and weedy ponds, spending the winter in the mud. The males can be distinguished by the thickened right tentacle which serves as a copulatory organ. The young are born fully formed, with a tiny shell.

The great pond snail *Lymnaea stagnalis* is the largest and most voracious species in its genus. The shape of the shell varies considerably according to the locality. There are several related species differing in size and shell form and some, such as the wandering snail *Lymnaea peregra,* release poisonous substances.

Lymnaea species which occur in weedy ponds and lakes are scarcely suitable for the home aquarium. They require a large amount of plant food and can destroy even dense vegetation in a very short time. If they are to be kept they should be fed regularly on dried food and blanched lettuce. When kept alone one of these snails can reproduce by self-fertilization.

Physa acuta is a remarkably pale snail which comes originally from the Mediterranean area. It breeds very rapidly in the aquarium and soon becomes a pest.

The great ram's-horn, *Planorbarius corneus,* is entirely suitable for the home aquarium. Some individuals lack shell pigment, and the red blood can be seen through the body wall; these red specimens are often available on the market and are particularly popular. In addition to this relatively large species there are also some smaller ram's-horns.

Tropical snails:

In place of endemic snails, which are only suitable for a cold-water tank, the tropical aquarist has at his disposal a few warm-water snails. These have been bred for a long time in the aquarium and so are undoubtedly free of parasites.

These snails are quite appropriate for the aquarium, but they must be kept under control, for they breed rapidly and are then very difficult to get rid of. They should not be used

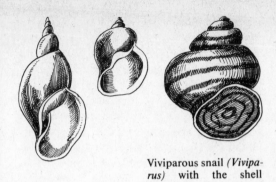

Shells of *Lymnaea*

Viviparous snail *(Vivipa-rus)* with the shell closed by the operculum

in a breeding tank because they attack fish spawn and fry that is not yet free-swimming.

The popular species are *Melanoides tuberculata,* which usually lives in the substrate, the Australian species *Physastra (Isidorella) proteus,* of which there is an attractive red form, and the small ram's-horn snail *Australorbis camerunensis,* which is also often red. All three species are warmth-loving, although they can tolerate a temporary decrease in temperature quite well. They must always be culled, as large numbers in a tank will attack the plants. In this respect *Melanoides* is regarded as harmless, but becomes a nuisance if allowed to multiply too much.

In such cases it is not difficult to bait the snails. Place a shallow saucer with some tablets of dried food on the substrate of the tank. This is best done in the evening shortly before the lights are switched off. After about an hour the lights are turned on again and masses of snails will be found in the saucer. They and the saucer can easily be lifted out of the water.

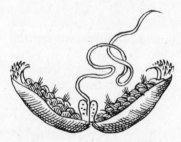

A glochidium, the young form of a freshwater mussel, which parasitizes fishes. Much enlarged

Tropical apple snails of the genus *Ampullaria,* which can grow up to the size of a fist, are often imported, and may even breed in the aquarium. They are very voracious, though opinions differ as to whether or not they attack the plants. In any case it is wise to feed these large snails separately on various dried foods, preferably those with a content of plant matter, and on blanched lettuce leaves. The pink to orange egg masses are laid out of the water on the upper edge of the glass or on the lid. A tank for these snails should never, therefore, be filled right up to the top.

Bivalve molluscs (Bivalvia):

Bivalves are not generally suitable for an aquarium, as they are not particularly interesting. Also they plough up the substrate as they move around, and uproot the plants. Anyone interested in having them should keep them in a separate tank.

The soft body of a bivalve mollusc is protected by two shells or valves which are joined together at the back by an elastic hinge. Externally, apart from the folded gill filaments, the only visible part is the muscular foot, which is used to move the mollusc through the substrate. The food, which consists of very small organisms and organic waste particles, is sucked in with the respiratory water current.

Only bivalves from standing waters are suitable for a cold-water tank, for example the swan mussel *Anodonta cygnea,* into which the female bitterling *(Rhodeus amarus)* inserts her ovipositor to lay eggs. Great care should be taken when keeping these relatively large bivalves, as they tend to die off very rapidly; this is seen when the shells remain open. Dead specimens must be removed promptly to avoid serious pollution. The larvae of the swan mussel and of related species, such as the painter's mussel, are known as glochidia, and they can swim. They live as temporary parasites on the skin and gills of fish, but fall off after a few weeks.

In fairly recent times the zebra mussel *(Dreissena polymorpha)* has found its way north from southern Europe. Its populations have suffered considerable fluctuations, as so often happens with immigrant animals. From time to time the larvae appear in lakes and rivers. These settle on the bottom, but are not parasitic. The zebra mussel can be watched in the aquarium because it does not hide away in the substrate, but likes to settle on the tank glass, attaching itself by byssus threads. When the bivalve is in this position it is possible to see the siphons (or openings) of the body when the shells are just agape and to watch the shells shut quickly when the tank is tapped. Zebra mussels are useful in the aquarium because they filter out infusorians and suspended algal cells, so that in a short time the water is brilliantly clear.

The care of aquatic plants

In the modern aquarium there is no doubt that water plants are of great importance, indeed they are almost essential. Healthy plants not only enhance the appearance of the tank, but are also beneficial to the fish. However, choosing and maintaining suitably adapted vegetation is not quite as simple as it might appear: although water plants may thrive in one place without artificial aids, they may well refuse to grow in another. Also, a general rule which is not always remembered by aquarists is that plants need the same care and attention as the fish themselves.

It is indisputable that fish are very dependent upon their environment, but not everyone realizes that plants are even more so, and will only grow if the environmental conditions are suitable. Thus the aquarist should be sure of the origin of each plant species so that he can reproduce suitable conditions in which it can thrive.

The decisive factor in the life of all green plants, including those in the water, is light. Green plants can only exist in light, because their most important nutritional process, the assimilation of carbon dioxide, is dependent upon its presence. In this process water plants extract the dissolved carbon dioxide from the water and, with the help of light and the green pigment chlorophyll, build up their living tissue. This involves the conversion of carbon into organic substances, such as fats, proteins and carbohydrates. This releases the oxygen used for respiration by both animals and plants, which produce carbon dioxide as a respiratory end-product. In light the plants again use the carbon dioxide to continue their metabolic processes, but animals get rid of it as a waste product.

These processes are, therefore, of great importance in the aquarium, so there must not only be sufficient light, but the numbers of fish and plants must be correlated and well balanced.

In cases where these requirements are not fulfilled, it is necessary to use technical means to establish an equilibrium, for example, using artificial lighting to increase the daily period of light, or aeration when the fish population is too large and the plant growth deficient. Artificial lighting provides a valuable substitute for natural light, indeed it is preferable in the tropical aquarium. It is particularly valuable during dull, overcast days in winter and sometimes at other times of the year.

Plant assimilation is minimal during dull days in autumn and winter, which is why many temperate aquatic plants die back in autumn. At such times, however, plant respiration still goes on, which means that the plants, like the fish, are using oxygen, but are not making use of the carbon dioxide produced by the fish and by the decomposition of animal and plant waste. This leads to oxygen deficiency and to an excess of carbon dioxide, and there may be heavy losses if these processes are not controlled. Countermeasures include a reduction in the fish population and pruning of any vegetation that is too luxuriant. If a reduction of the fish stock is undesirable, the situation can be controlled instead by vigorous aeration to compensate for the oxygen deficiency and to drive off the excess carbon dioxide. There should also be efficient filtration and regular replacement, preferably weekly, of a quarter of the water volume. In addition, it is essential that detritus is removed regularly by a mud-lifter or mulm bell, and that feeding should be sparse so that no food remains are left in the tank.

In general, submerse, or underwater, plants require less light, particularly sunlight, than emerse, or half-submerged, marsh plants. During their main period of growth aquatic plants from temperate regions are adapted to a daylength of fifteen to eighteen hours. They scarcely grow during winter when the light is poor and usually die back; some die completely even when given plenty of artificial light. Tropical plants, on the other hand, are adapted to a relatively uniform, short day, which along the equator is exactly twelve hours throughout the year, so they are subject to little or no seasonal fluctuation.

However, it should not be assumed that all tropical and subtropical plants require the same intensity of light; in the southern regions of the world, plant growth and competition between plants is so strong that many have to tolerate shade or half-shade, sometimes even twilight. In any case, it is not only the duration and intensity of light that are important; the angle of incidence can also be a factor. Overhead light is the most suitable for water plants, while light coming in at an angle is less suitable. A tank sited in a window may receive too much sunlight, and may require shading with, for instance, a sheet of green or white paper. As already mentioned, water filtered through peat has a brownish colour and this too reduces the amount of light reaching the plants.

For artificial lighting, ordinary tungsten lamps are sufficient for small tanks, but for larger sizes it is better to use fluorescent lamps, of which special types are available for aquarium use. These are more costly to buy but cheaper to run as they produce a higher light intensity for the same expenditure of current.

The second most important factor for plants is the substrate. In general, it can be said that most aquatic plants do best in a simple substrate of coarse sand with some loam in the lower layer. A substrate of ordinary soil is not recommended as it tends to encourage the growth of algae. The substrate should always have some nutrient content, even for those plants which only take nutrients from the water. This is because the nutrients in the substrate gradually dissolve in the water. The components of the substrate should be allowed to dry out in air before they are used. They should also not be too fine, to prevent the exclusion of air which leads to decomposition in the substrate. A mixture of coarse sand and boiled peat will produce a substrate with a sufficiently coarse texture.

Plants with special requirements can be planted in pots. One of the advantages of this method is that rare plants can be removed without disturbance to their growth when the tank has to be cleaned. The substrate surrounding the pot should not be too densely packed, and can well consist of coarse gravel or loose peat. The pots must, of course, be large enough to accommodate the expected growth of the plant, but they should not be too large.

The coarse sand used for a substrate must be well washed and rinsed in several changes of water. The last change should be checked for hardness if the tank is to have soft water. Naturally, any sand with a content of calcium will increase the hardness of the water. In such a case the most suitable substrate would be pure quartz sand.

The loam used should preferably be stored for some months, out of the rain. Only the top 2–3 cm (0·8–1·2 in) of loam, below the vegetable mould, should be collected.

Light and substrate are complementary

factors, and must be correlated. It would, for example, be wrong to compensate for deficient light by increasing the richness of the substrate. The plants should never be given more nutrient than the light conditions can deal with.

The qualitative composition of the water is also very important for many aquatic plants. In the wild the aquatic flora is much influenced by the type of water, and this depends to a large extent on the nature of the substrate. The presence in the water and substrate of trace elements may also affect plant growth. Some tropical plants like a soft, slightly acid water, others require a greater content of calcium for building up their tissues.

It must now have become evident that because of the varying requirements of the plants there are certain limits to the establishment of an attractive mixture of species, and choice becomes even more restricted when the requirements of the fish have to accord with those of the plants. In theory it would be possible to have an aquarium tank of fish and plants all from the same geographical area, but in practice this is seldom feasible. Some aquatic plants are thought to release substances which inhibit the growth of other species, but this has not been proved. To some extent the cultivation of aquarium plants depends upon the knowledge and experience of the aquarist, and on a certain element of luck, but it is hoped that the comprehensive lists that follow will enable aquarists to succeed with their chosen plants.

A trial-and-error method of choosing the correct species of plants and fish may well prove expensive and disappointing. It is important to choose fish and plants with complementary characteristics and not to take chances. Reputable plant suppliers are often a good source of advice. Once the tank community is established it will require careful monitoring; both the aesthetic and chemical balance can be maintained by careful control of plant growth. Plants that are too vigorous in their growth may be cut back periodically to allow others room to flourish.

Schedule of plants

Explanatory introduction

The schedule describes the principal plants used in the home aquarium, and also mentions a few plants suitable for a home marsh vivarium and a garden pond. The descriptions below list the most important characteristics, but detailed botanical identification is not attempted. Many of the plants are illustrated on pages 130 to 144.

The schedule is divided into two main groups:

I. Submerse plants and amphibious plants cultivated underwater.

II. Floating plants.

Within each group the plants are arranged according to families. To aid location of a particular plant, each description has a number which is indexed in the plant species list on page 106. Capital letters printed alongside the numbers in the descriptions refer to the illustrations on pages 130 to 144.

Synonyms are only given in so far as they have been used in recent years and are therefore familiar to many aquarists.

The following symbols refer to the warmth requirements of the individual plants:

▶ for use in the unheated cold-water aquarium

● for use in a moderately heated or, in summer, unheated aquarium

■ for use in a continuously heated tropical aquarium.

The following section explains certain technical terms:

adventitious	used of buds and small plants which grow from a fully developed plant
alternate	of leaves growing alternately on the stem, in contrast to 'opposite' (below)
amphibious	of plants growing half in water, half on land
annual	of plants growing from seed and flowering within a single year
axillary	placed in an axil, where a leaf base joins the stem
basal	of leaves growing directly from the base of a plant
culture	cultivation and care of plants
cutting	part of a plant inserted in soil to produce roots and a new plant
emerse	growing above water
marsh vivarium	tank with an area of wet land, for marsh plants
opposite	of leaves growing from the same node on opposite sides of the stem, contrast to 'alternate' (above)
perennial	of plants living for several years
rhizoid	root-like structures found in certain lower plants (cryptogams)
rhizome	rootstock
sessile	of leaves without a stalk, attached directly to the stem
spore	organ of reproduction in lower plants (cryptogams), e.g. mosses, ferns
submerse	submerged
synonym	another name for a plant, no longer valid
thallus	unsegmented body of certain lower plants (cryptogams).

Families, genera and species

Families and genera

Acanthaceae *(Hygrophila, Nomaphila, Synnema)*
Alismataceae *(Alisma, Echinodorus, Sagittaria)*
Amarantaceae *(Alternanthera)*
Aponogetonaceae *(Aponogeton)*
Araceae *(Acorus, Cryptocoryne, Pistia)*
Callitrichaceae *(Callitriche)*
Ceratophyllaceae *(Ceratophyllum)*
Characeae *(Chara, Nitella)*
Cruciferae *(Cardamine)*
Cyperaceae *(Heleocharis)*
Elatinaceae *(Elatine)*
Fontinalaceae *(Fontinalis, Vesicularia)*
Gentianaceae *(Nymphoides)*
Halorrhagaceae *(Myriophyllum)*
Hydrocharitaceae *(Elodea, Hydrilla, Hydrocharis, Lagarosiphon, Limnobium, Stratiotes, Vallisneria)*
Lentibulariaceae *(Utricularia)*
Lythraceae *(Peplis)*
Marsileaceae *(Marsilea)*
Najadaceae *(Najas)*
Nymphaeaceae *(Barclaya, Cabomba, Nuphar, Nymphaea)*
Oenotheraceae *(Ludwigia)*
Parkeriaceae *(Ceratopteris)*
Polypodiaceae *(Bolbitis, Microsorium)*
Pontederiaceae *(Eichhornia, Heteranthera)*
Potamogetonaceae *(Potamogeton)*
Primulaceae *(Lysimachia)*
Ranunculaceae
Ricciaceae *(Riccia)*
Salviniaceae *(Azolla, Salvinia)*
Scrophulariaceae *(Bacopa, Limnophila)*
Umbelliferae *(Hydrocotyle)*

Species

Acorus gramineus	29	*Echinodorus amazonicus*	4	*Nymphaea*	
Alisma plantago-aquatica	19	≈ *aschersonianus*	5	*daubenyana* hort	88
Alteranthera reineckii	104	≈ *bleheri*	6	≈ *lotus*	89
≈ sp. "lilacina"	105	≈ *cordifolius*	7	*Nymphoides humboldtiana*	60
≈ sp. "rosafolia"	106	≈ *horizontalis*	8	≈ *indica*	61
Aponogeton crispus	22	≈ *latifolius*	9	*Peplis diandra*	79
≈ *distachyus*	23	≈ *major*	10	*Pistia stratiotes*	107
≈ *elongatus*	24	≈ *osiris*	11	*Potamogeton gayi*	97
≈ *longiplumulosus*	25	≈ *parviflorus*	12	*Riccia fluitans*	112
≈ *madagascariensis*	26	≈ *tenellus*	13	*Sagittaria eatonii*	14
≈ *ulvaceus*	27	*Egeria densa*	74	≈ *filiformis*	15
≈ *undulatus*	28	*Eichhornia azurea*	95	≈ *montevidensis*	20
Azolla caroliniana	114	≈ *crassipes*	111	≈ *platyphylla*	16
Bacopa amplexicaulis	99	*Elatine macropoda*	57	≈ *sagittifolia*	21
≈ *monniera*	100	*Elodea canadensis*	75	≈ *subulata*	17
Barclaya longifolia	82	*Fontinalis antipyretica*	58	≈ *teres*	18
Bolbitis heudelotii	93	*Heleocharis acicularis*	56	*Salvinia auriculata*	113
Cabomba aquatica	83	*Heteranthera zosteraefolia*	96	*Stratiotes aloides*	76
≈ *caroliniana*	84	*Hydrilla verticillata*	73	*Synnema triflorum*	3
Callitriche stagnalis	49	*Hydrocharis morsusranae*	108	*Utricularia gibba*	77
Cardamine lyrata	55	*Hydrocotyle verticillata*	103	≈ *vulgaris*	78
Ceratophyllum demersum	50	*Hygrophila corymbosa*	2	*Vallisneria americana*	68
≈ *submersum*	51	≈ *difformis*	3	≈ *gigantea*	69
Ceratopteris cornuta	110	≈ *polysperma*	1	≈ *neotropicalis*	70
≈ *thalictroides*	92	*Lagarosiphon muscoides* var.		≈ *spiralis*	71
Chara foetida	52	*major*	72	*Vesicularia dubyana*	59
≈ *fragilis*	53	*Limnobium stoloniferum*	109		
Cryptocoryne affinis	30	*Limnophila aquatica*	101		
≈ *balansae*	31	≈ *sessiliflora*	102		
≈ *beckettii*	32	*Ludwigia arcuata*	90		
≈ *blassii*	33	≈ *palustris* × *repens*	91		
≈ *ciliata*	34	*Lysimachia nummularia*	98		
≈ *cordata*	35	*Marsilea crenata*	80		
≈ *griffithii*	36	*Microsorium pteropus*	94		
≈ *lingua*	37	*Myriophyllum brasiliense*	62		
≈ *lucens*	38	≈ *elatinoides*	63		
≈ *minima*	39	≈ *hippuroides*	64		
≈ *nevillii*	40	≈ *pinnatum*	65		
≈ *parva*	41	≈ *spicatum*	66		
≈ *petchii*	42	≈ *verticillatum*	67		
≈ *purpurea*	43	*Najas microdon*	81		
≈ *siamensis*	44	*Nitella flexilis*	54		
≈ *tonkinensis*	45	*Nomaphila stricta*	2		
≈ *usteriana*	46	*Nuphar pumilum*	85		
≈ *wendtii*	47	≈ *sagittifolium*	86		
≈ *willisii*	48	≈ *japonicum*	87		

Plant groups

The following twelve plant groups are intended to help in the selection of suitable aquatic plants for certain groups of fish. In the tables of ornamental fish towards the end of the book they are referred to in the 'Maintenance' column under the abbreviatron Pg. They are not based on geographical considerations, but rather on the temperature requirements of both plants and fish.

1. Plants for labyrinth fish:

Aponogeton species (22, 24, 25, 27, 28), *Cabomba* species (83, 84), *Ceratopteris* (92), *Cryptocoryne* species (30–48), *Hygrophila* species (1–3), *Limnophila* species (102, 103), *Microsorium* (94), *Vesicularia* (59); floating plants: *Ceratopteris* (110), *Salvinia* (113).

2. Plants for barbs that burrow:

Acorus (29), *Marsilea* (80), *Bacopa* species (99, 100), *Echinodorus* species (4–13), *Hygrophila* species (1–3), *Vallisneria* species (68–71), *Sagittaria* species (14–18), *Nuphar* and *Nymphaea* species (85–89).

3. Plants for barbs that do not burrow:

As in Group 2 with the addition of plants with finely divided leaves, e.g. *Ceratopteris* (Sumatra form, 92), *Limnophila* species (101, 102), *Cabomba* species (83, 84), *Vesicularia* (59), *Aponogeton* species (22, 24, 25, 27, 28), *Cryptocoryne* species (30–48), *Potamogeton* (97).

4. Plants for egg-laying toothcarps:

Aponogeton species (22, 24, 25, 27, 28), *Barclaya* (82), *Cabomba* species (83, 84), *Ceratopteris* (92), *Cryptocoryne* species (30–48), *Echinodorus* species (4–13), *Heteranthera* (96), *Hygrophila* species (1–3), *Limnophila* species (101, 102), *Microsorium* (94), *Nuphar* and *Nymphaea* species (85–89), *Vesicularia* (59); floating plants: *Ceratopteris* (110), *Salvinia* (113), *Riccia* (112), *Limnobium* (109), *Utricularia* (77).

5. Plants for livebearing toothcarps:

Cabomba species (83, 84), *Egeria* (74), *Heleocharis* (56), *Hygrophila* species (1–3), *Limnophila* species (101, 102), *Najas* (81), *Peplis* (79), *Vesicularia* (59), *Microsorium* (94), *Vallisneria* species (68–71), *Sagittaria* species (14–18), *Echinodorus* species (4–13); floating plants: *Riccia* (112), *Utricularia* (77), *Ceratopteris* (110), *Salvinia* (113).

6. Plants for various fish species from shady, tropical forest waters:

Acorus (29), *Cryptocoryne* species (30–48), *Sagittaria* species (14–18), *Echinodorus latifolius* (9), *Marsilea* (80); floating plants: *Ceratopteris* (110).

7. Plants for characins:

Cabomba species (83–84), *Echinodorus* species (4–13), *Egeria* (74), *Heteranthera* (96), *Hydrilla* (76), *Najas* (81), *Hydrocotyle* (103), *Myriophyllum* (62), *Peplis* (79), *Nuphar* and *Nymphaea* species (85–89), *Sagittaria* species (14–18), *Vallisneria* species (68–71), *Heleocharis* (56), *Vesicularia* (59), *Hygrophila* species (1–3).

8. Plants for small cichlids, burrowing or not, and other related small fish:

Echinodorus species (4–13), *Heteranthera* (96), *Cryptocoryne* species (30–48), *Hygrophila* species (1–3), *Microsorium* (94), *Ceratopteris* (92), *Nuphar* and *Nymphaea* species (85–89), *Vallisneria* species (68–71).

9. Plants for *Pterophyllum, Symphysodon* and similar, non-burrowing larger cichlids:

Vallisneria species (69, 70), *Echinodorus* species (4–13), *Sagittaria* species (14–18), *Microsorium* (94), *Hygrophila* species (1–3), *Cryptocoryne* species (30–48); floating plants: *Ceratopteris* (110).

10. Plants for actively burrowing larger cichlids:

Robust, tough plants in pots, e.g. *Acorus* (29), *Echinodorus* species (6, 7); free-floating shoots of *Egeria* (74); floating plants:

Ceratopteris (110), possibly aerial roots of *Monstera* hanging down into the water.

11. Plants for certain perch-like fish and other non-burrowing fish requiring little warmth:

Acorus (29), *Ceratophyllum* (50, 51), *Elatine* (57), *Elodea* (75), *Fontinalis* (58), *Lagarosiphon* (72), *Ludwigia* species (90, 91), *Lysimachia* (98), *Marsilea* (80), *Myriophyllum* species (63–67), *Nuphar* (85), *Sagittaria* species (14, 15, 18), *Vallisneria* (71).

11a. Plants for actively burrowing fish requiring little warmth:

Acorus (29), *Elodea* (75), *Lagarosiphon* (72), *Ludwigia* species (90, 91), *Lysimachia* (98), *Marsilea* (80), *Nuphar* (85), *Sagittaria* species (14, 15, 18), *Vallisneria* (71).

12. Plants for fish which occasionally eat parts of water plants:

Acorus (29), *Cryptocoryne* species (30–48), *Echinodorus* species (4–8, 11, 12), *Microsorium* (94), *Sagittaria* species (14–18), *Vallisneria* (69).

I. Submerse and amphibious plants

The following are the submerse plants, or those usually cultivated underwater in the aquarium (although amphibious in the wild), as well as plants rooted in the substrate that have floating leaves.

Family Acanthaceae

● ■ *Hygrophila polysperma* (A) 1
South-east Asia, in swamps and shallow waters, along river banks, frequently emerse.

The attractive pale green leaves are opposite on the more or less branched stem. The plant is usually cultivated submerse, but in dense groups or shallow water it may easily grow up above the water surface. A very undemanding plant which does well in a substrate of unwashed sand, although with the addition of a little loam the leaves grow rather larger. Propagation is by cuttings, and even single leaves floating near the surface will grow roots and new shoots. The plant requires good light, preferably with some sunlight, and any temperature between 18 and 30 °C (64 and 86 °F), but has no special water requirements.

● ■ *Nomaphila stricta* (Also known as *Hygrophila stricta* and *H. corymbosa*) (H) 2
South-east Asia, first introduced from Thailand.

The leaves, which feel rough to the touch, are narrow- to broad-lanceolate and opposite with short petioles attached to the rather fragile stem. The nerves are clearly seen on the underside of the leaves, which vary in form and size. They are bright green above but somewhat paler on the underside.

This is really an amphibious plant, which can, however, be cultivated submerse, although when the light is poor it often sheds the lower leaves. In shallow water the shoots will grow up above surface. Propagation by planting side shoots. The plant should be grown in good light with some sun, at 10–25 °C (50–77 °F), in water that is not too hard.

● *Synnema triflorum* (Also known as *Hygrophila difformis*) (H) 3
South-east Asia in swamps, along the banks and in paddy fields; originally introduced from Thailand.

A stout, extremely vigorous plant. The leaves are variable in shape, usually with irregular edges when grown submerse, but ovate and more or less entire when emerse. The pale green leaf rosettes look particularly attractive in a large aquarium. In smaller tanks the plants will require pruning to prevent them growing up above the surface.

This species should be grown in good light with some sun, at a temperature of 20–25 °C (68–77 °C), in a sandy substrate containing some loam. If possible the water should not be too hard (8–15 °dH).

Family Alismataceae

Perennial plants widely distributed in the temperate, subtropical and tropical regions of the world. Of the species of *Echinodorus* and *Sagittaria* described here some live completely submerse, some are amphibious marsh plants; in the aquarium, however, they are cultivated almost exclusively as submerse plants.

Genus *Echinodorus:*
The sword plant species described here have a short stout rootstock, from which the linear to lanceolate, sometimes ovate leaves arise. They are either basal or stalked. In some species the leaves are curved and sickle-like. The leaf nerves appear prominently on the underside of the leaves. Some species of *Echinodorus* grow up above the water surface, particularly when the water is shallow and the substrate rich in nutrients.

The smaller, always submerse species produce runners from which they can be propagated. In the larger species the long-stalked inflorescence is often produced underwater and adventitious plants may appear on the flower stalk. These can be pressed into the substrate and anchored with glass rods. Once they have formed roots they can be separated from the parent plants.

Genus *Sagittaria:*
The species described here are similar to the species of *Vallisneria*. The leaves are narrow and linear and usually slightly curved. Some species (9–12) also form long-stalked floating leaves. The inflorescence of the submerse species grow up above the water surface on long stalks. In general, propagation is by runners.

The members of the family Alismataceae have no special requirements, although they prefer water that is not too soft. In order to prevent them growing too vigorously the species of this family are best grown in a substrate of unwashed sand mixed with some loam.

■ *Echinodorus amazonicus* (Also known as *E. brevipedicellatus*) (F) 4
In Brazil, in shallow waters, swamps and along the banks of lakes, growing submerse or emerse.

The leaves, up to 25 cm (9·8 in) long, are sickle-shaped with slightly recurved edges. They are bright green with paler leaf nerves. Propagation by the adventitious plants produced on the flower stalks.

This sword plant should always be cultivated submerse. When conditions are favourable it is extremely vigorous, so it is not suitable for small tanks. The leaves remain small when the temperature is too low. The species does best at 18–30 °C (64–86 °F), preferably 20–25 °C (68–77 °F), with good light and medium-hard water (but not too soft).

■ *Echinodorus aschersonianus* (M) 5
Southern South America.

A medium-sized undemanding plant. Grown under long-day conditions the leaves are pointed and ovate to roundish, but under short-day conditions they are pointed and spatulate to broadly lanceolate. The plant only grows up above the surface in very shallow water and with a long day. The inflorescences grow erect and their stalks produce young plants which can be used for propagation when they have at least five leaves.

The plant requires bright light, a temperature of 18–30 °C (64–86 °F), preferably around 24 °C (75 °F), and medium-hard to hard water.

■ *Echinodorus bleheri* (Also known as *E. paniculatus*) (H) 6
Tropical South America, in similar locations to those of the other sword plants.

This is a large plant with leaves arranged in rosettes, suitable for a spacious tank. In favourable conditions the attractive, bright green leaves may reach a length of up to 35 cm (13·7 in) and a breadth of 8 cm (3 in). The petioles are relatively short. Each individual forms a broad clump, so no other plants should be planted in the vicinity.

This species should be cultivated like *E. amazonicus*. Propagation is by means of daughter plants which are produced from the rootstock or from adventitious plants on the flower stalk. The plant should be grown in good light at 22–30 °C (71–86 °F), in water that is not too soft.

● *Echinodorus cordifolius* (I) 7
Southern United States and Mexico.

A very large plant with broad, bright green ovate leaves, which are rather rough. The nerves on the underside of the leaves are prominent. Propagation by young plants produced on the flower stalks, at the nodes.

This species, which is only suitable for a very large aquarium tank, should be pruned regularly when grown submerse, to prevent it appearing above the water surface. The substrate should contain no nutrient if growth is to be kept in check. The plant should be kept in good light at 20–28 °C (68–82 °F), in medium-hard water.

■ *Echinodorus horizontalis* (M) 8
Central Amazon region.

The pointed, cordate leaf blades grow at an angle to the stalk so that they lie horizontally in the water. The flower stalks are stiff and grow vertically. Propagation is by plantlets produced at the nodes, but they must have well developed roots before they are removed and planted out.

The plant requires moderately good light, a temperature of 20–30 °C (68–86 °F) and water that is medium-hard to hard.

● *Echinodorus latifolius* (Dwarf Amazon sword plant—also known in the trade as *E. magdalenensis*, *E. intermedius* and *E. grisebachii*) (K) 9
Central and South America, probably in the same places as the other sword plants.

A very attractive plant which is even suitable for a small tank. Under favourable conditions the runners spread all over the substrate. In a shady position the leaves grow larger.

Large bushy plants can be obtained by the regular removal of the runners.

This species has no special water requirements, but is best grown at a temperature of 25–30 °C (77–86 °F), although it will grow slowly at 15–20 °C (59–68 °F).

■ *Echinodorus major* (Also known as *E. martii*) (H) 10
Brazil.

A large decorative plant with lanceolate, pale green leaves borne on short petioles. The leaves, which are 30–50 cm (11·8–19·6 in) long and 5–10 cm (2–4 in) broad, have wavy edges and conspicuous nerves. Propagation is by adventitious plants.

This species is particularly suitable for a spacious tank receiving good light. The water should be slightly soft at a temperature of 22–30 °C (71–86 °F).

● *Echinodorus osiris* (Also known in the trade as *E. rubra*) (M) 11
Eastern Brazil.

A very decorative large sword plant with bright green leaves which become reddish to red-brown when grown in bright light. The flowers are only produced by strong plants which must be kept submerse. The flower stalks develop numerous plantlets which should not be removed for planting too soon. Plantlets may also be produced from the parent rootstock.

The species should be grown in bright light at 15–30 °C (59–86 °F) in medium-hard to hard water.

■ *Echinodorus parviflorus* (Also known in the trade as *E. peruensis* and *E. tocanthius*) (M) 12
The species probably comes originally from western Brazil, Peru and Bolivia.

This is a leafy, medium-sized dark green plant which thrives under most aquarium conditions. The flowers are only produced when the plant is grown under short-day conditions. Young plants appear at the nodes but they should not be removed until they have good roots.

The species is best kept in light to moderately light conditions at a temperature of 18–30 °C (64–86 °F). The water should be medium-hard to hard.

■ *Echinodorus tenellus* (F) 13
Temperate and tropical regions of the American continent, in sandy places with shallow water.

This is a small sword plant with narrow linear to lanceolate leaves, which usually reaches a height of about 10 cm (4 in). In the aquarium only the tropical forms are cultivated submerse, in a substrate of fine sand mixed with some loam and sieved peat. Numerous runners are produced which soon form a dense mat.

The species is best grown in good light, possibly with some sunlight, at a temperature not below 20 °C (68 °F). The water composition is not critical, but it should not be too hard.

▶ *Sagittaria eatonii* 14
Northern United States.

An undemanding, slow-growing plant with grass-like leaves which in time forms dense mats of runners. In a sunny position the inflorescences grow up above the surface and sometimes produce fertile seeds. These can be strewn on the surface of a 5 cm (2 in) thick layer of fine sand and covered with 5 cm (2 in) of water. At a temperature of 20–25 °C (68–77 °F) the seeds will then germinate quite quickly.

The species can be grown in bright light to half shade, but it requires some sunlight for flowering. The most suitable temperature is 18–25 °C (64–77 °F), but the composition of the water is not critical.

● *Sagittaria filiformis* 15
Southern United States, forming dense mats in quiet waters.

This very attractive species has narrow, almost filamentous submerse leaves. It is propagated from runners. The floating leaves are roundish. The flowers do not grow above the surface. In other respects it can be treated like the preceding species, but at a slightly higher temperature.

● *Sagittaria platyphylla* (F) 16
Southern United States, Mississippi area.

A stately, broad-leaved plant, requiring plenty of space if large specimens are to be produced. Propagation by runners.

The plant requires bright light, otherwise dwarfed forms may appear. The temperature should be in the range 15–30 °C (59–86 °F), and the water compositon is not critical.

● *Sagittaria subulata* (Often known as *S. natans,* with three forms: *natans, pusilla* and *gracillima*) 17
Eastern United States, in shallow standing or slow-flowing waters.

An undemanding, fast-growing plant which is very similar to *Vallisneria spiralis,* from which it differs in having fewer leaf nerves and in producing floating leaves. Also it does not require so much light as *Vallisneria.* The stalk of the inflorescence does not grow up above the surface. Floating leaves are linear or elliptical. The plants do better in a sandy substrate with an admixture of some loam. The form *pusilla* is suitable for very small tanks.

The light should be bright, although slightly subdued light is tolerated. The water is best kept at 15–20 °C (59–68 °F), but its composition is not critical.

▶● *Sagittaria teres* (Also known as *S. graminea* var. *teres*) 18
Eastern United States.

A very popular small species with white flowers and almost circular leaves which are 5–15 cm (2–6 in) across. It can be cultivated like the preceding species.

▶ *Alisma plantago-aquatica* 19

▶● *Sagittaria montevidensis* 20
Southern South America.

▶ *Sagittaria sagittifolia* 21
Distributed throughout many parts of the world.

It can be cultivated as a marsh plant, either emerse or half-emerse, becoming very large. It is particularly suitable for large, damp vivaria and for garden ponds. The rootstock is often thickened and forms roundish overwintering resting bodies. The basal leaves which grow up above the surface are cordate, spear-shaped or arrow-shaped. The white or pink flowers are borne above the water surface on tall stems.

Family Aponogetonaceae

The members of this family are beautiful aquarium plants from the tropical and sub-tropical regions of Africa, south-east Asia, Australia and Madagascar. They have a stout, spherical to cylindrical rootstock from which the leaves and inflorescences grow up verti-cally. The leaf shape varies from linear to longish-oval. They are often wavy and bright green to reddish-green. Some species also have floating leaves. The longitudinal nerves are usually connected by prominent transverse nerves. In many cases the leaf tissue between this network of nerves is partially or com-pletely absent. The petioles are more or less long. The inflorescences are borne on long stalks above the water surface. The densely packed tiny flowers are white, yellowish or pink.

As a rule the rootstock cannot be divided and it seldom produces daughter plants, so propagation has to be by seeds. For seed pro-duction the flowers have to be pollinated, us-ing a soft watercolour brush. This pollination has to be repeated several times as the flowers open in succession. The tank should have a well-fitting lid to protect the flowers from draughts and the fruiting parts should be en-closed in a pouch of muslin. After a few days the fruits/seeds fall into the muslin. Germina-tion is best carried out in special tanks with a 2 cm (0·8 in) thick substrate containing a mix-ture of fine loamy sand and boiled peat. At in-tervals of 3 cm (1·1 in) the substrate should be pricked out with a series of 5 mm (0·2 in) deep holes, using the blunt end of a pencil, and a seed should be dropped into each hole. Water should then be added drop by drop un-til it is 1 cm (0·4 in) above the substrate. The temperature should be 20–25 °C (68–77 °F) and the tank placed in a light but not sunny position. Depending upon the growth the wa-ter level should be gradually increased. When the plantlets start to touch one another they should be planted out in their final position in the aquarium.

Most members of the genus *Aponogeton* grow best in soft water. This must always be free of algae and of floating particles of detri-tus as these should never be allowed to settle on the leaves. The substrate should consist of a mixture of ten parts of coarse sand with one part of loam. An admixture of a little acti-vated charcoal is advantageous.

● ■ *Aponogeton crispus* (Often erroneously known in the trade as *A. undulatus,* and usually hybridized with other species)

(G) 22

Sri Lanka (Ceylon) in clear shallow waters.

Tall, slender plants with narrow wavy leaves. In pure sand the leaves are green and thin, with the addition of loam they become darker and thicker. The leaf tissue is com-plete. Tolerates more sun than No. 13, and soft water is not absolutely necessary.

▶ ● *Aponogeton distachyus* 23

Southern Africa, naturalized in Peru and southern France. In standing and slow-flow-ing waters.

This species develops floating leaves almost exclusively, and it is particularly suitable for a garden pond. If the rootstock is protected from cold it may be hardy in the winter. In an indoor tank it requires plenty of overhead light, particularly sunlight. Propagation as de-scribed in the family description. The species requires good light, preferably sunlight. The temperature should be 5–10 °C (41–50 °F) in winter, otherwise 18–21 °C (64–69 °F), and 25 °C (77 °F) for flowering.

There are no special requirements as re-gards the water.

● ■ *Aponogeton elongatus* (Often confused with *A. undulatus*)   24
Australia, in shallow backwaters of the rivers.

A large species with broad linear, olive-green leaves which are slightly wavy at the edges. The leaf tissue between the nerves is complete. A fast-growing plant suitable for a medium-sized tank, and rarely producing floating leaves. It flowers well, and is not particularly delicate.

This species can be grown in light that is not too bright, otherwise there may be a risk of algal growth. The temperature should be up to 26 °C (78 °F), falling to 18–20 °C (64–68 °F) during the winter. Soft water is preferable, but medium-hard water can be tolerated.

● ■ *Aponogeton longiplumulosus*   25
North-western Madagascar.

A large species with broad, transparent brownish-green leaves, which may have wavy edges depending upon the cultural conditions. It only thrives in a large, spacious tank. Flowering takes place fairly freely, but it is best to pollinate with pollen from another plant.

The light can be bright or moderately bright and the temperature a little over 25 °C (77 °F), but 18–20 °C (64–68 °F) during the resting period. The water should be slightly hard rather than too soft.

● *Aponogeton madagascariensis* (Madagascar lace plant)   26
Madagascar, in slow-flowing waters, in the deep shade of overhanging trees.

A difficult plant with longish-ovate, dark green to reddish-green leaves. The leaf tissue between the nerves is completely lacking.

The species is particularly sensitive to the settlement of algae and to old water. It is, therefore, essential that a proportion of the water should be renewed at regular intervals. If the tank is to be placed in a window it should preferably face north or the illuminated side can be shaded with transparent paper. In artificial light the water surface can be covered with floating plants. Direct sunlight is injurious. If necessary, fish that consume algae can be introduced.

Propagation can be by division of the rhizome or by seeds, as given in the family description. The seedlings must be supplied with fresh water at the same temperature every three to seven days.

Apart from subdued light this species requires a temperature of 18–22 °C (64–71 °F) in summer, falling to 15–18 °C (59–64 °F) during the resting period from January to March. The water should be soft and slightly acid.

● ■ *Aponogeton ulvaceus*   27
Madagascar, in quiet backwaters of the rivers.

A large species with long, linear, slightly wavy leaves, which is only suitable for a spacious aquarium tank. It grows very rapidly in summer and flowers twice a year. Some specimens will even grow in slightly hard water.

● ■ *Aponogeton undulatus*   (N) 28
India and south-east Asia.

This is a rather small species with wavy leaves which show irregular, translucent areas. In a tank that is too tall the plant tends to grow very long leaf petioles. The flower stalk usually produces plantlets which can be removed and planted out once they have sufficient roots. This is probably the most undemanding of all the *Aponogeton* species. It prefers bright or moderately bright light, and a temperature of 20–25 °C (68–77 °F), dropping to 16–18 °C (60–64 °F) during the resting period. Water can be medium-hard to hard.

Family Araceae

Of the two genera described below, namely *Acorus* and *Cryptocoryne,* the latter is probably the most popular for aquarium purposes. Most of them can scarcely be surpassed by other aquatic plants as a decorative feature in the well-furnished aquarium tank.

▶ ● *Acorus gramineus*   (I) 29
In addition to the main form there are some varieties on the market, of which the dwarf

variant *pusillus* is particularly attractive. A green and white striped form is especially suitable for the garden pond.

The species comes from the temperate regions of eastern Asia, where it occurs in shallow and swampy waters and also on land. The stiff, grass-like, bright green plant has basal leaves arranged like a fan, and a horizontal, creeping rootstock. It is hardy and undemanding. Grown submerse it is suitable for a temperate or slightly warm tank, when half-emerse for a marsh aquarium. The substrate should be unwashed sand with a little loam. Propagation by division of the rootstock. The species does not require bright light, although it grows more slowly in subdued light. The temperature should be 15–21 °C (59–64 °F), and the water composition is not critical.

Genus *Cryptocoryne*:

The inflorescence and the basal leaves arranged in a rosette arise from the creeping and often branched rootstock. The leaves, which are entire, vary in shape: linear, elliptic, longish or broadly ovate. They are usually pale green to dark green, often even brownish, sometimes with darker speckling. The underside of the leaves frequently has reddish or red spots. The leaf edges are often wavy.

The inflorescence consists of a tubular section at the bottom which contains the female and male flowers, a long, fairly thin rod-like spadix and a sheath-like spathe which is usually brightly coloured. The whole structure is very similar to the inflorescence of the related common European plant *Arum maculatum,* known colloquially as cuckoo-pint or lords-and-ladies. Most species of *Cryptocoryne* flower when grown emerse but some do so when submerse. The inflorescence usually grows up above the water surface but some remain underwater.

All species of *Cryptocoryne* are warm-water plants, and most can be cultivated emerse or submerse. The substrate should be coarse sand with some loam and a proportion of peat to give an open texture; it should be 8–15 cm (3–6 in) deep. These plants do not like being

moved, and so far as possible changes in light intensity should be avoided. Any attempt to move submerse specimens on to the land should be carried out very gradually.

Propagation is mainly by runners produced quite freely from the rootstock.

Most species do not require a great amount of light, but almost all thrive better when not kept in dim light. Some like an occasional period of sunlight. The water should normally be fairly soft, possibly slightly acid, and at a temperature of 24–30 °C (75–86 °F).

Unfortunately there is still a certain amount of confusion over the correct naming of many species of *Cryptocoryne*.

■ *Cryptocoryne affinis* (For a long time this species was known in the trade as *C. haerteliana)* (C) 30
Malay Peninsula.

In this species the longish leaves are dark green with a silky sheen, their undersides reddish to bright red. The leaf nerves appear pale on the upperside. There are two forms of this species, one with erect leaves, the other with leaves lying along the bottom. This is a vigorous *Cryptocoryne* which produces numerous runners, so that under favourable conditions the plants spread over the whole substrate. Flowering takes place in shallow water and the spathe is dark red with a long tip.

The light need not be too bright. The temperature is best kept around 24 °C (75 °F) and the water should not be too hard.

■ *Cryptocoryne balansae* (Also known in the trade as *C. somphongsi)* 31
Thailand and northern Vietnam.

The leaves, which grow to a length of up to 30 cm (11·8 in), are narrow, strap-like and green or brownish, with wavy and crimped blades. This is a fast-growing species which, under favourable conditions, can be propagated rapidly by runners; these must be allowed to become well rooted in the substrate before they are separated from the parent plant. The substrate should be deep, with some loam, and the water soft and slightly acid.

114

The species likes a moderate amount of light and a temperature of 22–30 °C (71–86 °F).

■ *Cryptocoryne beckettii* (C) 32
Sri Lanka.

This is a very variable species. The best-known form has submerse, longish, pointed leaves with slightly wavy edges. The coloration is brownish-green, the undersides usually somewhat reddish with a matt sheen. The leaves are up to 12 cm (4·7 in) long, 4 cm (1·5 in) across.

Another form has narrower pale green to olive-green leaves with purplish-red undersides; they are up to 8 cm (3 in) long and 2·5 cm (1 in) across.

The species scarcely ever flowers when grown submerse and is, in fact, very suitable for growing emerse. There is no need for bright light and the plant does perfectly well in half shade. The water should preferably be soft and kept at a temperature of 20–30 °C (68–86 °F), mainly around 24 °C (75 °F).

■ *Cryptocoryne blassii* (I) 33
Southern Thailand, in standing or slow-flowing waters, often in half shade.

This is a handsome species which develops to the full in an aquarium tank that is sufficiently spacious.

The leaves are ovate and pointed, the base heart-shaped. Leaf size is variable but in good specimens it may be up to 15 cm (6 in) long and 6 cm (2·3 in) across. The upperside of the leaves is dented, and shiny grey-green, the underside dark wine-red. This species requires a substrate rich in nutrients and moderately soft to hard water, at a temperature of 22–25 °C (71–77 °F). The light should be subdued and there should be no sunlight.

■ *Cryptocoryne ciliata* (N) 34
India, Thailand, Malay Peninsula, Indonesia; also in brackish water areas.

This is a suitable plant for a large tank or for a marsh aquarium. It only remains submerse in deep water. The leaves are narrow to broadly lanceolate, sometimes truncated at the end. The uppersides are pale green in submerse plants, rather darker in those growing emerse. The undersides are always paler. The spathe is yellow in the middle, becoming purplish-red at the edge which has thread-like outgrowths. Propagation is mainly by runners.

This species grows fairly rapidly, hence the need for a large tank, preferably with an area of land. When kept submerse it grows more slowly, but lasts longer. It requires bright light and a temperature of 20–30 °C (68–86 °F). It tolerates hard and even brackish water.

■ *Cryptocoryne cordata* 35
Malay Peninsula, Indonesia.

The large, broad leaves are heart-shaped at the base, slightly pointed at the tips, dark green above and sometimes reddish on the underside. The spathe is purple, becoming yellow inside; the yellow colour may sometimes extend over the whole of the spathe. Propagation is by runners. The species can be cultivated like *C. beckettii*.

■ *Cryptocoryne griffithii* (B) 36
Malay Peninsula.

This species is not commonly seen in the aquarium (the plant formerly grown as *C. griffithii* is now thought to be *C. purpurea*).

C. griffithii is very similar to *C. cordata*, differing only slightly in a few details, mainly of the leaf shape. In *C. griffithii* the spathe has a narrow tail-like tip.

■ *Cryptocoryne lingua* (I) 37
Kalimantan (Borneo).

A small plant, about 12 cm (4·7 in) tall, with rough, fleshy leaves leaves up to 5 cm (2 in) long, 2·5 cm (1 in) broad, and bright green with dark markings on the underside. They are spatulate and pointed.

This species grows rather slowly when emerse or submerse. It requires a substrate of coarse sand with some nutrient and should be grown in subdued light, without sunlight. The temperature can be in the range 22–28 °C

115

(71–82 °F), and the composition of the water is not critical.

■ *Cryptocoryne lucens* (B) 38
Probably from Sri Lanka

This species can be cultivated like *C. nevillii,* but it is considerably larger, and in particular has longer petioles. The shiny spathes are characteristic.

Growth is much faster than in *C. nevillii,* up to a height of 20 cm (7·8 in), but when too crowded it tends to produce elongated, often insignificant growth. Propagation by runners.

■ *Cryptocoryne minima* 39
Malay Peninsula and Borneo.

A small plant, only 10 cm (4 in) tall, with ovate leaves which have pointed tips. It grows better when emerse and requires bright light. It will then cover large areas with mat-like growth.

■ *Cryptocoryne nevillii* (In botanical literature there is considerable confusion about this species. Some authorities maintain that it is a form of *C. willisii.*) (B) 40
Sri Lanka.

A small species with rough, dark green, slightly curved leaves, varying in breadth. The spathe is blackish-purple. Growth is very slow when the substrate contains insufficient nutrient.

Under favourable conditions, when it has been grown undisturbed over a long period, this species will produce numerous runners, forming an extensive mat. It is particularly suitable for planting in the foreground of an aquarium tank. It requires a moderate amount of light and a temperature of 22–30 °C (71–86 °F).

■ *Cryptocoryne parva* 41
Probably from Sri Lanka.

A very small plant which some authorities consider to be a dwarf form of *C. nevillii* or *C. willisii.* It grows to a height of less than 10 cm (4 in). An ideal plant for the tank foreground.

■ *Cryptocoryne petchii* (N) 42
Sri Lanka.

An attractive plant, very similar to *C. beckettii,* which has olive-green leaves, with reddish undersides. It can be cultivated like *C. affinis* and propagated by runners.

■ *Cryptocoryne purpurea* 43
Malay Peninsula.

This species is very similar to *C. cordata* and *C. griffithii* and difficult to distinguish. It is yet another species of *Cryptocoryne* which has been involved in the nomenclatural confusion that bedevils the genus.

■ *Cryptocoryne siamensis* 44
South-east Asia.

A similar plant to *C. blassii* but the leaves are narrower with green uppersides (*C. blassii* has a greyish tinge above). The undersides of the leaves are red-brown to deep coffee-brown. In recent years *C. blassii* has been considered to be a form of *C. siamensis.* Cultivation as given for *C. blassii.*

■ *Cryptocoryne tonkinensis* (N) 45
India and south-east Asia.

A tall species, up to 60 cm (23·6 in) which differs considerably in appearance from other species of *Cryptocoryne.* The leaves are very long, narrow and olive-green or olive-brown, sometimes with wavy edges. Cultivation as for *C. affinis.*

■ *Cryptocoryne usteriana* (Formerly known as *C. aponogetonifolia*) (I) 46
Philippines.

A very attractive plant with pale green, lanceolate, much dented leaves which may be up to 50 cm (19·6 in) long. It requires plenty of light and is not difficult to propagate by runners. Leaves lying along the water surface may tend to shade other plants.

■ *Cryptocoryne wendtii* (O) 47
South-east Asia.

A widely distributed species of *Cryptocoryne,* with considerable variation in leaf form and coloration. The leaves are usually pale olive-green above, pink to reddish below. The uppersides of the leaves are characterized by a pattern of V-like grey markings, which are even discernible in the red-brown variant known as C. 'rubella'.

■ *Cryptocoryne willisii* (K) 48
Sri Lanka.

Recently this plant has acquired two new synonyms, *C. undulata* and *C. axelrodi*, which merely add to the confusion surrounding the species.

The narrow, brownish leaves with distinctly wavy edges are up to 25 cm (9·8 in) long.

This is a good plant for the aquarium, and can be cultivated like *C. affinis*.

Family Callitrichaceae

The members of this family, known as starworts, are delicate water plants, which do not always survive for long in an aquarium tank. The leaves are linear or spatulate and arranged opposite one another on the fragile, much branched stem. They are undemanding plants which remain green throughout the winter but they cannot be kept together with very active fish. The substrate can be loamy sand and propagation is by cuttings.

▶ *Callitriche stagnalis* (D) 49
Europe, North Africa, northern and central Asia to India, in standing and flowing waters.

They require bright light and a moderate temperature of 15–18 °C (59–64 °F). The composition of the water is not critical.

Family Ceratophyllaceae

The hornworts are somewhat fragile, usually rootless water plants. The finely feathered stiff leaves have tiny spines on the underside and are arranged in whorls around the stem. This is normally a floating plant, but pieces can be anchored to the bottom of an aquarium tank with glass rods. Endemic hornworts will die down in autumn and form winter buds, but specimens from warmer regions, if procurable, should remain green. Propagation by division of the shoots.

▶ *Ceratophyllum demersum* (Hornwort)
(E) 50
Cosmopolitan.

This is a very variable plant, best kept in bright light but without too much sun; algae tend to develop on the leaves. The plants from temperate regions can be kept at 14–22 °C (57–71 °F), but those from the tropics usually do well at 22–26 °C (71–78 °F). The water should not be too soft.

▶ *Ceratophyllum submersum* 51
Cosmopolitan.

A very similar plant to *C. demersum*, but the leaves are thinner and they have fewer spines. Also the stems are even more fragile.

Cultivation as for *C. demersum*.

Family Characeae

These are algae with no true roots. The species described here have a stem 30–40 cm (11·8–15·7 in) long which carries a whorl of needle-like leaves. The plants are usually rather fragile and more or less covered with a calcareous incrustation. They are annuals or perennials, mostly the latter. In the aquarium they can be propagated from cuttings. The endemic species of *Chara* are not much cultivated nowadays, but the more cosmopolitan *Nitella* is still used. They are particularly valuable as spawning sites for fish which spawn at random or in among dense vegetation. Identification of the individual species is mostly a matter for the specialist.

▶ *Chara foetida* (G) 52
Widely distributed in many parts of the world, in quiet shallow waters.

This species is useful as a spawning plant when not too much encrusted. It likes subdued light, with not too much sun, and cold water.

▶ ● *Chara fragilis* 53
With much the same distribution as *C. foetida*, but extending into brackish water and into the eastern Baltic Sea.

This species appears more often on the market. It should be cultivated like *C. foetida*, but tolerates rather warmer water.

▶ ● *Nitella flexilis* (G) 54
Europe, Asia, North America, particularly in small bodies of water with a muddy bottom.

For decorative purposes this species can be anchored in the bottom, but as a spawning plant it can be kept in loose bundles, which also provide good shelter for fish fry. The light should be bright, without too much sun which encourages algae. The composition of the water is not critical and the temperature can be around 20–22 °C (68–71 °F), but not above 25 °C (77 °F).

Family Cruciferae

▶ ● *Cardamine lyrata* (N) 55
Eastern Siberia, northern and eastern China, Korea, Japan, normally emerse but sometimes submerse, in similar places to the bittercress (*Cardamine* sp.) of Europe.

This is a delicate plant which is usually cultivated submerse in the aquarium. The creeping, branched rootstock produces fragile stems which carry roundish leaves on long petioles. The submerse plants do not flower. Propagation is by division of the rootstock or by cuttings. This is a good plant for the garden pond where it is grown emerse. The delicate flowers must be protected from snails.

The light should be bright, with some sun for those in the garden, and the temperature 15–20 °C (59–68 °F). The plant has no special requirements as regards the water composition, but the leaves grow larger when the water is not too hard.

Family Cyperaceae

▶ ● *Eleocharis acicularis* (Needlegrass, Hairgrass) (E) 56

Europe, Asia, Australia, America, in standing waters, especially near the banks.

An undemanding perennial plant with stiff, pale green, needle-like leaves. The creeping rootstock produces shoots which can cover the whole of the bottom. Such dense growths provide good shelter for the eggs of random-spawners. The submerse form does not flower. Propagation by division of the rootstock. Plants from temperate regions can be kept in good light, at room temperature.

Family Elatinaceae

The species of *Elatine*, of which *E. macropoda* is described here, are annual or perennial marsh plants. They can be found submerse in flooded areas, half-emerse or as land plants.

▶ ● *Elatine macropoda* (A cultivated form is known in the trade as *E. macropoda* forma *submersa*.) (E) 57
France, Spain, North Africa, Malta, Sicily.

This is a small plant which can be grown in a substrate containing a mixture of fine, unwashed sand and loam; it requires a resting period, during which the tank should contain no fish that might upset the plants. The plants should initially be distributed over the whole of the substrate as this helps the formation of a dense mat. This is a plant which provides good shelter for fish eggs.

The light should be bright and it must reach down to the bottom. The water is best kept at 18–21 °C (64–70 °F).

Family Fontinalaceae (Water-mosses)

These have an almost cosmopolitan distribution. The true water-mosses are highly adapted for underwater life. The stem is round or angular and usually much branched. The small scale-like leaves are green to brownish or reddish. The plant is attached by root-like filaments, the rhizoids, to firm objects such as rocks or timber, but it can also live floating free in the water.

▶ *Fontinalis antipyretica* (G) 58
Europe, northern Asia, North America, North Africa, in clear flowing or standing waters.

This is more suitable for a cold-water tank than mosses from warmer regions, mainly because it can become acclimatized more easily to the changed conditions. It is best to collect a plant that is attached to a small piece of rock. In a cold-water tank this moss will remain green throughout the winter. It will survive for some time in a heated tank and will then serve as a spawning site. Propagation is by cuttings.

This moss is best kept in light that is not too bright, to avoid the risk of algal settlement, and should not be kept for any length of time at temperatures above 18–20 °C (64–68 °F). It likes clear, clean water.

■ *Vesicularia dubyana* (Java moss) 59
Indonesia, Malaya, Philippines.

An attractive, much branched plant belonging to the moss family Hypnaceae. In the wild it lives mainly emerse on the damp edges of rivers and lakes, but it is highly adaptable and will live submerse for a long time.

When grown submerse the plant produces small, delicate, bright green leaves. When attached to a rock or the aquarium the richly branched plant spreads out in all directions, but it also thrives floating free in the water. Propagation is by cuttings.

Java moss is susceptible to the settlement of algae and to detritus stirred up by burrowing fish.

This moss should be kept in slightly subdued light at 16–26 °C (60–78 °F), and it does not require any special type of water.

Family Gentianaceae

The two species of *Nymphoides* described here produce floating leaves on very long petioles, from which adventitious shoots and inflorescences appear. The flowers are white with hairy petals and they are arranged in groups. These plants only thrive in a home

aquarium when kept in a tank receiving very bright light. The substrate should be sand mixed with loam and a little peat. Overwintering is difficult. It is best, in summer, to plant some strong specimens in pots with a mixture of loam and peat and gradually acclimatize them to shallow water. Then keep them in a well-lit position at 15–18 °C (59–64 °F); the tank should have a glass lid.

■ *Nymphoides humboldtiana* (Often known in the trade as *Villarsia humboldtiana* or *Limnantherum humboldtianum*) (B) 60
Tropical South America, in shallow waters.

This is an attractive but demanding plant. When kept outside in summer it is sensitive to periods of cool weather. Propagation is by the rooted adventitious plants or by seeds. The light should be very bright with some sun, and the temperature, including the air temperature, 20–30 °C (68–86 °F) in summer. The plant does best in soft water.

In general, the members of this genus are difficult to keep in a home aquarium. In the United States, *N. aquatica* is popularly known as the Banana plant.

■ *Nymphoides indica* 61
India, China, Japan, Australia, Fiji, Africa.

To be cultivated like the preceding species.

Family Halorrhagaceae

The species of *Myriophyllum* (milfoils) described here are mainly submerse perennial plants with a creeping rootstock and fine, branched roots. The feathery leaves are green, dark green to reddish, usually arranged in whorls, more rarely alternate or opposite. At flowering time, shoots with aerial leaves grow up above the surface and small flowers appear in the leaf axils. Propagation is by cuttings.

These are decorative, undemanding aquarium plants which can be grown in a substrate of unwashed sand with a small content of loam. Most species have no special requirements as regards temperature, although they are sensitive to water that is too warm. They should not be kept with actively burrowing fish or with aeration as the disturbed detritus settles on the leaves which then die off. Any detritus that does appear should be removed at regular intervals.

● ■ *Myriophyllum brasiliense* (Also known in the trade as *M. proserpinacoides*)   (D) 62
South America and southern United States.

Delicate green, feathery plants that grow up above the surface. They will grow in a substrate of sand, preferably in bright or very bright light. The temperature should be 18–25 °C (64–77 °F).

Like all the milfoils, this is a good spawning plant.

▶ *Myriophyllum elatinoides*   63
South and Central America, in cold freshwater lakes.

This is a plant for the cold-water aquarium, to be grown in clear, clean water. It is best kept in a good depth of water to allow full development. The light should be bright, but too much sunlight may encourage algal growth. The water, which should not be too hard, can be kept at 15–20 °C (59–68 °F) or less.

▶ *Myriophyllum hippuroides* (Also known in the trade as *M. scabratum, M. mexicanum* and *M. affinis elatinoides*)   64
North America to Mexico, in clear water.

This plant can be cultivated like the preceding species, but it also thrives in hard water. It is characterized by the regularly formed leaf whorls.

● *Myriophyllum pinnatum* (Also known in the trade as *M. eggelingi, M. tritoni, M. scabratum* and *M. nitsehei*)   65
Eastern North America and Mexico, Cuba, in clear waters that are not too deep. As the water level falls the plants become emerse.

This milfoil requires rather more warmth than the other species. It is particularly suitable for the breeding tank on account of its branched and irregular growth. Any piece of the plant with a few adventitious roots can be used as a cutting. The leaves may be opposite or alternate or more rarely in whorls. This species can be cultivated like the other members of the genus, but at 15–18 °C (59–64 °F) in winter, and up to 25 °C (77 °F) in summer.

▶ *Myriophyllum spicatum* (Spiked milfoil) 66
Occurs almost everywhere, except in Central and South America, Central Africa and Australia, in clear quiet waters, and also in brackish water.

This species can be cultivated like the other milfoils, but only thrives in cold water, which can be hard. Regular pruning in the summer will give bushy growths which remain green during the winter. This is not a particularly suitable species for the aquarium.

▶ *Myriophyllum verticillatum* (Whorled milfoil)   67
Europe, Canada, parts of Asia and Africa, particularly in waters with a low calcium content.

Cultivation as for the other milfoils. This species remains green in winter when kept at a relatively low temperature. Propagation is from winter buds. Does not like hard water.

Family Hydrocharitaceae

A family of purely aquatic plants, many of which are much appreciated in the aquarium. The pollination mechanisms are particularly interesting. The female flowers usually float at the surface, attached to the parent plant by a thin stalk. The male flowers, formed at the base of the male plants, break loose at the right time and rise to the surface where wind and waves carry them to the female flowers.

● *Vallisneria americana* (Often known in the trade as *V. torta*)   68
Southern United States, California, Nevada.

A relatively small species with strap-like, spirally twisted leaves. The leaf edges are entire but finely toothed. A species which requires a certain amount of warmth. When kept too cool the leaves remain smaller.

■ *Vallisneria gigantea* (The trade often offers hybrids between this species and *V. spiralis*. A red form known as *V. neotropicalis* is very similar to *V. gigantea,* but it has slightly red leaves which may be even longer − over 2 m [2·2 yd].) (F) 69
New Guinea, Philippines and other tropical areas of south-east Asia, in standing and flowing waters.

A handsome plant with broad, linear leaves which reach a length of over 1 m (1 yd). The true form of this species has three nerves on each side of the central nerve. Propagation is by the profusely produced runners. The parent plants usually die in the second year.

This large plant should be grown in a rich substrate (half coarse sand, half loam) at a temperature of 25−30 °C (77−86 °F), not below 18 °C (64 °F). The light should be bright and the water not too soft.

■ *Vallisneria neotropicalis* 70
Florida, Cuba.

Cultivation as for *V. gigantea*. The intense red colour is enhanced by bright light.

● ■ *Vallisneria spiralis* (F) 71
Southern areas of the north temperate zone and the subtropics, forming dense mats in flowing and standing waters.

The strap-like leaves reach a length of 30 cm (11·8 in) and a width of 1 cm (0·4 in). This is a very decorative and undemanding plant which can be grown in a substrate of unwashed sand mixed with some loam. Propagation is by runners which are produced profusely when the conditions are favourable.

The light should be very bright, as the plant becomes pale in dim light. The temperature can be kept at 17−24 °C (62−75 °F), and certainly not below 15 °C (59 °F) for any length of time. Growth is inhibited in water that is too soft.

▶ ● *Lagarosiphon muscoides* var. *major* (For many years known in the trade as *Elodea crispa*) 72
Southern Africa, in clear waters.

Very similar to the species of *Elodea,* but the leaves, which are attached close to the stem, are rolled into little coils, rather like curly hair. This is a perennial plant which can be cultivated floating free in the water or anchored with glass rods in the substrate; it is a good oxygen producer. Nutrients are taken up exclusively through the leaves. The plant requires bright light and a temperature of 18−23 °C (64−73 °F).

▶ ● *Hydrilla verticillata* 73
North-eastern Europe, southern and eastern Asia, Australia, Madagascar, West Africa, in standing and flowing waters, preferably with a muddy bottom.

A perennial plant, very similar to *Egeria,* but the leaves are distinctly toothed and the central stem is reddish. Plants from temperate parts of the range can be used in a cold-water aquarium, but they die down in winter and form resting bodies. Cultivation as for *Elodea* (No. 75).

● ■ *Egeria densa* (E) 74
Southern United States, Central and South America, in standing waters or in quiet backwaters of rivers.

This is a very decorative bright green plant with closely packed leaves. It should be cultivated like *Elodea canadensis,* but at a slightly higher temperature (18−26 °C or 64−78 °F). It does well in summer in a garden pond. The light should be bright and the water not too soft.

▶ *Elodea canadensis* (Canadian waterweed − the genus *Elodea* has also been known as *Helodea, Egeria* and *Anacharis*) 75
North America, Canada.

This species has been introduced into many temperate zone areas. The leaves are arranged in whorls of two to three around the stem.

This is an undemanding plant which can be cultivated floating free in the water or anchored in the substrate with glass rods. It is a good oxygen producer which can be propagated by simple division of the stem. It prefers bright light, but should be kept cool, preferably 5–21 °C (41–69 °F). The composition of the water is not critical.

▶ *Stratiotes aloides* (Water-soldier)   (C) 76
Europe, northern Asia, in standing waters, growing either rooted in the bottom or floating free in the water.

This plant is only suitable for a cold-water aquarium, where it can be grown from winter buds collected in the autumn, kept cool during the winter and planted out in spring. The light should be bright with some sunlight.

Family Lentibulariaceae

The two species of bladderwort described here are perennial submerse plants. They have root-like structures and finely divided leaves. They mostly float free in the water, forming dense tangles of branches. Flowers arise out of the water on leafless flower stems. The remarkable thing about the bladderworts is that, in addition to normal photosynthesis, they also derive nourishment from animals, and are in effect carnivorous, catching small aquatic invertebrates in small air-filled bladders, or vesicles. The prey is digested within the bladders.

● ▶ *Utricularia gibba* (Bladderwort – also known in the trade as *U. eroleta* and *U. minor*)   77
Europe, Africa, parts of Asia and Australia, in waters of all kinds.

These plants have very thin stems and tiny bladders. Alongside each leaf there are one or two bladders which on account of their small size can only catch tiny live food. In the absence of animal food the bladders degenerate and the plants generally become thinner. The shoots grow irregularly and float free below the surface, forming dense thickets. Propagation is by pieces of stem which rapidly grow new plants. This plant provides an excellent spawning site for fish that lay near the surface and also gives shelter for fish fry. The light should not be too bright, to avoid the risk of algal settlement. The temperature should not be less than 18 °C (64 °F), and the plant thrives best in soft water, provided it is not too deficient in live food.

▶ *Utricularia vulgaris*   (D) 78
Europe, North Africa, North America, in clear, soft water.

A very attractive cold-water plant with pale green, finely divided alternate leaves on long stems. There may be 10–200 bladders alongside each leaf, and these catch small planktonic animals such as water-fleas, and may be dangerous to fish fry.

The plant can be cultivated floating free in the water or it can be anchored to the bottom by glass rods. Propagation is by cuttings. The light should be subdued to avoid algal settlement, and the temperature 15–20 °C (59–68 °F). The water should preferably be soft and slightly acid.

Family Lythraceae

● *Peplis diandra* (= *Didiplis diandra*)   (K) 79
South-eastern North America.

A marsh plant which can be successfully cultivated underwater, sending up shoots above the surface. It is somewhat similar in general appearance to *Elodea*, but the narrow leaves are arranged much more densely on the stem, which branches profusely. According to the water level the shoots may grow up to a length of 40 cm (15·7 in). Propagation is by division.

The plant requires bright light, a temperature of 15–25 °C (59–77 °F) and water that is not too soft.

Family Marsileaceae

Marsh plants with a long, creeping rootstock. The leaves have four clover-like leaflets and long, erect stalks. These may lie along the surface or grow up above it.

These plants, which belong among the fern family, will grow submerse or emerse. The spore-bearing bodies develop at the base of the leaf stalks, but only in plants growing emerse.

The substrate can be sand with a little loam. Propagation in the aquarium is by division of the rootstock.

● ■ *Marsilea crenata* (Often confused in the trade with *M. quadrifolia*)   (D) 80
Central and southern Australia in muddy waters which sometimes dry up.

A hardy plant which does not require too much warmth, growing best at 18–22 °C (64–71 °F). It becomes stunted and dies back when grown only underwater. It requires a moderate amount of light.

Family Najadaceae

Annual or perennial plants with finely branched roots. The mainly opposite leaves are dark green, the edges with tiny teeth. The inconspicuous flowers appear in the leaf axils.

● ■ *Najas microdon* (= *N. guadelupensis*) (Also known in the trade as *N. flexilis*)
(G) 81
Mainly North America.

A pale green plant which forms dense submerse bushes. It is simple to keep. The substrate should be sand that is not too coarse, mixed with a little loam. When the light is sufficient the clumps do not die back in winter. Propagation is by cuttings which should be inserted in the sand so that the two lowermost leaf nodes are covered.

The light should be bright and the temperature not below 20 °C (68 °F), preferably around 24 °C (75 °F). The water must not be too soft.

Family Nymphaeaceae

The plants described here are submerse members of the genera *Barclaya* and *Cabomba* and also of *Nuphar* and *Nymphaea* (water-lilies), which can be cultivated underwater over a long period.

■ *Barclaya longifolia*   (K) 82
Burma, Thailand, Vietnam, in shady places near the banks.

The very long strap-like leaves are greenish-brown above, reddish below. They are very delicate and translucent, with conspicuous leaf nerves. The plants reach a height of up to 30 cm (11·8 in), so they require a tall tank. They are prone to attack by snails. Propagation is by cuttings or from seeds. The substrate should be sand with loam to provide nutrients. The water must not be too hard, and it should be kept at 20–28 °C (68–82 °F). Subdued light is recommended, possibly in a shady corner of a densely planted tank.

Genus *Cabomba*:
The members of this genus are perennial plants with opposite, finely-divided, fan-shaped or kidney-shaped leaves. At flowering time, but rarely in the aquarium, floating leaves with entire edges are formed, which carry the flowers above the water surface on short stalks. The underwater shoots may grow very long. The leaves are pale to bright green, but the colour may vary according to the light.

These are delicate plants which require care. If possible they should be planted in pots, in a one to one mixture of coarse sand and loam. Propagation is by cuttings. The plants are very sensitive to the settlement of detritus and algae.

■ *Cabomba aquatica*   83
Mexico in the north to central Brazil in the south, in standing waters or the backwaters of rivers.

The very long shoots grow below the surface, occasionally producing floating leaves. Cultivation as given above.

This species requires bright light in summer and winter, but sunlight is not recommended as it increases the chance of algal settlement. For the same reason soft water, if possible below 6 °dH, should be used as this discourages algae. The temperature can be around 25 °C (77 °F) in summer and not below 18 °C (64 °F) in winter.

● *Cabomba caroliniana*   (E) 84
In the same range as the preceding species, but extending further to the north and south.

Cultivation as for the preceding species, but with a slightly lower temperature. A red-leaved form only retains its colour when given sufficient overhead light in summer and winter. Temperature: 15–18 °C (59–64 °F) in summer, 18–22 °C (64–71 °F) in winter.

In addition to these two species of *Cabomba* there are others on the market in which the stalks or the undersides of the leaves are reddish.

Genus *Nuphar*:

The submerse forms of this genus are either juvenile plants or those from deep water which may not produce floating leaves. They all require a substrate rich in nutrient. The rootstock is best planted in a pot and placed in position as soon as it starts to develop leaves. Specimens from water plant nurseries have usually been raised from seed and they are particularly suitable. All water lilies require bright light.

▶ ● *Nuphar pumilum*   85
Europe, western Siberia.

The roundish, lettuce-like, relatively large underwater leaves are delicate pale green and translucent.

These are decorative plants which last a long time, even in high temperatures, although growth is rather slow.

● ■ *Nuphar sagittifolium*   86
Southern Carolina.

The leaves are long and arrow-shaped with wavy edges and long stalks. They are a beautiful pale green. Floating leaves are not produced. Cultivation as given above.

● ■ *Nuphar japonicum*   87
Japan.

An attractive plant with broad, deeply incised, arrow-shaped submerse leaves. These are normally bright green and there is also a reddish-brown variety.

Genus *Nymphaea*:

Two species have proved suitable for the warm-water aquarium. They only flower when several floating leaves have been produced and these, of course, tend to shade any underwater plants.

● ■ *Nymphaea daubenyana* hort. (A hybrid between *N. micrantha* and *N. caerulea)* (L) 88

At first this form produces very decorative and delicate submerse leaves, which die back when the first floating leaves appear. These are followed by the flowers, which are sterile. Propagation is by adventitious plants produced at the bases of the leaf blade. Growth is encouraged by a substrate containing loam.

■ *Nymphaea lotus*   (L) 89
West Africa.

This water-lily appears on the market in three forms, with green, pale reddish-violet or deep red leaves, sometimes with dark markings. The submerse leaves are very broad and slightly wavy. Floating leaves and flowers are rarely produced in the aquarium. Propagation is by runners which should only be separated from the parent rootstock after they have formed good roots.

Family Onagraceae

The two species of *Ludwigia* described here are suitable for submerse cultivation in cold or slightly warm tanks, or for emerse cultivation in garden ponds and a marsh aquarium. They are both perennial with broad, lanceolate, pointed leaves, which are arranged alternate or opposite on the more or less branched stem. The leaves are dark green to brownish-green above, reddish below. The plants tend to grow up above the water surface and this can be prevented by regular pruning. The small flowers only appear on emerse shoots.

▶ ● *Ludwigia arcuata*   90
South-eastern United States (Virginia, Carolina).

The leaves are narrow-lanceolate and relatively long. The plant does well when submerse and forms dense thickets. It requires bright light and a temperature of 18–22 °C

(64–71 °F), or slightly higher. The composition of the water is not critical.

▶ ● ■ *Ludwigia palustris × repens* (Hybrid Ludwigia – also known in the trade as *L. natans*, *L. palustris* or *L. mullerti*)   (B) 91

Ludwigia palustris is widely distributed as a wild plant throughout Europe, northern Asia and the Mediterranean area. It does well when grown submerse, but does not tolerate high temperatures.

L. repens is a species that occurs in the south-western United States. It develops a number of very different growth forms, depending upon the light and substrate. It also tolerates higher temperatures – up to 30 °C (86 °F). Hybrids between *L. palustris* and *L. repens* are often offered on the market under one of the two names.

The hybrids have large leaves which are green above, red below. Apart from bright light they have no special requirements. Propagation is by cuttings. Regular pruning will keep the plants from growing up out of the water.

Family Parkeriaceae

One species of this fern family is widely distributed throughout the tropics, growing submerse, half-emerse or on land. There is a floating fern of the same genus with broad, lobed floating leaves which is nowadays often regarded as a separate species, *Ceratopteris cornuta*.

Depending upon origin and locality the large basal leaves are broad with lobed edges to finely feathered or antler-like. In the emerse form the leaf tissue may be completely lacking. The stem and leaf nerves are easily damaged.

Numerous adventitious plants form on the leaves, and new plants can be raised from these. Spores only appear on the leaves of emerse plants.

■ *Ceratopteris thalictroides*   (C) 92
Cosmotropical, in marshes, flooded areas or river banks, where, depending upon the water level, it develops several very different forms.

The submerse cultivated form may grow very large and need plenty of space. It can be planted, preferably in a substrate of coarse sand with some loam. The daughter plants can be removed as soon as they have formed roots. The light should be as bright as possible and the water soft, preferably not above 10 °dH, at a temperature not below 24 °C (75 °F).

The plant can be overwintered as a marsh plant in a shallow, covered dish at 18–20 °C (64–68 °F).

A form with finely divided leaves is known in the trade as Sumatra fern.

Family Polypodiaceae

So far only two species of this fern family have proved really suitable for cultivation in the aquarium. These are marsh ferns, which in the wild grow in damp places or along river banks. In the aquarium they do well when cultivated submerse but are even more suitable for a marsh aquarium.

■ *Bolbitis heudelotii*   (O) 93
Tropical West Africa from Guinea to Angola.

A decorative plant which requires very bright light and only develops fully after a long period of cultivation. Rhizome division should not be carried out too early, otherwise both pieces will die back or remain small for a long time.

The water should be medium-hard, even hard, rather than soft, and the temperature can be 18–28 °C (64–82 °F).

■ *Microsorium pteropus*   (L) 94
Widely distributed in tropical south-east Asia.

The leaves are lanceolate, bright green to dark green and growing one behind the other from a creeping rootstock. In the aquarium they may reach a length of up to 20 cm (7·8 in), but are usually smaller. It is best to tie the plant on to a rock until it has become attached by its own fibrous roots. Propagation is by division of the rootstock or from daughter plants produced on the leaves. In favourable conditions this fern may flourish, but in poor conditions it may stop growing and gradually die back. It thrives under the most varied light conditions and prefers water that is not too hard, at a temperature of 22–26 °C (71–78 °F).

Family Pontederiaceae

■ *Eichhornia azurea* (O) 95
Tropical and subtropical America, rooted along the banks or in flooded areas.

The submerse form differs considerably from the emerse form. Plants cultivated underwater have narrow, linear, pale green leaves arranged in two rows along the stem. The lower leaves become detached very easily. Before the plants reach the water surface they must be pruned and the shoots planted in the substrate where they will soon take root. Emerse plants have roundish-ovate shiny leaves on slightly thickened stems. The inflorescence is dark blue.

This plant requires bright light, with sunlight for the emerse form at flowering time. The temperature should be 22–28 °C (71–82 °F), but the composition of the water is not critical.

● ■ *Heteranthera zosteraefolia* (B) 96
Tropical America, in swamps and flooded areas.

An attractive water and marsh plant with narrow, lanceolate pale green leaves, arranged alternately on the brittle stem. This species is usually cultivated submerse, but is also suitable for emerse cultivation in a marsh aquarium. The substrate can be unwashed sand. In the right conditions growth is very rapid. The tips of the shoots can be cut off before they reach the water surface and inserted in the substrate. In this way dense thickets can be produced quite quickly.

The light should be bright, with not too much sun. The water should be medium-hard, preferably around 8–10 °dH, and the temperature 18–30 °C (64–86 °F), if possible 22–24 °C (71–75 °F).

Family Potamogetonaceae

These are perennial cosmopolitan plants with submerse and floating leaves of the most diverse form, and emerse spike-like inflorescences. They have a long rootstock creeping on or in the substrate. Only a few tropical species are suitable for cultivation in the aquarium. Species from temperate areas grow well in a garden pond.

■ *Potamogeton gayi* (L) 97
Widely distributed in tropical and subtropical America.

This exclusively submerse plant has very long thin stems with narrow-linear, olive-green to brownish leaves. The inflorescence, which rises above the surface, is only a few centimetres long. The shoots may branch so profusely below the surface that a dense thicket is formed. Propagation is by cuttings. The substrate can be unwashed sand.

The light should be bright, and the water preferably not too hard, at a temperature of 20–25 °C (68–77 °F).

Family Primulaceae

▶ *Lysimachia nummularia* (Moneywort, Creeping Jenny) (A) 98
Europe, eastern North America, Japan, usually as an emerse plant in damp places.

The creeping or erect stems carry roundish, pale green, opposite leaves on short stalks. The plant only flowers when emerse, but it can be kept completely submerse and gradually becomes acclimatized to higher temperatures.

Family Ranunculaceae

The water and marsh plants of this family are not particularly suitable for the home aquarium, where they do not survive for very long. The leaves are finely divided and resemble those of *Cabomba*. The flowers are usually white and carried above the surface.

126

Family Scrophulariaceae

The species of *Bacopa* described here have a somewhat stiff, fragile stem with thick, fleshy ovate leaves. The small flowers sit in the axils of the emerse leaves. The plants can be cultivated emerse or submerse.

▶ *Bacopa amplexicaulis* (Also known as *B. caroliniana*)   (A) 99
Southern and central North America, usually emerse in swamps and flooded areas.

These are marsh plants suitable for an unheated home aquarium or a marsh aquarium. The substrate can be unwashed sand, possibly with a little loam.

The light must be bright with a little sunshine and the water preferably soft. The temperature should be 18–20 °C (64–68 °F), possibly a little higher in summer.

● *Bacopa monniera*   (P) 100
Tropical and subtropical areas of Africa, Asia, Australia and America, in swamps and flooded areas.

Distinguished from the preceding species by the smaller leaves; it also tolerates more warmth.

The two species of *Limnophila* described below are perennial, submerse water plants which are superficially very similar to the species of *Cabomba*. The leaves are finely divided and arranged in whorls around the stem. At the start of the flowering season the plants grow up above the surface and develop emerse leaves in whose axils the small flowers appear. Both species are undemanding and grow well in a substrate of unwashed sand with a little loam. Vigorous aeration is not recommended as this stirs up detritus which settles on the leaves and may kill them. For the same reason burrowing fish should be excluded from the tank. Propagation is by cuttings, which take root very rapidly. In artificial light the plants will remain in growth throughout the year.

The genus was formerly known as *Ambulia*.

● ■ *Limnophila aquatica*   101
Tropical south-east Asia.

The much divided pale green submerse leaves are arranged in whorls which may attain a diameter of 10 cm (4 in). In general the plant requires abundant light and regular changes of a proportion of the water.

● ■ *Limnophila sessiliflora*   102
India, south-east Asia, Japan.

Cultivation as given for the preceding species, but it does not require so much light.

This species is not poisonous like, for example, *L. indica*, which smells of turpentine and has a sap which is poisonous to fish.

Family Umbelliferae

▶ ● *Hydrocotyle verticillata*   (L) 103
North and central America, West Indies.

A marsh plant with a creeping rootstock which normally grows on the damp banks of rivers and lakes. It is suitable for a garden pond, but can also be cultivated successfully underwater. The circular pale green to dark green leaves are carried on fairly long, erect stems. The diameter of the leaves is up to 4 cm (1·5 in), and the plant itself is 5–15 cm (2–6 in) tall. In shallow water the leaves lie on the surface or grow up above it.

This plant requires abundant light and a temperature of 10–24 °C (50–75 °F).

Family Amaranthaceae

Several amphibious species of this South American family have been introduced to the aquarium in recent years. The light must be bright and the substrate should preferably have some peat, but growth is generally quite slow.

■ *Alternanthera reineckii*   104
Tropical South America.

An attractive plant which can be cultivated like the species of *Ludwigia*, but at a slightly higher temperature. Propagation is by cuttings which take a long time to form roots.

■ *Alternanthera* sp. *'lilacina'* 105
Tropical South America.
   Cultivation as for *A. reineckii.*

■ *Alternanthera* sp. *'rosafolia'* (P) 106
The exact origin of this plant is unknown, but
it almost certainly comes from tropical South
America.
   Cultivation as for *A. reineckii,* but growth is
rather more rapid.

II.   Floating plants

These are never, or only rarely, rooted
in the substrate.

Family Araceae

■ *Pistia stratiotes* (Water lettuce) (K) 107
Tropical and subtropical areas in many parts
of the world.
   A floating plant with velvety, grey-green
leaves arranged in rosettes. The roots are
finely divided, whitish to bluish. The tiny
flowers are in the leaf axils. This is not a good
plant for the home aquarium where it usually
dies off in the winter. It can be overwintered
more successfully as a marsh plant in a pot
with a mixture of sand and peat. Propagation
is by runners.
   This plant requires warm, damp air, very
bright light with some sunshine and preferably soft water at a temperature of 20–28 °C
(68–82 °F).

Family Hydrocharitaceae

▶ *Hydrocharis morsusranae* (Frogbit) (A) 108
Europe, Asia, Australia, North Africa, in shallow, standing waters, along the banks of
ponds and lakes, often in reed-beds, and
rooted in the bottom when the water level is
low.
   The round leaves on shortish stalks are arranged in rosettes. The white flowers grow up
above the surface. The plant, which somewhat

resembles a miniature water-lily, dies down in
autumn and forms resting bodies. It can be
kept in a home aquarium tank throughout the
summer in good light with some sunshine but
not too much heat. A good plant for outdoors,
but those taken from the wild must be carefully washed as they are easily injured by
pests such as snails. Propagation is by runners
in the summer.
   The temperature can be 18–20 °C (64–
68 °F), or slightly higher in summer. The water
composition is not critical.

■ *Limnobium stoloniferum* (Also known as *L.
laevigatum* and *Trianea bogotensis*) (A) 109
Tropical and subtropical parts of South America, on the surface of standing waters.
   In the aquarium this species must be protected from reflected sunlight, but in ordinary
bright light it does not die back much, even in
winter. It is a good plant for outdoors during
the summer. Propagation is by runners.
   The species prefers soft water, at a temperature of 22–28 °C (71–82 °F).

Family Parkeriaceae

■ *Ceratopteris cornuta* (This fern is regarded
by some botanists as a separate species, and
by others as a floating form of *C. thalictroides*)
(D) 110
Tropical Africa and many other places.
   The very large pale green floating leaves are
broad with incised edges. The petioles and
leaf nerves are spongy and very fragile, and
the much branched roots form beard-like
tufts. These plants should be kept beneath the
cover-glass of the tank which should slope
slightly so that no condensation water can
drop on to the leaves.
   This fern is useful for tanks with fish which
like to swim just below the surface, also for
bubble-nest builders for generally shading the
tank.
   The light should be bright without too
much sunshine and the water not too hard
and at a temperature of 22–30 °C (71–86 °F).

Family Pontederiaceae

■ *Eichhornia crassipes* (Water hyacinth)
(P) 111
Widely distributed in the tropics, forming
dense carpets which may even hinder naviga-
tion.

The shiny green, heart-shaped leaves are
borne on swollen, air-filled stalks which are
full of spongy tissue and serve as floats. The
bluish-black roots are very dense and hairy.
The flowers are pale blue. When the water
level is low the plants take root in the mud.

Water hyacinths do not normally thrive in a
home aquarium tank, but they do well in a
tropical marsh aquarium where their roots can
reach the substrate. Flowering is encouraged
by cutting off the side shoots at the right time.
The plants can be overwintered in artificial
light, while floating at the surface. In daylight
they are best kept in peat-filled pots in a separate tank.

The light must be bright, with some sunshine, and the water temperature 20–25 °C
(68–77 °F).

Family Ricciaceae

▶ ● *Riccia fluitans* (Crystalwort)   (G) 112
Distributed throughout most temperate and
warm regions, particularly in shallow,
swampy waters.

These are small, rootless, pale green,
branched liverworts, which usually float in
dense cushions below the surface. Buoyancy
is maintained by air spaces in the tissues (thallus), but the plants may also become rooted
among rocks on the bottom. These are good
spawning plants and they also help to shade
the tank from too much sun. They can be
propagated throughout the year from small
pieces of thallus. They require very bright
light with some sunshine and preferably soft
water at 15–25 °C (59–77 °F).

Family Salviniaceae

■ *Salvinia auriculata*   (A) 113
Tropical South America, often forming thick
cushions on the surface of bays and backwaters in rivers and lakes.

These are floating ferns in which the leaves
develop in threes, two floating at the surface,
the third submerse and root-like. The upperside of the leaves is hairy and water-repellent.

These small plants like fresh, warm and
rather damp air, and the tank lid should be
sloping so that condensation water does not
drop onto the leaves. The plants quickly die
back if cultivated in poor light. They are useful as a means of providing shade and also
protection for fish fry. Some anabantids use
them as a support for the bubble-nest. They
require bright light and water that is not too
hard, at a temperature of 18–28 °C (64–82 °F).

● *Azolla caroliniana* (Lesser fairy moss)   114
Tropical and subtropical areas of America, in
the same kind of habitat as *Salvinia*.

In spite of the popular name, this is actually
a floating fern. The small grey-green leaves lie
one above the other like roof tiles. The long
root fibres are not feathery. These are plants
which grow well in a garden pond, but gradually die off in a home aquarium. They are difficult to overwinter, but can be kept on mud in
a shallow saucer at 12–15 °C (53–59 °F). In
summer they require bright light and soft water at 18–25 °C (64–77 °F).

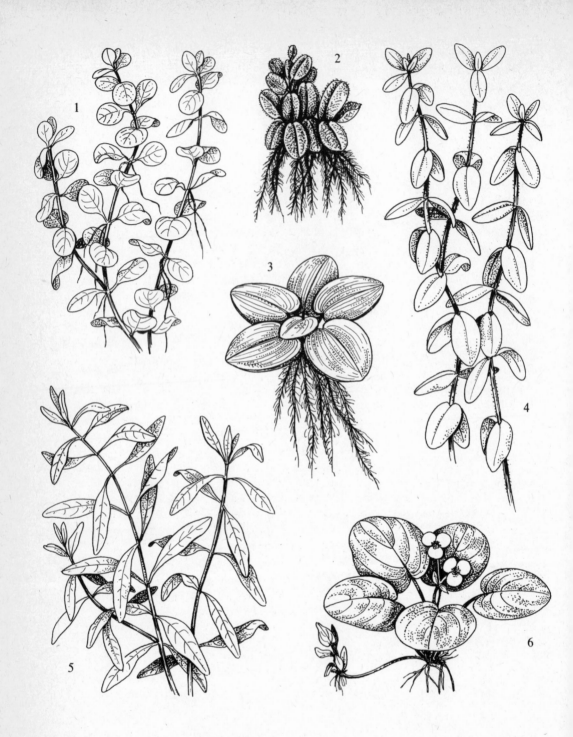

Plate A

1 *Lysimachia nummularia* (98) **2** *Salvinia auriculata* (113) **3** *Limnobium stoloniferum* (109) **4** *Bacopa caroliniana* (99) **5** *Hygrophila polysperma* (1) **6** *Hydrocharis morsusranae* (108)

Plate B

1 *Heteranthera zosteraefolia* (96) 2 *Cryptocoryne griffithii* (36) 3 *Nymphoides humboldtiana* (60)
4 *Cryptocoryne 'nevillii* (40) 5 *Cryptocoryne lucens* (36) 6 *Ludwigia palustris* × *repens* (91)

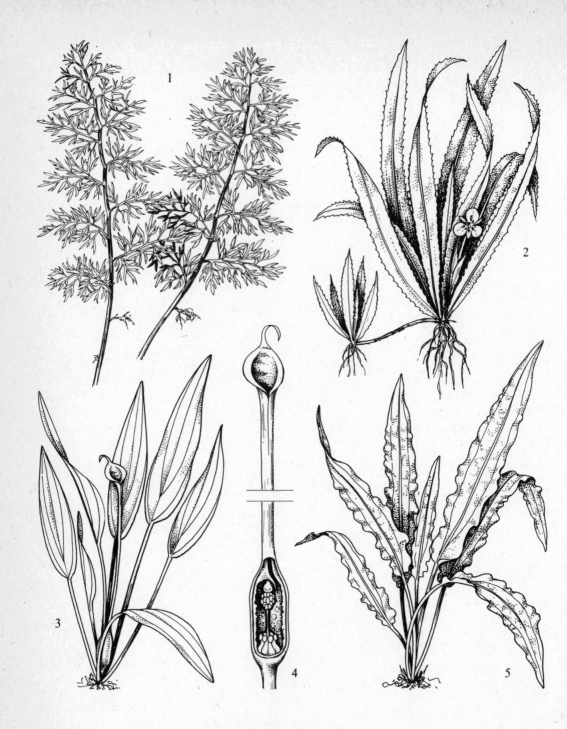

Plate C

1 *Ceratopteris thalictroides* (92) **2** *Stratiotes aloides* (76) **3** *Cryptocoryne affinis* (30) **4** Inflorescence of a *Cryptocoryne* **5** *Cryptocoryne beckettii*

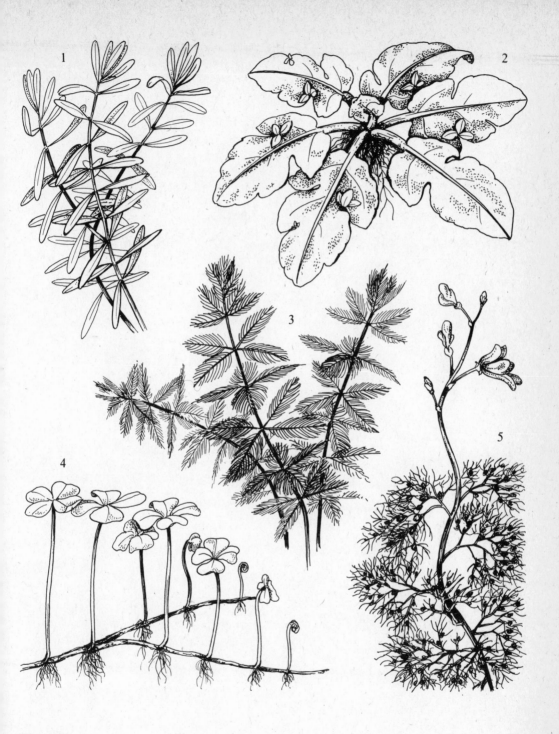

Plate D

1 *Callitriche stagnalis* (49) **2** *Ceratopteris cornuta* (110) **3** *Myriophyllum brasiliense* (62) **4** *Marsilea crenata* (80) **5** *Utricularia vulgaris* (78)

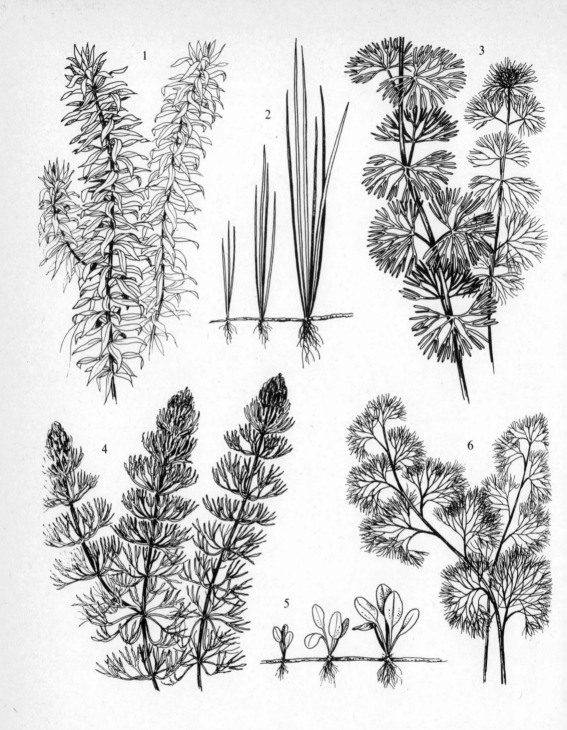

Plate E

1 *Egeria densa* (74) **2** *Heleocharis acicularis* (56) **3** *Cabomba caroliniana* (84) **4** *Ceratophyllum demersum* (50) **5** *Elatine macropoda* (57) **6** *Ranunculus aquatilis* (−)

Plate F

1 *Vallisneria gigantea* (69)   **2** *Vallisneria spiralis* (71)   **3** *Echinodorus amazonicus* (4)   **4** *Echinodorus tenellus* (13)   **5** *Sagittaria platyphylla* (16)

135

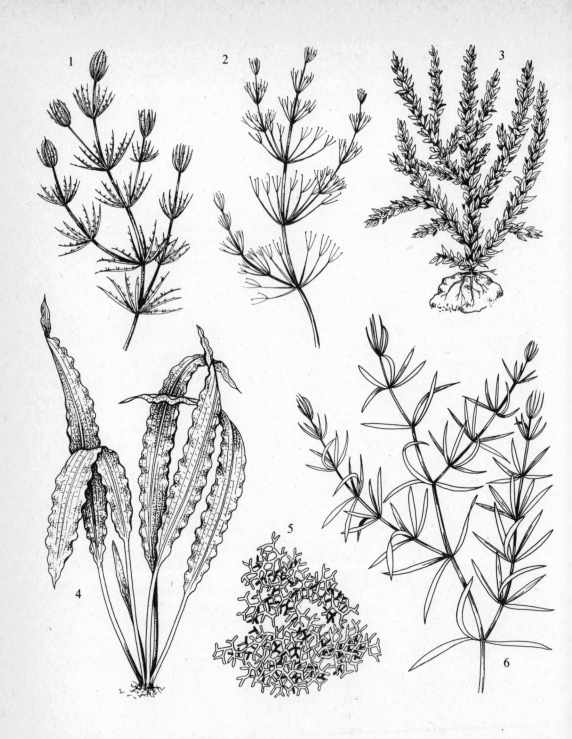

Plate G

1 *Chara foetida* (52) **2** *Nitella flexilis* (54) **3** *Fontinalis antipyretica* (58) **4** *Aponogeton crispus* (22) **5** *Riccia fluitans* (112) **6** *Najas microdon* (81)

136

Plate H

1 *Nomaphila stricta* (2)   **2** *Synnema triflorum* (3)   **3** *Echinodorus major* (10)   **4** *Echinodorus bleheri* (6)

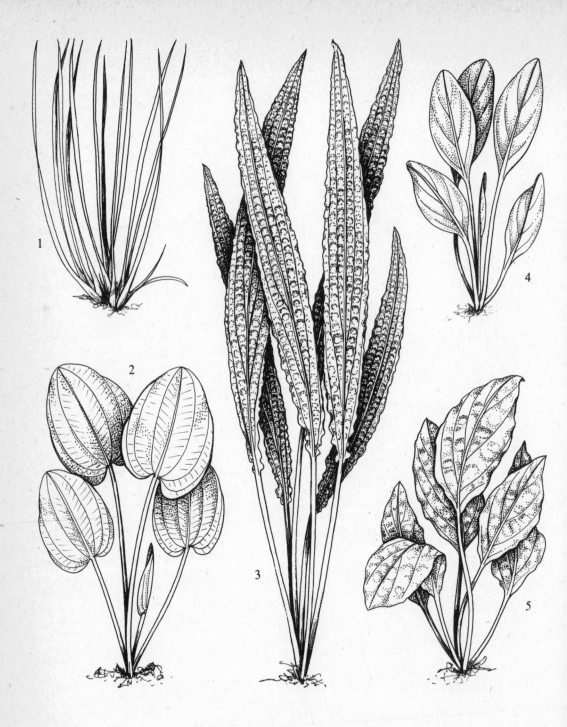

Plate I

1 *Acorus* *gramineus*, dwarf form (29) 2 *Echinodorus* *cordifolius* (7) 3 *Cryptocoryne* *usteriana* (46) 4 *Cryptocoryne lingua* (37) 5 *Cryptocoryne blassii* (33)

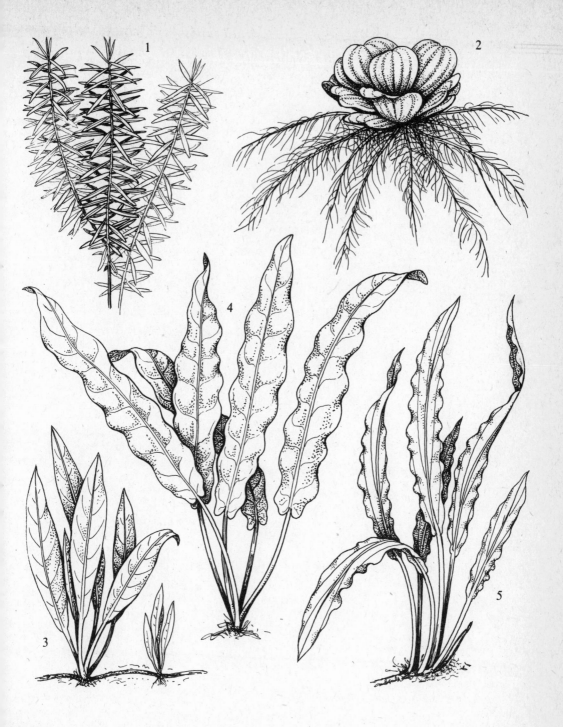

Plate K

1 *Peplis diandra* (79) **2** *Pistia stratiotes* (107) **3** *Echinodorus magdalenensis* (9) **4** *Barclaya longifolia* (82) **5** *Cryptocoryne willisii* (48)

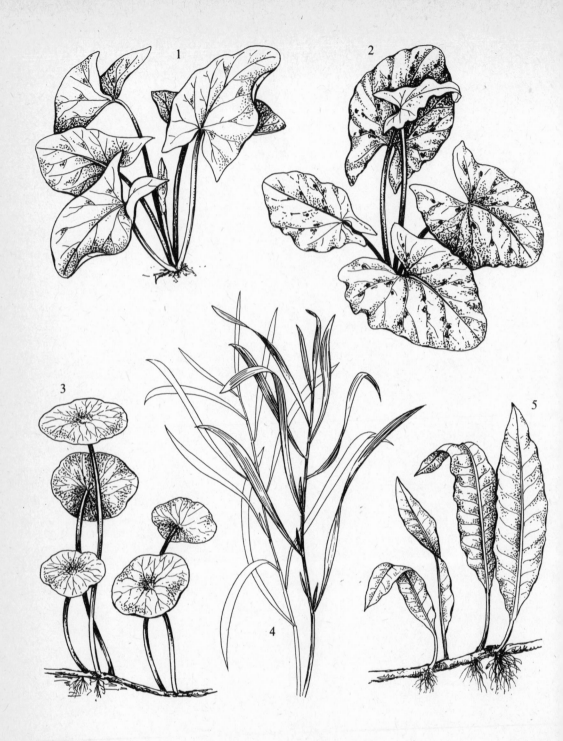

Plate L

1 *Nymphaea daubenyana* (88) **2** *Nymphaea lotus* (89) **3** *Hydrocotyle verticillata* (103) **4** *Potamogeton gayi* (97) **5** *Microsorium pteropus* (94)

Plate M

1 *Echinodorus horizontalis* (8)   **2** *Echinodorus aschersonianus* (5)   **3** *Echinodorus osiris* (11)   **4** *Echinodorus parviflorus* (12)

Plate N

1 *Aponogeton undulatus* (28) **2** *Cryptocoryne ciliata* (34) **3** *Cryptocoryne tonkinensis* (45) **4** *Cryptocoryne petchii* (42) **5** *Cardamine lyrata* (55)

Plate O

1 *Cryptocoryne wendtii* (47) **2** *Bolbitis heudelotii* (93) **3** *Vesicularia dubyana* (59) **4** *Eichhornia azurea*, submerse form (95) **5** *Eichhornia azurea*, emerse form (95)

Plate P

1 *Bacopa monniera* (100)　**2** *Eichhornia crassipes* (111)　**3** *Alternanthera 'lilacina'* (105)　**4** *Alternanthera 'rosafolia'* (106)

The Fishes

Notes on fish biology

Structure, shape and colour

Fish are the oldest group in the long line of vertebrates, and from them have evolved the land animals of today. Even in our own age fish are still evolving in this way, developing organs which make life on land possible.

The normal body form of the fish is spindle-shaped, either circular in cross-section or laterally compressed. This shape is common to many fish, but other shapes have also evolved in response to habitat, either on the bottom, at the surface or in fast-moving waters. The evolution of these different shapes in response to environmental conditions has been taking place over a period of millions of years, and undoubetly still is.

It is, in fact, possible to deduce from the shape of the fish the type of environment it has inhabited in the wild, and this helps the aquarist to work out the kind of conditions in which each shape, or each species, should best be kept.

Most of the small aquarium fish come from standing or slow-flowing waters, from the banks or backwaters of rivers, from flooded areas, lakes, ponds and ditches, with varying amounts of vegetation.

The greatest change from the basic spindle shape occurs in fish which have become adapted to life on or near the bottom. These have a straight belly profile, a ventrally positioned mouth often surrounded by sensory barbels which serve to detect food. The body is frequently flattened. Variations in shape are found in many different families, and particularly among the bottom-living catfish. The most extreme development is seen among the flatfish, which are mostly marine, though there are a few small species suitable for the freshwater aquarium. Fish which burrow in the bottom often have a band-like, worm-like or serpentine shape.

Most aquarium fish belong among the group known as the teleosts, or bony fish; cartilaginous fish, such as sharks and rays, are only to be found as exhibits in large public aquaria. A bony fish has a skeleton with a central moveable axis, the backbone or vertebral column, which protects the delicate spinal column and gives the body a certain degree of rigidity and support. Fish, unlike mammals, do need a great deal of support because the water provides buoyancy.

The ribs attached to the vertebral column surround and protect internal organs, and there are bony supports for the fins. The strongly ossified skull encloses the brain, the most important sense organ. The jaw bones, lips, pharynx, tongue and other parts of the mouth may carry teeth or tooth-like horny or bony plates.

Usually, the body and tail are to varying degrees visibly separated from one another, the body ending at the anal opening. In some fish the body cavity is further forward, and in others it may even extend into the tail region. There is no clear division between head and

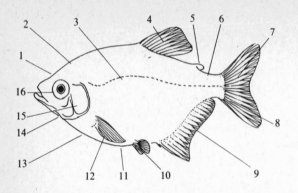

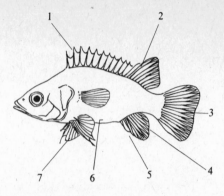

External characteristics of a characin

Fins of a nandid

1 Forehead	9 Anal fin
2 Nape	10 Ventral fins, paired
3 Lateral line	11 Belly
4 Dorsal fin	12 Pectoral fins
5 Adipose fin	13 Breast
6 Caudal peduncle	14 Throat
7 Caudal fin	15 Gill cover
8 Root of tail	16 Head

1 Spiny part ⎫
2 Soft-rayed part ⎬ Dorsal fin
3 Caudal fin
4 Soft-rayed part ⎫
5 Spiny part ⎬ Anal fin
6 Pectoral fins, paired
7 Ventral fins, paired

body, the former ending at the rear end of the gill-cover (operculum).

The musculature of a fish is relatively powerful. Its division into individual segments, the myotomes, which fit into one another, enables the body to move smoothly when swimming. Muscles also serve to move the jaws. The fins, also moved by muscles, consist of bony or cartilaginous rays and spines which are usually connected to one another by soft skin. The caudal fin almost always has soft rays. The dorsal and anal fins may have soft rays, but sometimes also spiny rays. In all perch-like fish the front part of the dorsal fin has spiny rays, the rear part soft rays. In some fish the dorsal fin spine and the front spine of the pectoral fin are sharply pointed. The fin spines can be used as defensive weapons, and in certain fish they can be locked into an erect position.

In a few species the unpaired fins form a fold or fringe extending from the dorsal fin round the rear part of the body to the anus. The position on the body of the ventral fins may vary. They are either in the centre of the belly or below the pectoral fins. In the ar-

moured catfish the ventral fins have an auxiliary function in reproduction; in gobies they are fused together to form a suction organ, and in labyrinth fish they are elongated and thread-like and serve as tactile and taste organs. The anal fin of male live-bearing toothcarps is modified with a copulatory organ, the gonopodium, which serves to inseminate the female.

The development of the pectoral fins can also vary considerably. Normally they serve as steering and balancing organs. Fast swimmers often have powerful pectoral fins, while in some surface-living fish they are elongated and wing-like, enabling the fish to leap or 'fly' over the water surface, as for example in the flying barb *Esomus* of southern Asia and the South American hatchetfish. The pectoral fins serve as supports in some bottom-living fish, sometimes being modified to leg-like structures which aid progression. Finally, there is the ray-less adipose fin situated between the dorsal and caudal fins in the Salmonidae, most characins and numerous catfish.

The fins are primarily locomotory organs.

The beats of the caudal fin and the caudal peduncle drive the fish forwards, and the other fins serve for steering and maintaining equilibrium. In some fish the ventral fins act as brakes, as can be seen so well in fighting fish. The gentle gliding movements of certain fish are carried out by fins other than the caudal fin, for example in the species of *Nannostomus* in which the undulations of soft rays move the fish forwards like a matchstick through the water.

The fins of many fish also serve to alter the external appearance; they can be spread out as a symbol of threat. Ostentatious fins often play a part in male courtship behaviour, for instance in fighting fish, paradise and other labyrinth fish, in the tall fins of mollies and the elongated fin rays in *Apistogramma* and *Telmatherina*.

Fish skin consists of two layers: an outer slimy, transparent epidermis and an inner corium with pigment cells, blood vessels and scales. Scales may be roundish (cycloid) or comb-like (ctenoid). The age of many fish can be estimated from a count of the annual rings formed in the scales. The shiny appearance of the scales is due to the presence of guanine crystals. The iridescence of the scales in many shoaling fish serves as a form of protective coloration, as light from above serves to break up the outline of the fish's body into numerous glittering spots which confuse an attacking predator, which finds it difficult to pick out an individual fish in the shoal.

Fish colours are of two kinds, structural and pigmentary. In the former, the guanine crystals in the skin break up the incident light in various ways, producing what are known as structural colours. According to the angle of incidence of the light, the silvery iridescence may appear greenish, bluish or like mother-of-pearl. The other type of colour is produced by pigments deposited in special pigment cells. In some cases considerable changes in coloration can occur, according to whether the pigments in these cells are concentrated or diffused. Pigments may produce black, blue, red and yellow or various mixed tones. Colour change is related to the mood or degree of excitement of a fish, and is often very striking. Iridescent colours, such as those in neon tetras, are due to a combination of structural and pigmentary colours.

The surroundings also have an influence on coloration. As most aquarists know, many fish are more brightly coloured on a dark background than they are on a pale one. In most cases sexual excitement also leads to an intensification of colour. Courtship behaviour in both males and females is almost always accompanied by a brilliant play of colours.

A complete lack of pigments, particularly of black pigments, leads to the condition known as albinism. The eyes then appear red due to the blood vessels at the back of the eyes. An excess of black pigment causes melanism, while a preponderance of yellow or reddish pigment results in gold coloration.

The significance of fish colours is not always absolutely clear. It now seems that they may not actually have a strong effect on other fish, for instance as a sexual display, as even in shallow depths, red tones are no longer seen as such. It is possible, therefore, that the colours of fish are more arbitrary than we are tempted to believe, and that bright colours may often simply be an external manifestation of an inner change in mood.

Internal organs, sense organs and sensory functions

Fish are poikilothermal (loosely speaking 'cold-blooded') animals, which maintain the same temperature as the surrounding water. In general, their living functions are slowed down by cold water, and speeded up by warm. This certainly happens in the case of tropical and subtropical aquarium fish. Depending upon their origin, each fish species is adapted for a certain mean temperature, so it follows that fish from the temperate zone should not be kept too warm, and tropical fish not too cool. The dependence of body temperature on the temperature of the surroundings means that care must be taken to avoid over-rapid changes in water temperature, as this can cause injury or even death.

Respiration is primarily the function of the gills. These lie on each side of the head behind protecting bony gill-covers, and consist of the gill arches which carry delicate, highly vascularized gill filaments. Here the blood takes up dissolved oxygen from the water and releases unwanted carbon dioxide. The water needed for respiration flows continuously in at the mouth, passes over the gills and flows out again through the gill-covers. Respiration is a rhythmic activity which can be clearly seen. In addition to gill respiration some fish have a form of accessory respiration. They can take in atmospheric air at the surface and use it for respiration in the alimentary tract (loaches, some catfish), in lung-like sacs (lungfish), or in other organs in association with the mouth (labyrinth fish). Because of this, such fish are able to remain hidden for a long period in dried mud, to survive in water deficient in oxygen or to leave the water for short periods.

The orientation of the fish in water is primarily the function of the lateral line organ, the swimbladder and the organ of balance in the inner ear.

The lateral line is discernible as a row of tiny pits extending to varying degrees over the flanks of the fish. The appearance of a lateral line is due to the scales of a longitudinal row

Mouth positions in fishes

a) dorsal

b) terminal

c) ventral

being pierced, producing a series of tiny holes. The latter contain sensory cells which serve to detect vibration, currents and movements. There are similar sensory units on the head and sometimes also on other parts of the body. The lateral line may be interrupted or may be only quite short, and is sometimes completely lacking. The sensory cells are extraordinarily sensitive, and to a large extent carry out the functions of eyes, which in fish are not always very efficient. For instance, with the help of its lateral line, the blind cave characin *(Astyanax mexicanus = Anoptichthys jordani)* is able to orientate very efficiently and even to differentiate between fish of its own species and other fish species.

The gas-filled swimbladder functions as a hydrostatic organ which enables the fish to compensate for the water pressure and to swim at any depth. Adjustments in the amount of gas in the swimbladder are carried out through connections to the gut or by passing excess gas into the blood system. During their first days of life fish fry have to fill the swimbladder before it becomes functional. This is done partly by taking up air at the water surface. This is why the water level in a breeding tank should be kept as low as possible. In some fish the swimbladder amplifies sound waves and transmits them to the organ of balance (audio-equilibration). Such fish, as for example the weatherfish *(Misgurnus),* react strongly to changes in air pressure. In certain fish species, particularly bottom-living fish, the swimbladder is not necessary, and it is then either reduced or completely absent.

The organ of balance is situated in the inner ear. It has numerous sensory cells which detect changes in the fish's position in water, so that righting movements can be made.

The eyes are also important sense organs, but they do not play the largest role in orientation. Many fish use their eyes to detect colour, form and movements, but the shape of the lens of the eye cannot be altered, and it is normally focused for near vision. In certain fish, the eyes are used to detect the colour of the surroundings, and the fish will change colour accordingly. Blinded fish are usually dark coloured, having lost this ability.

The senses of smell and taste are very well developed, and fish can detect substances dissolved in the water at considerable distances. The ability to do this is obviously very important in finding food. The so-called 'fright substances' released by wounded or dead specimens of some fish species are probably detected by the sense of smell; minnows, for example, are warned of danger by these substances. The olfactory organ consists of paired pits lined with sensory cells, and it communicates with the exterior by the two nasal openings or nostrils. These have nothing to do with respiration, and in most cases they are not connected with the mouth. The sense of taste is not localized in any one part of the body: although naturally, taste buds are found mainly in the mouth and near to it, on the lips and barbels, they also occur in smaller numbers on the belly, the ventral fins and on other parts of the body.

It has not been established whether fish in general can hear sounds. Some fish, such as bullheads and minnows, can certainly hear, but they may be exceptions. It is well known, however, that many fish species can produce sounds, which often have important biological functions, so it seems quite probable that such sounds can be dedected by other fish.

'Mind' and behaviour

The mental abilities of fish, that is, their memory and their ability to evaluate experiences, vary considerably according to the species or even the individual. The old idea that fish have no mental abilities and react almost entirely by instinct has now been disproved by scientific investigations.

From aquarium investigations it would appear that such mental faculties are poorly developed in shoaling fish, because here individuality is less important than mass behaviour and reactions. Thus, shoaling fish take little notice of the person looking after them, although they may remember feeding times and feeding places. The situation is quite different among fish which live either alone, with a mate, or in small communities. For example, cichlids appear to be particularly intelligent, and it is always astonishing how they appear to follow what is going on outside their aquarium tank. One often has the impression that they even recognize their keeper, although this may, of course, be a case of recognizing certain movements during feeding and maintenance which are characteristic of that keeper. It has been demonstrated in experiments that the memory of some fish is very well developed, and that they even have an outstanding ability to differentiate form and colour. This is especially necessary for brood-protecting fish, which have to find their breeding site when they have moved a long way away from it, and in captivity they are known to select prominent external features to define their territory or breeding site. Brood-protecting fish may become disturbed when these features are removed or displaced.

On the whole it seems that many fish have a well-developed memory for places, for example, aquarium fish which have been temporarily moved out of a tank for cleaning will quickly feel at home when returned to the same tank with its original arrangement. Thus it appears that fish learn quickly from experience. One aquarist was known to be on such good terms with his cichlids that he was able to stroke them on the back, and even to lift them out of the water, where they would then lie motionless in his hand without any sign of distress.

One must, however, avoid ascribing to fish the ability to base their actions on logical thought in the human sense of the term. Most of their behaviour, particularly during the breeding period, is dictated by innate instincts, stimulated by external influences and backed up in many cases by the action of hormones. These instincts, which have evolved over an almost immeasurable period of time, will even prescribe the behaviour of newly hatched fish fry. Thus, young mouthbrooders have a well-established 'internal' picture of the mother's head, and are aware of the importance of certain movements they have to make in order to seek shelter in her mouth.

But one should not regard the concept of instinct as entirely mechanical; individual experiences in a changing environment play an important part in their development. Fish which have been much chased are more wary than those members of their species which have not suffered in this way. Aquarium practice yields numerous examples of individual differences, for instance, among individuals of the same species there are some which take the greatest care in preparing for spawning and in tending the brood, whereas others are extremely negligent. Some male paradise fish are extraordinarily pugnacious and inconsiderate towards their mates, whereas other individuals show exactly the opposite behaviour.

This raises the question of the choice of mate, as even shoaling fish will not spawn with just any member of the opposite sex. Observations in the aquarium may, of course, be influenced by the fact that the fish are in captivity, but it does appear that partners which have once spawned together will continue to do so. It is not known whether fish in the wild have any long-lasting association between sexes, but in the aquarium there is no doubt that such associations do exist in cases where the fish have a choice of several partners.

Another interesting question concerning fish behaviour is their method of sleeping. There is little doubt that fish do spend part of each day in what we would term a sleep-like state, and indeed some specimens have been removed from the water by hand while apparently asleep. Some species slumber vertically, some lie on their sides on the bottom, some float to the surface while others remain still, suspended in mid-water.

Most well-fed fish tend to sleep during the hours of darkness. Fishes' late-night behaviour can be a fascinating study and simply observed by leaving on a low-power night-light so that the fish are undisturbed.

Some basic rules for keeping tropical fishes

1. There should be a reasonable relation between the number of fish and the volume of water. As a rough guide, use 1 litre (1·75 pints) of water for 1 cm (0·4 in) of fish length. Overpopulated aquarium tanks quickly develop oxygen deficiency, and over a period of time they cannot be kept hygienic. The fish should never hang at the surface and snap for air because the tank is too crowded.

2. The water temperature should be in accordance with the origin and requirements of the fish concerned. For temperate zone fish the temperature should only exceptionally exceed 20–21 °C (68–70 °F), although it can fall to about 4 °C (39 °F) in winter. On the other hand, warm-water fish should not be hardened off, and tropical fish should not be kept unless the water can be maintained at the proper temperature. At night and during a resting phase, preferably in winter, the temperature can be allowed to fall a few degrees, even for tropical fish, as this is what happens in the wild.

3. Fish should never be transferred suddenly from warm to cold water or vice versa. Before being introduced into the aquarium the temperature of the tank water must be the same as that of the water in the transport container. The best way to do this is to suspend the container in the tank until the temperatures correspond.

4. Fish which are to be kept together must have the same characteristics and living requirements. In particular, those requiring spe-

cial food should not be part of a community tank.

5. Any unnecessary disturbance must be avoided, and this includes superfluous handling. Cleaning should be restricted for as long as possible to the unavoidable minimum, removal of detritus with a mulm bell and cleaning the front pane with a glass-cleaner. As a routine, about one-fifth of the water should be removed every week and replaced by fresh water at the same temperature.

6. The fish must be fed regularly, but not overfed. Too much dried food pollutes the water, even when it does not cause cloudiness. Live food, such as water-fleas, should only be given in quantities which will be consumed within a few hours. Uneaten food animals remove oxygen from the water, while dead animals quickly lead to fouling. Diets should be varied and in accordance with the fishes requirements.

7. Always bear in mind that in most cases fish diseases are hard to cure, and sometimes cannot be cured at all. Prevention is better than cure.

Hints on the breeding of aquarium fishes

Here are a few general rules for breeding ornamental fish. More detailed information is given in the tables on pages 192 to 277.

1. The well-being of the fish and their chances of breeding in the aquarium depend upon proper methods of maintenance, as given in the preceding section, 'Some basic rules for keeping tropical fishes'.

2. The aquarist wishing to breed should obtain some young fish and rear them on. This gives him a sufficiently long period to observe them and to find out which specimens are compatible with one another. These fish will be better for breeding than adults, as older fish are usually more difficult to acclimatize than young ones. As a general rule the dealer will not part with his best breeding pair.

3. For breeding use only those fish which are strong and healthy with a good shape and colour.

4. Set up the breeding tank some time before the start of the proposed breeding attempt, and in such a way that it corresponds with the requirements of the fish and the aim of the breeding programme. Depending upon the species concerned the fish may be introduced into the breeding tanks weeks in advance or perhaps only a few days or hours. After acclimatization and at full maturity, spawning can usually be brought about by a partial or complete change of water, using the same type of water or sometimes a rather different type.

5. Ensure that the breeding tank is free from all injurious pests, such as snails, planarians, water insects, water mites and small crustaceans, particularly *Cyclops*, also freshwater polyps *(Hydra)* and excessive numbers of infusorians.

6. In cases where the number of offspring is not important, breeding can be allowed to take place in a fully established aquarium tank. For planned breeding, however, the conditions must be quite different. It is then usually best to have no bottom substrate. If sand or gravel are suitable as spawning substrates they should be steeped in boiling water to render them as near as possible germ-free.

7. Fish that are difficult to breed are usually those whose spawning habits in the wild are unknown or those with special requirements regarding water (for example the pH), or

those which require a special diet. It is often difficult to get recently imported fish to breed. Tropical rain-forest fish can often be stimulated to spawn by soft water (up to about 4 °dH), combined with a low pH value (about 6·5), peat filtration and natural food, such as mosquito larvae.

For species sensitive to infusorians, the breeding tank must be scrupulously cleaned. All containers and equipment must be washed in hot water and rinsed. Plants should be given a bath for half an hour in a pale pink solution of potassium permanganate and then rinsed in water that has been boiled and then cooled. Every care must be taken to avoid infecting the spawning tank water with infusorians. For example, the breeding fish should be transferred into the spawning tank using a clean glass bell, so as to leave any water behind. The cover-glass of the tank must also be scrupulously cleaned.

After they have been filled with clean water, breeding tanks for fish that are sensitive to infusorians should always be left in semi-darkness for a few days. Any water, including rain and distilled water, will become free of infusorians if kept for a time in a cool, darkened glass container.

Some fish which require soft water for breeding should not be reared in water that is too hard in case they are later required for breeding. There is, however, no firm rule, because it is sometimes a change in water composition which stimulates spawning, and over the course of several generations some stock may become acclimatized to harder water. In every case, however, it is essential to avoid transferring fish too suddenly into water with a different degree of hardness. This should be done gradually over a period of several hours at least.

The pH value plays an indirect role, because many infusorians and bacteria, including those that damage fish spawn, do not thrive at a pH below 7. As already mentioned, micro-organisms multiply more rapidly with increasing alkalinity, whereas acid water is poor in such organisms.

8. Before spawning, the breeding fish should be copiously fed, making sure that no food scraps remain in the tank. Particular care should be taken to exclude any *Cyclops* with egg-sacs from the diet.

9. After spawning, the breeding pair should again be well fed. Fish that practise brood protection can be given dried food or live food which will not damage the eggs or fry, for example whiteworms or earthworms. At the end of spawning the pair will require rest, and are best separated, unless they both take part in brood protection.

10. Only healthy young fish should be reared. No attempt should be made to rear any crippled or obviously sick offspring.

Breeding is the peak of a fish's life, and indeed of the art of aquarium keeping. The aquarist learns a great deal about his fish during their period of courtship, the preparation for spawning, the actual mating and, in some cases, brood protection.

There are two main types or methods of breeding in the aquarium. In the first, the aim is to produce large numbers of offspring, often using all kinds of strategems. At first sight this method does not appear to have much in common with natural breeding, although it must, of course, be based on fulfilling the principal requirements of the fish species concerned. In the second type an attempt is made to allow the fish, so far as possible, to breed in natural surroundings. Here the aquarist is less concerned with the numbers of young fish reared than with observation of interesting breeding behaviour.

Unfortunately, the breeding of aquarium fish has not to date been based on scientific principles (except perhaps among the live-bearing toothcarps, where the rules of genetics are useful). As a result there is a tendency for fish stocks to degenerate. The best way to avoid this is to breed only from stock which is without blemish, and to rear only those young fish which are healthy and are the best examples of the species concerned.

Plate I   Characins, Characoidea

1 *Aphyocharax rubripinnis*, bloodfin (4)   2 *Prochilodus insignis*, flagtail (−)   3 *Gymnocorymbus ternetzi*, black tetra (15)   4 *Hyphessobrycon ornatus*, ornate tetra (30)   5 *Hyphessobrycon flammeus*, flame tetra (25)   6 *Pyrrhulina rachoviana*, fanning characin (−)   7 *Hemigrammus nanus*, silver-tipped tetra (19)   8 *Paracheirodon innesi*, neon tetra (44)   9 *Hemigrammus ocellifer*, beacon fish (20)   10 *Pristella riddlei*, X-ray fish (48)   11 *Hyphessobrycon pulchripinnis*, lemon tetra (31)   12 *Copella arnoldi*, spraying characin (11)   13 *Petitella georgiae*, false rummy-nose (45, see also 22)   14 *Hemigrammus caudovittatus*, Buenos Aires tetra (−)   15 *Hemigrammus pulcher*, pretty tetra (21)   16 *Hemigrammus erythrozonus*, glowlight tetra (16)   17 *Hyphessobrycon heterorhabdus*, flag tetra (29)   18 *Hyphessobrycon callistus*, blood characin (24)   19 *Copeina guttata*, red-spotted copeina (10)

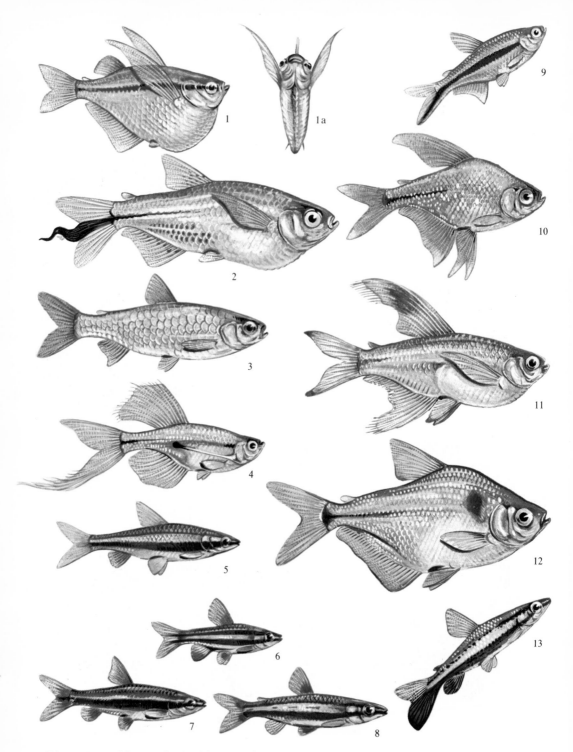

Plate II   Characins, Characoidea

1 and 1a *Pterodiscus levis*, silver hatchetfish, side and front view (−)   2 *Chalcinus elongatus*, elongated chalcinus (−)   3 *Chalceus macrolepidotus*, pink-tailed characin (−)   4 *Corynopoma riisei*, swordtail characin (12)   5 *Nannostomus beckfordi beckfordi*, golden pencilfish (−)   6 *Nannostomus marginatus*, dwarf pencilfish (40)   7 *Nannostomus beckfordi aripirangensis*, golden pencilfish (38)   8 *Nannostomus trifasciatus*, three-banded pencilfish (41)   9 *Thayeria boehlkei*, Boehlke's penguin fish (50)   10 *Moenhausia pittieri*, diamond tetra (35)   11 *Pseudocorynopoma doriae*, dragon-finned characin (−)   12 *Ctenobrycon spilurus*, silver tetra (13)   13 *Nannostomus eques*, tube-mouthed pencilfish (37)

Plate III   Characins, Characoidea and Atherines, Atherinidae

1 *Chilodus punctatus*, spotted headstander (9)   **2** *Leporinus affinis*, affinis leporinus (−)   **3** *Anostomus anostomus*, striped anostomus (3)   **4** *Abramites hypselonotus*, headstander (1)   **5** *Telmatherina ladigesi*, Celebes sailfish (255)   **6** *Nematocentris maccullochi*, dwarf rainbow fish (252)   **7** *Metynnis hypsauchen*, Schreitmuller's metynnis (34)   **8** *Metynnis roosevelti*, Roosevelt's metynnis (−)

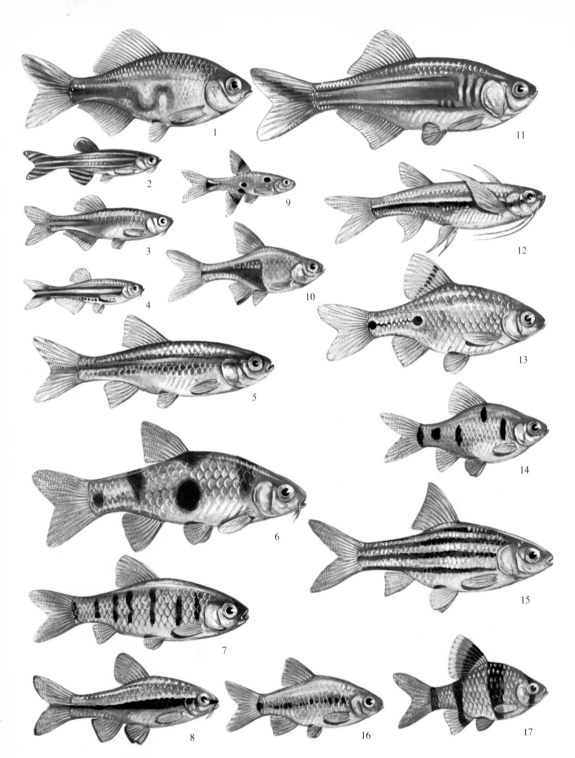

Plate IV   Barbs, Cyprinidae

1 *Danio devario*, Bengal danio (74)   2 *Brachydanio rerio*, zebra danio (72)   3 *Brachydanio albolineatus*, pearl danio (68)   4 *Brachydanio nigrofasciatus*, spotted danio (71)   5 *Rasbora einthoveni*, Einthoven's rasbora (–)   6 *Barbus everetti*, clown barb (53)   7 *Barbus semifasciatus*, green barb (61)   8 *Barbus titteya*, cherry barb (66)   9 *Rasbora maculata*, spotted rasbora (80)   10 *Rasbora heteromorpha*, harlequin fish (79)   11 *Danio aequipinnatus*, giant danio (73)   12 *Esomus lineatus*, striped flying barb (–)   13 *Barbus terio*, one-spot barb (–)   14 *Barbus phutunio*, dwarf barb (–)   15 *Barbus fasciatus*, striped barb (–)   16 *Barbus 'schuberti'*, golden barb (62)   17 *Barbus tetrazona*, Sumatra barb (63)

Plate V Barbs, Cyprinidae

1 *Barbus ticto*, two-spot barb (64) **2** *Barbus cumingi*, Cuming's barb (–) **3** *Barbus oligolepis*, island barb (59) **4** *Tanichthys albonubes*, White Cloud Mountain minnow (83) **5** *Barbus conchonius*, rosy barb (52) **6** *Barbus nigrofasciatus*, black ruby (58) **7a–c** Selected forms of *Carassius auratus*, goldfish (67)

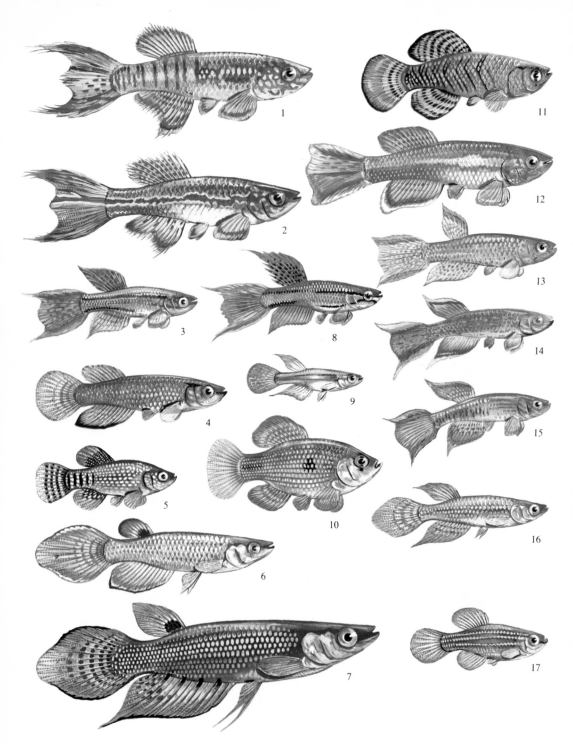

Plate VI Egg-laying toothcarps, Cyprinodontidae

1 *Aphyosemion sjoestedti*, blue gularis (96)   2 *Aphyosemion gulare*, yellow gularis (92)   3 *Aphyosemion bivittatum* ('*multicolor*'), red lyretail (85)   4 *Pachypanchax playfairi*, Playfair's panchax (125)   5 *Aphanius dispar*, dispar killifish (−)   6 *Aplocheilus panchax*, blue panchax (104)   7 *Aplocheilus lineatus*, panchax lineatus (103)   8 *Aphyosemion bivittatum*, red lyretail (85)   9 *Aplocheilichthys macrophthalmus*, lamp-eye panchax (99)   10 *Jordanella floridae*, American flagfish (121)   11 *Nothobranchius rachovi*, Rachov's nothobranchius (124)   12 *Roloffia occidentalis*, red aphyosemion (135)   13 *Aphyosemion cognatum*, red-speckled killy (see 88)   14 *Aphyosemion australe*, lyretail (84)   15 *Aphyosemion calliurum*, blue-chinned aphyosemion (87)   16 *Aplocheilus blocki*, green panchax (101)   17 *Cubanichthys cubensis*, Cuban killifish (−)

Plate VII   Egg-laying toothcarps, Cyprinodontidae
and Livebearing toothcarps, Poeciliidae

1 *Cynolebias belotti*, Argentine pearlfish (109)   2 *Rivulus cylindraceus*, Cuban rivulus (129)   3 *Epiplatys dageti monroviae*, panchax chaperi
(115)   4 *Poecilia (Mollienesia) sphenops*, pointed-mouth molly: ♂ the black molly, ♀ the chequered form (145)   5 *Phalloceros caudimaculatus*,
caudo, ♂/♀ (148)   6 *Poecilia (Limia) vittata*, Cuban limia ♂ (143)   7 *Poecilia (Limia) melanogaster*, black-bellied limia ♂/♀ (141)   8 *Epiplatys chevalieri*, Chevalier's epiplatys (114)   9 *Rivulus urophthalmus*, golden rivulus (–)   10 *Poecilia (Mollienesia) velifera*, Mexican sailfin
molly ♂ (146)   11 *Phallichthys amates*, merry widow ♂/♀ (147)   12 *Girardinus metallicus*, girardinus ♂/♀ (138)   13 *Heterandria formosa*,
least killifish ♂/♀ (139)

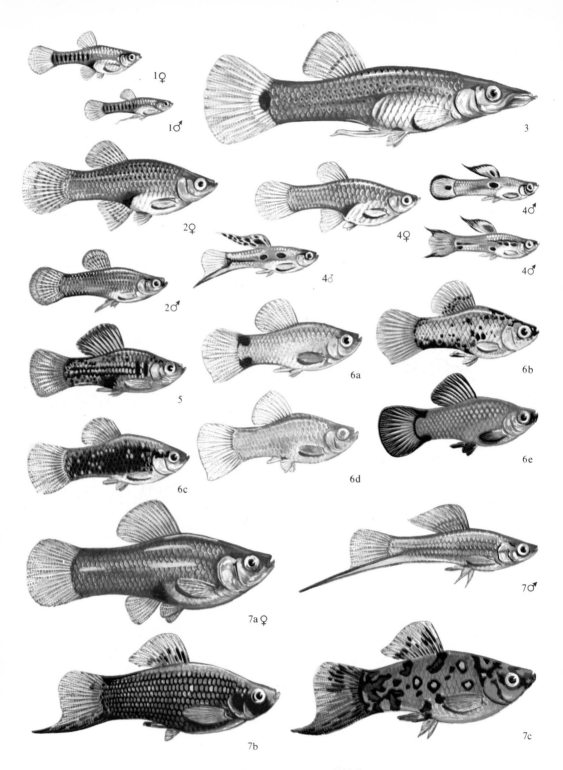

Plate VIII Livebearing toothcarps, Poeciliidae

1 *Cnesterodon decemmaculatus*, ten-spotted livebearer ♂/♀ (–) **2** *Gambusia puncticulata*, blue gambusia ♂/♀ (–) **3** *Belonesox belizanus*, pike-top minnow ♂ (136) **4** *Poecilia (Lebistes) reticulata*, guppy ♂♂♂/♀ (140) **5** *Xiphophorus variatus*, variatus platy ♂ (152) **6a–e** *Xiphophorus maculatus*, platy, selected forms ♂♂ (150) **7** *Xiphophorus helleri*, swordtail, green wild form ♂ (149) **7a–c** Selected forms and hybrids of the genus *Xiphophorus* (149–152)

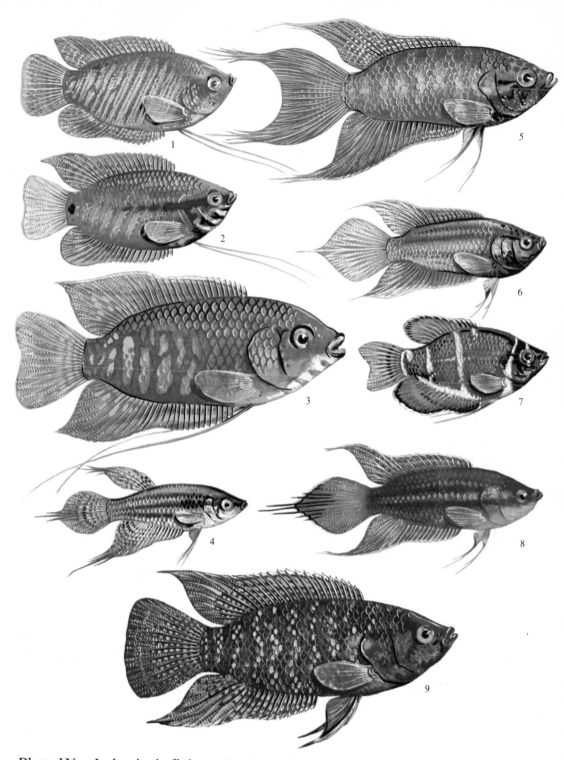

Plate IX   Labyrinth fishes, Anabantoidea

1 *Colisa lalia*, dwarf gourami (161)   **2** *Colisa labiosa*, thick-lipped gourami (160)   **3** *Colisa fasciata*, banded gourami (159)   **4** *Trichopsis vittatus*, croaking gourami (177)   **5** *Macropodus opercularis*, paradise fish (166)   **6** *Pseudosphromenus c. cupanus*, spike-tailed paradise fish (169)   **7** *Sphaerichthys osphromenoides*, chocolate gourami (171)   **8** *Pseudosphromenus cupanus dayi*, brown spike-tailed paradise fish (170)   **9** *Ctenopoma fasciolatum*, Banded climbing perch (162)

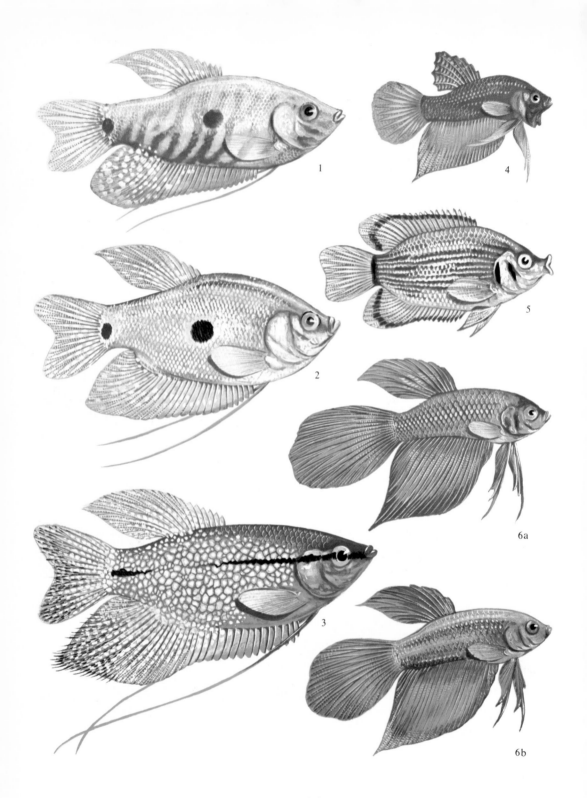

Plate X   Labyrinth fishes, Anabantoidea

1 *Trichogaster trichopterus sumatranus*, blue gourami (175)   **2** *Trichogaster t. trichopterus*, three-spot gourami (175)   **3** *Trichogaster leeri*, pearl gourami (172)   **4** *Betta splendens*, fighting fish, wild form (157)   **5** *Helostoma temmincki*, kissing gourami (164)   **6a–b** *Betta splendens*, fighting fish, selected forms (157)

Plate XI   Cichlids, Cichlidae

1 *Cichlasoma facetum*, chanchito (191)   2 *Cichlasoma severum*, banded cichlid (196)   3 *Pseudocrenilabrus multicolor*, Egyptian mouthbrooder ♂
(226)   4 *Nannacara anomala*, golden-eyed dwarf cichlid ♂/♀ (220)   5 *Apistogramma ramirezi*, Ramirez's dwarf cichlid ♂ (185)   6 *Etroplus
maculatus*, orange chromide (200)   7 *Apistogramma agassizi*, Agassiz's dwarf cichlid ♂/♀ (183)

Plate XII   Cichlids, Cichlidae

1 *Cichlasoma festivum*, festivum (192)   2 *Crenicichla lepidota*, pike cichlid (199)   3 *Sarotherodon mossambicus*, Mozambique mouthbrooder
(233)   4 *Pelvicachromis pulcher*, kribensis (223)   5 *Geophagus acuticeps*, earth-eater (see under 202)

Plate XIII Cichlids, Cichlidae

1 *Cichlasoma meeki*, firemouth cichlid (193) **2** *Pterophyllum scalare*, angelfish (232) **3** *Apistogramma reitzigi*, yellow dwarf cichlid ♂/♀ (186) **4** *Aequidens pulcher*, blue acara (182) **5** *Symphysodon aequifasciata axelrodi*, brown discus (235)

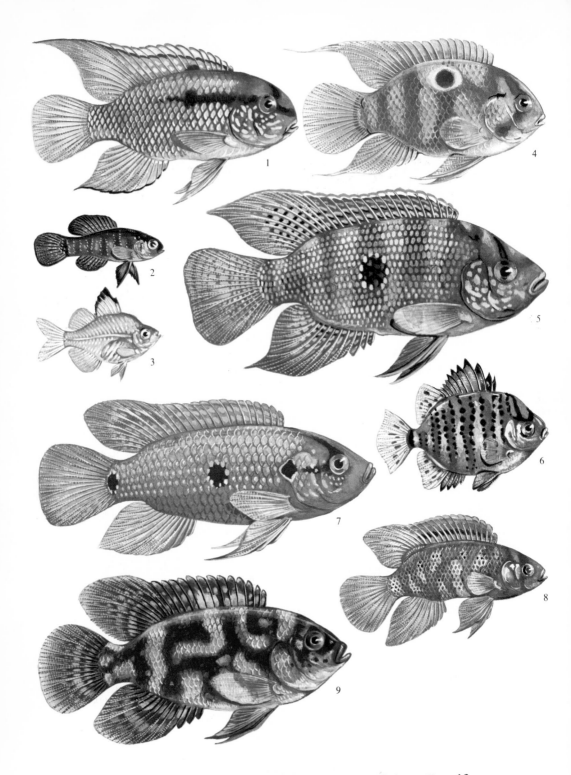

Plate XIV   Cichlids, Cichlidae and Perch-like fishes, Perciformes

1 *Aequidens curviceps*, flag cichlid (178)   2 *Elassoma evergladei*, Everglades pygmy sunfish (243)   3 *Chanda ranga*, Indian glassfish (242)
4 *Aequidens maronii*, keyhole cichlid (180)   5 *Cichlasoma octofasciatum*, Jack Dempsey (195)   6 *Scatophagus argus 'rubrifrons'*, argusfish (248)
7 *Hemichromis bimaculatus*, jewel cichlid (206)   8 *Badis badis*, badis (240)   9 *Astronotus ocellatus*, oscar (188)

Plate XV Perch-like fishes, Perciformes

1 *Polycentrus schomburgki,* Schomburgk's leaf-fish (247) **2** *Enneacanthus obesus,* blue-spotted sunfish (244) **3** *Mesogonistius chaetodon,* black-banded sunfish (245) **4** *Periophthalmus barbarus,* mudskipper (287) **5** *Brachygobius* (sp.), bumblebee fish (283) **6** *Monocirrhus polyacanthus,* South American leaf-fish (–) **7** *Toxotes jaculator,* archerfish (250) **8** *Eleotris marmorata,* marbled goby (285) **9** *Mogurnda mogurnda,* Australian gudgeon (–)

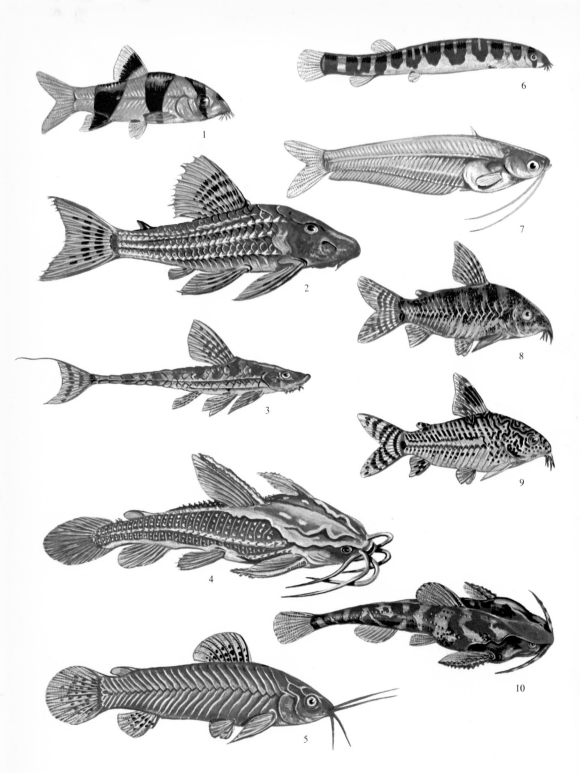

Plate XVI   Loaches, Cobitidae and Catfishes, Siluriformes

1 *Botia macracantha*, clown loach (280)   **2** *Plecostomus commersoni*, suckermouth catfish (274)   **3** *Loricaria parva* (?), dwarf whiptail (271)   **4** *Acanthodoras spinosissimus*, spiny catfish (256)   **5** *Callichthys callichthys*, armoured catfish (259)   **6** *Acanthophthalmus semicinctus*, coolie loach (277)   **7** *Kryptopterus bicirrhis*, glass catfish (270)   **8** *Corydoras paleatus*, peppered corydoras (264)   **9** *Corydoras punctatus julii*, leopard corydoras (265)   **10** *Bunocephalus* (sp.), banjo catfish (258)

Tables of fishes

Explanation of the tables

The following tables contain a selection of the most commonly kept and interesting aquarium fish with information on their nomenclature, country of origin, size, characteristics, sex differences, maintenance, breeding and diet. The information on maintenance and breeding is based on the observations of experienced aquarists, but this does not preclude the possibility that others may have different experiences.

The majority of the fish mentioned in the tables are illustrated, and all the species have been given a number which also appears by the side of the fish in the illustrations. Species shown in the illustrations, but rarely imported at present and not mentioned in the text, are given the symbol (–). Species shown in the colour photograph section (pp 33–56) have an asterisk*.

The species in the tables are arranged according to families or sub-orders, and in one case according to habitat (bottom-living fish). The species in each group are arranged alphabetically according to the scientific name; the genera are also arranged alphabetically within each group.

The scientific names consist of two parts, the first denoting the genus, the second the species, e.g. *Brachydanio* (genus) and *rerio* (species). Scientific names are based on Latin, which is international, and words derived from other languages are suitably latinized.

The popular names given are those in general use among aquarists, but they have no scientific validity. Some species have no suitable popular name.

Abbreviations

Temperatures are average values
MT   Minimum possible temperature
♂   Male
♀   Female
-/-   Breeding stock required, thus: male/ female
Pg. 1–12 Plant groups (see p. 107)
TS   Tank size is given thus:
   I = smallest tanks, 15–20 cm (6–7·8 in) long
   II = small tanks, 20–30 cm (7·8–11·8 in) long
   III = medium-sized tanks, 30–50 cm (11·8–19·6 in) long
   IV = medium-large tanks, 50–80 cm (19·6–31·6 in) long
   V = large tanks, 100 cm (39 in) and over
   VI = large special tanks
pH   pH value
°dH   degrees of hardness (German)

Exotic fishes

Characins and relatives (Characoidea)

The sub-order Characoidea contains a number of fish families known to aquarists as characins. These families, with species from the fresh waters of Africa, South and Central America, and the southernmost part of the United States, comprise small to medium-sized fish with the most varied appearance and habits. Many of them have an adipose fin, a characteristic they share with the salmon family (Salmonidae). They are related to the barbs (Cyprinidae) which, however, lack an adipose fin and have rather poorly developed dentition. Most characins have variously shaped small teeth but a few have a dangerous sharp dentition capable of tearing up the prey, or needle-like teeth for catching it.

I. The true characins, family Characidae

These are mostly good swimmers, which tend to live in shoals. Some species live in open, standing or flowing waters, others prefer areas of dense vegetation. As a rule they all keep to the upper and middle waters, and there are almost no bottom-living species.

In accordance with the large distribution range – the Characidae occur in Africa and also America – the body form varies from a very slender spindle-like shape to an almost circular profile. The throat region is often distended, so that the front part of the body appears overladen. In most species the fins are relatively small, but in some they are more or less enlarged and lobe-like or drawn out to a point.

Bright colours are rare within the family, or are concentrated as brilliant spots or streaks. In the shoaling species of open water the scales may show brilliant iridescence, often in various colour tones.

In the aquarium most true characins like bright light with shaded areas, clear water and sufficient vegetation, leaving enough space for swimming. Coloration is enhanced by a dark substrate.

Feeding habits vary considerably, from vegetarian to predatory. Most species are, however, undemanding and will take live and dried food. Temperature requirements are somewhat variable, but the majority are content with a temperature of 22–24 °C (71–75 °F), although some species do better at 20–22 °C (68–71 °F).

Breeding can sometimes be very easy, though requiring some care, but in other cases is very difficult. Most species are random spawners, releasing their sexual products into the open water or among or above the plants. Mating involves the pair coming close to one another, sometimes lying on their sides or even turning on their backs. Some male characins have fine hooklets on the anal fin which help to hold the pair together during mating and the fertilization of the eggs. Each spawning consists of several separate matings, each releasing ten to thirty eggs. The total number depends upon the species and the condition of the fish.

So far as possible fairly young fish should be used for breeding, as there may be difficulties when using older specimens. Quite often old females produce eggs that are not viable. The sexes are, as a rule, not difficult to distinguish. The males are smaller and more slender, and often more colourful. In many species their fins are larger and more pointed and in some the anal fin hooklets become entangled with the net when they are being caught up. Experienced aquarists can differentiate the sexes by structural differences in the translucent internal organs.

In one group of characins the female stores sperm received during a mating. These sperm are stored in a small pocket in the female's body, and they are sufficient to fertilize eggs at several subsequent spawnings without the presence of a male.

Brood protection is only rarely practised. In some species of *Pyrrhulina* the eggs are laid on the broad leaves of water plants, on rocks or in pits. The spraying characin, *Copella arnoldi*, is particularly noteworthy. At spawning time both parents leap out of the water and the female lays her eggs on leaves (or on the tank glass) where they are simultaneously fertilized by the male. After this the eggs are regularly sprayed with water by beats of the male's tail. This goes on until the eggs hatch and the fry drop into the water.

In most true characin species the eggs hatch in eighteen to thirty-six hours. The fry either move up to the water surface or hang by fine filaments from plants, the aquarium glass or other objects. They can be reared on powdered dried food or on very tiny live food.

Occasionally, breeding may be successful in a fully established aquarium or even in a community tank. However, for more efficient breeding the breeding fish should be put into a separate tank. The following remarks on this type of breeding may be useful; they are referred to in the 'Breeding' column of the tables by their Z number.

Z 1: Random-spawning characins without special water requirements

The breeding stock should be put into an all-glass, plastic or angle-iron tank without substrate and without rooted water plants. The volume of the tank will vary according to the number of offspring expected. To protect the eggs from being eaten (many characins are spawn-eaters) the bottom can have a layer of marble-sized pebbles. The same objective can be achieved by having a coarse-mesh plastic mop or a few feathery plants anchored to the bottom by glass rods. The composition of the water is not critical and there is no need to lower the pH as the eggs and fry are generally not very sensitive to bacteria or to infusorians.

The effect of light on the breeding fish varies. Some species like bright light for spawning, for example morning sun, while others prefer subdued light. In general, it is best to have the light slightly shaded. After spawning the lighting can be restored to normal as the eggs and fry are not light-sensitive.

The breeding fish do not always spawn at clearly defined spawning periods. In the aquarium they can be put together at intervals of one to three weeks. When they are fully mature, some characins spawn immediately after they have been together, others need a few days before they are ready to spawn, or these may have to be put back and tried again later.

The eggs hatch in fifteen to thirty hours. When there are large numbers of newly hatched fry the water should be treated with a very weak dose of a commercial bacteriostat.

The fry can be fed on *Paramecium,* rotifers, powdered dried food, and somewhat later on newly hatched brine shrimps.

Group Z 1 contains table numbers 4, 13, 15, 18, 20, 23, 25, 27, 32, 35, 36, 48, 50.

Z 2: Random-spawning characins with special water requirements

a) The breeding fish should be put together in well-cleaned (or sterilized in potassium permanganate) all-glass tanks, or for highly productive species, in angle-iron tanks. The water should be soft (2–5 °dH), slightly acid (pH 6·5 or a little less) and filtered through peat. The equipment and plants must be thoroughly washed as the eggs and fry are usually sensitive to the attacks of bacteria and infusorians (see also 'Hints on the breeding of aquarium fishes'). There should be no substrate. A few feathery plants can be anchored to the bottom with glass rods, or a coarse mop of plastic can be placed on the bottom. The breeding tank should be slightly darkened during spawning and for a few days after hatching. Eggs and fry may be light-sensitive. The light can be restored to normal as soon as the fry are free-swimming. To prevent the multiplication of infusorians the breeding pair should not be fed during spawning. If they have not spawned after a few days they should be removed from the breeding tank and a further attempt can then be made a little later on.

Group Z 2a contains table numbers 16, 17, 19, 21, 22, 24, 26, 28, 31, 33, 44.

b) Some African characins have special water and food requirements. They should be put together in a spacious angle-iron tank without substrate. A small amount of water-moss can be laid on the bottom, although these fish generally do not attack their own spawn. The water should be soft (under 3 °dH) and filtered through peat. The parent fish will only spawn if they have been fed on spiders, insects and their larvae, e.g. gnat larvae, flies, ant pupae and mealworms.

Group Z 2b contains table numbers 2, 5, 47.

Z 3: Characins with storage of sperm

In an ordinary aquarium tank containing several pairs of these fish or one male and three females, the latter are almost always fertilized. When they appear ready to spawn they should be put into a tank without substrate and treated like those in group Z 1. Feathery plants will serve as a spawning substrate. Some species attach their eggs to the broad leaves of water plants.

Group Z 3 contains table number 12.

II. Headstanders, family Anostomidae

A South American family of fish with a moderately high-backed to elongated, sometimes even spindle-shaped, body. Some of them have thick, fleshy lips which are provided with fine tooth-like structures for rasping algal films from plants. The popular name refers to the fact that some species live and swim at an oblique angle with the head down. They only give up this position for short periods, as for example in flight. Some headstanders are brightly coloured or they at least have a striking pattern. Certain species are rather expensive to buy, because in their country of origin they are rare or difficult to catch. Only a single species, *Chilodus punctatus,* is regularly bred in the aquarium, so the trade has to rely exclusively on imports. Now and then other species have laid eggs but the young have not been reared. In the aquarium the diet consists of plant fragments, algae, gnat or mosquito larvae and small crustaceans which are taken from the bottom. Little is known of their life in the wild, although certain species carry out long migrations at spawning time to reach their spawning grounds. This behaviour may in some measure account for the difficulties experienced in attempts at captive breeding.

III. Hatchetfish, family Gasteropelecidae

These are relatively short fish, with marked lateral compression and an almost straight dorsal profile. The ventral profile is much expanded and curved to produce a boat-like appearance. The pectoral fins are enlarged. Hatchetfish usually live close to the surface where they catch insects that have landed on the water. When chased they beat the pectoral fins and glide rapidly along the surface and for short distances can even leave the water in a form of flight.

Hatchetfish are not easy to keep in the aquarium, and breeding is very difficult. Some species of *Carnegiella* have been successfully bred, and their spawning behaviour is similar to that of other characoids. They are not particular as regards diet, but the food must be offered at the surface or at least swimming free in the middle water layers.

IV. Family Hemiodontidae

A relatively small family of South American fish. Some species, such as the pencilfish (*Nannostomus, Poecilobrycon* and others) are now often classified in the family Lebiasinidae.

In the wild these attractive fish live along the water's edge and in flooded areas, especially among the vegetation.

The family consists almost exclusively of awl-shaped species with moderate lateral compression and a very small mouth. Members of the genera *Nannostomus* and *Poecilobrycon* swim either in the normal position or obliquely with the head pointed upwards. Feeding is not difficult as they take both live and dried food provided it is fine enough for the small mouth. They do not normally take food from the bottom.

They spawn at random or lay adhesive eggs, but rearing is sometimes difficult. Here are some general points:

Z 4

As for Z 1 the fish should be placed in an all-glass tank, which can be quite small, a volume of about 10 litres (2 gals) being sufficient. The water can be slightly soft, with a hardness not exceeding 6–12 °dH, but there are individual differences. There is no need to make the water acid, but it must be clean and clear. Both the eggs and fry are sensitive to infusorians.

These fish are notorious spawn robbers, so there must be a grating at the bottom, through which the eggs can fall, and also a few feathery plants anchored with glass rods. A clump of plants should be placed in the centre of the tank and for *Poecilobrycon* there can be a broad-leaved plant of e.g. *Cryptocoryne.* In every case the light should be somewhat subdued.

The number of offspring is not particularly large and an average of fifty fry can be regarded as a good result. During the spawning period the fish can be put together for breeding every eight to fourteen days. Otherwise treat as given for Z 1 and Z 2.

V. Family Citharinidae

An exclusively African family of fish with very varied form. Some species are high-backed and much laterally compressed, others are elongated and spindle-shaped, while the members of the genera *Nannaethiops* and *Neolebias* usually kept in the aquarium are more like barbs than characins. These are small, active fish, somewhat timid and best kept in a species tank or at least with other similar species. Feeding is not always easy, as some, particularly the species of *Neolebias*, require very fine food and preferably live food, such as *Artemia* and Grindal worms.

Breeding of *Nannaethiops* should be carried out as recommended in Z 1, and of *Neolebias* as given in Z 2. In both cases, however, the water should not be so soft.

Remarks on characoid classification
The opinions of experts on the systematic position of the species described change from time to time with the publication of new scientific material. Furthermore, the validity of such taxonomic changes is often of short duration. For various reasons these developments cannot always be followed in aquarium literature. In the present context any new names are only used when they have become established in aquarium practice and appear to be reliable.

No.	Scientific name	Popular name	Distribution	Length cm	Characteristics	Sex differences
1	*Abramites hypselonotus* (formerly *A. microcephalus*)	Headstander	Amazon region and Guyana	12 (4.7 in)	Not always entirely peaceful. Often also swims in normal body position	♂ darker and with distinct edge to fins
2	*Alestes longipinnis*	Long-finned characin	Tropical West Africa in flowing waters	10–12 (3.9–4.7 in)	Active shoaling fish, likes to jump. Good for community tank with other African characins	Dorsal fin rays elongated, filamentous in ♂ and reddish, but yellowish in ♀
3	*Anostomus anostomus*	Striped anostomus	Amazon region, Guyana, in water with rich vege-tation	15 (5.9 in)	Typical headstand-er, only swimming in normal position when disturbed. In restricted space sometimes aggres-sive, particularly towards other mem-bers of its own spe-cies	Unknown
4	*Aphyocharax rubropinnis*	Bloodfin	Argentina, La Plata region	4.5 (1.7 in)	Active, tolerant shoaling fish	♂ more slender, more intense red. Caught in a net the anal fin hooklets of ♂ become en-tangled
5	*Arnoldichthys spilopterus*	Red-eyed characin	Tropical West Africa	10 (3.9 in)	Active fish. Likes to jump. Suitable for community tank with other African characins	♂ more brightly coloured, the anal fin with black and red pattern
6	*Astyanax mexicanus* (formerly *Anoptichthys jordani*)	Blind cave characin	Subterra-nean caves in central Mexico	3–8 (1–3 in)	Peaceful, always on the move. Swims well	♂ more slender, ♀ stouter and some-what larger
7	*Carnegiella marthae*	Black-winged hatchetfish	Upper Peruvian Amazon, Orinoco region	3.5 (1.3 in)	Peaceful, relatively hardy, surface fish. Jumps	Seen from above ♂ more slender, ripe ♀ considerably stouter

Maintenance	Breeding	Diet	Page/ Figure
TS IV/V. Pg. 12. Dark substrate and decorative roots. 23–28 °C (73–82 °F)	Not yet bred	Bottom-living food: *Tubifex*, midge larvae, algae, lettuce, dried food	III/4
TS V. Pg. 7. 22–25 °C (71–77 °F). Scattered plant clumps and sufficient swimming space. Soft, clear water rich in oxygen. Good tank lid	Z 2b. Difficult, only bred occasionally	Live and dried food, including insects	186/4
TS IV/V. Pg. 7, with strap-like plants or sword plants. 22–28 °C (71–82 °F), preferably about 24 °C (75 °F)	Not yet bred in the home aquarium	As for No. 1	III/3
TS III. Pg. 7, plant clumps to leave sufficient swimming space. 18–23 °C, (64–73 °F) will tolerate down to 15 °C (59 °F)	Z 1. Surface spawner, 23–26 °C (73–78 °F), in small shoal or 1 ♂ and 2 ♀. Bad egg-eater; remove parents as soon as possible. 300–400 eggs hatch in 24–30 hours. Fry free-swimming at 5 days, feed on live and dried food. Fast-growing	Live and dried food	I/1
TS V. Pg. 7, with plants leaving sufficient swimming space. 22–25 °C (71–77 °F). Soft, clear, oxygen-rich water, and a good tank lid	Z 2b. Difficult, only bred occasionally	Live and dried food, including insects	186/2
TS III/IV, with rocks, roots, no plants. Aeration and filtration. 18–24 °C (64–75 °F). No special water	Not difficult. Spawns near surface. Eggs hatch in 3–4 days, fry free-swimming 6 days later. Easy to rear on brine shrimps and dried food. Fast-growing	Live and dried food, often taken from bottom	186/1
TS III. Pg. 7. Good swimming space, and plant clumps for shelter. Long, well-covered tank. Leave sufficient space between water surface and lid. Subdued light. 24 °C (75 °F)	Probably not yet achieved. Possibly requires soft, slightly acid water	Insects (wingless fruitflies, mosquito larvae, waterfleas) at the surface. Dried food	187/8

No.	Scientific name	Popular name	Distribution	Length cm	Characteristics	Sex differences
8	*Carnegiella strigata*	Marbled hatchetfish	Amazon region and northern South America	1 (0.4 in)	Peaceful surface fish, does well in aquarium. Jumps	Seen from above ♂ more slender, ripe ♀ much stouter
9	*Chilodus punctatus*	Spotted headstander	Northern South America	8 (3 in)	Peaceful, relatively quiet	♂ somewhat more slender, ♀ much stouter at spawning time
10	*Copeina guttata*	Red-spotted copeina	Central Amazon, in open water	up to 12 (4.7 in)	Peaceful, very active shoaling fish. Likes to jump	♂ with bright red fins, ♀ with black spot on dorsal fin
11	*Copella arnoldi*	Spraying characin	Lower Amazon, Rio Para, in backwaters with dense vegetation	♂ 8 (3 in) ♀ 6 (2.4 in)	Lively, tolerant. Likes to jump	♂ larger and more brightly coloured, with larger elongated fins
12	*Corynopoma riisei*	Swordtail characin	Venezuela, Trinidad, Colombia, in lakes and ponds	♂ 7 (2.75 in) ♀ 5.5 (2.2 in)	Very active, sociable, swimming in open water	♂ with larger fins and a spoon-shaped extension of gill cover
13	*Ctenobrycon spilurus*	Silver tetra	Northern South America, in fresh water near coasts	8 (3 in)	Peaceful, active, occasionally somewhat aggressive towards smaller fish. Good in community tank with fish of same size. Sometimes attacks plants	♂ smaller, more slender, with red sheen on anal fin
14	*Gasteropelecus sternicla*	Common hatchetfish	Guyana and Amazon region	6 (2.4 in)	Peaceful, active shoaling and surface fish	Seen from above, ♂ narrower, possibly somewhat more elongated

Maintenance	Breeding	Diet	Page/Figure
As for *C. marthae*	Once achieved. Spawns beneath the surface, like other random spawning characins (Z 1). At 26 °C (78 °F) eggs hatch in 36 hours, fry free-swimming 5 days later	As for *C. marthae*	188/3
TS IV. Pg. 12, plants as tall as possible, densely planted in places. 24 °C (75 °F)	Occasionally successful. Planned breeding in large tank, water up to 10 °dH, 25 °C (77 °F), peat filtration, clear and clean, subdued light. Spawning among roots or feathery plants, either near bottom or below surface. Eggs hatch in 36 hours, fry free-swimming 4 days later, assuming typical headstander position immediately. Rearing with brine shrimps not difficult. Fast-growing	Live food on bottom, *Tubifex*, midge larvae, plant matter, dried food	III/1
TS IV/V. Pg. 7, with some plant clumps. No special water requirements. 23–25 °C (73–77 °F). Well-fitting lid, as they jump.	TS V. One of each sex. Spawns in fine sand or on smooth rock. 1,000 or more very adhesive eggs, guarded by ♂ (remove ♀). Rearing as for Z 1. 24–25 °C (75–77 °F)	Live and dried food	I/19
TS III/IV. Pg. 7, with some dense vegetation, and floating plants. MT 18 °C (64 °F), otherwise 22–25 °C (71–77 °F)	Not difficult. Even spawns in community tank. But 1/1 fish can be spawned in all-glass tank. At spawning they jump up and lay eggs on a leaf or tank lid. Leave 6–8 cm (2.4–3 in) between water surface and lid. 50–200 eggs regularly sprayed with water by beats of male's tail. Rear fry after they fall into water as given in Z 1. 24–26 °C (75–78 °F)	Live and dried food	I/12
TS III. Pg. 7, dense vegetation, but plenty of swimming space. Clear, clean water and bright light. MT 15 °C (59 °F), otherwise 22–26 °C (71–78 °F)	Z 3. ♀ lays eggs, already fertilized, in rows on leaves; they hatch in 24–26 hours. Rearing not difficult with brine shrimp and powdered dried food. Fast-growing. Not particularly productive, 50–100 fry	Live and dried food	II/4
TS IV. Pg. 12, leaving sufficient swimming space. 20–23 °C (68–73 °F) falling to 18 °C (64 °F)	Z 1. TS IV/V. 22–26 °C (71–78 °F). 1 ♂/1 ♀. Attractive courtship followed by spawning among dense, feathery plants. Very productive, 600–2,000 eggs. Rearing not difficult	Live and dried food	II/12
TS IV. Pg. 7, leaving sufficient swimming space. 24–26 °C (75–78 °F). MT 20 °C (68 °F). Likes more light than *Carnegiella*	As for *Carnegiella*. Only once bred in captivity	As for *C. marthae*	

No.	Scientific name	Popular name	Distribution	Length cm	Characteristics	Sex differences
15	*Gymno-corymbus ternetzi*	Black tetra	Paraguay, northern La Plata region	6 (2.4 in)	Active, tolerant, good for community tank	♂ smaller, more slender, white tips more intense on caudal fin
16	*Hemigrammus erythrozonus*	Glowlight tetra	North-eastern South America in forest areas	4 (1.5 in)	Lively, peaceful, suitable for tank with other forest fish	♂ more slender
17	*Hemigrammus hyanuary*	Green neon	Western Amazon, Lake Hyanuary	3.5 (1.3 in)	Peaceful, shoaling fish, preferring middle water layers	♂ more slender. Anal fin hooklets are caught up in nets
18	*Hemigrammus marginatus*	Black-tailed tetra	Brazil	5 (1.9 in)	Active, shoaling fish. ♂ sometimes rather aggressive	♂ more slender. Fin tips more intense white
19	*Hemigrammus nanus* (formerly *Hasemania marginata*)	Silver-tipped tetra	East Brazil	5 (1.9 in)	Active, tolerant and sociable	♂ more slender, with coppery over-tones
20	*Hemigrammus ocellifer*	Beacon fish	Northern South America, Amazon	6 (2.4 in)	Active, peaceful, sociable	♂ more slender and somewhat smaller
21	*Hemigrammus pulcher*	Pretty tetra	South America, Amazon	5 (1.9 in)	Peaceful, sociable, not particularly active. Good for tank with other forest fish	♂ more slender, more brightly coloured
22	*Hemigrammus rhodostomus*	Red-nosed tetra	Lower Amazon	6 (2.4 in)	Active, peaceful shoaling fish	♂more slender
23	*Hyphessobrycon bifasciatus*	Yellow tetra	South-eastern Brazil	4.5 (1.7 in)	Active, sociable, more peaceful than No. 25	♂ smaller, more slender, more brightly coloured
24	*Hyphessobrycon callistus*	Blood characin	Rio Para-guay (Mato Grosso area)	4 (1.5)	Active, peaceful, playful. Suitable for community tank	♂ more slender, usually also smaller, more brightly coloured, the white in the fins more intense

(*H. callistus* has some subspecies, distributed throughout tropical South America. A deep red selected form is sold as *H. 'minor'*, but *H. callistus minor* is a subspecies scarcely imported as yet.)

178

Maintenance	Breeding	Diet	Page/Figure
TS II/III. Pg. 7, with some plant clumps for shelter. 23–26 °C (73–78 °F)	Z 1. Very productive, so TS IV. 25–28 °C (77–82 °F). Rearing easy. Halfgrown individuals particularly attractive. A veiltail now on the market	Live and dried food	I/3
TS III. Pg. 6. Lighting not too bright. Dark background enhances coloration. Soft water, up to 8 °dH. 24 °C (75 °F)	Z 2a. 23 °C (73 °F). Water must not be acidified. Eggs not so light-sensitive as in neon tetra. 300 fry are a good result. Rearing not difficult	Live and dried food	I/16
TS II/III. Pg. 7, with plant clumps and sufficient swimming space. Soft water, 20–24 °C (68–75 °F)	Z 2a. 22–25 °C (71–77 °F). Water up to 3 °dH. Rearing not difficult	Live and dried food	186/5
TS III. Pg. 7. 22–24 °C (71–75 °F)	Z 1. 24 °C (75 °F). Only rarely bred	Live and dried food	186/12
TS II/III. Pg. 7. 20–25 °C (68–77 °F)	Z 2a. 23–24 °C (73–75 °F). Notorious spawn robber. Not very productive, 150–200 fry, fed at first on *Paramecium*.	Live and dried food	I/7
TS II/III. Pg. 6. 23–26 °C (73–78 °F), not very sensitive to lower temperatures. Dark substrate enhances iridescent spots	Z 1. 25 °C (77 °F). No special water requirements, but not too hard (up to 12 °dH). Fairly productive	Live and dried food	I/9
TS III. Pg. 6. 24–27 °C (75–80 °F). Dark substrate enhances coloration	Z 2a. 26–28 °C (78–82 °F). Water up to 5 °dH, slightly acid, peat filtration. Not very easy to breed. 400–600 eggs. Rearing rather difficult, fry require very fine food	Live and dried food	I/15
TS III. Pg. 7. 23–26 °C (73–78 °F). Soft, clear, clean water	Z 2a. Breeding difficult, see also *Petitella georgiae*	Live and dried food	
As for *H. flammeus*	Z 1. As for *H. flammeus*. Not very productive	Live and dried food	187/3
TS II/III. Pg. 6/7. Soft water, up to 6 °dH (or more if breeding not required). Dark substrate. 23–26 °C (73–78 °F)	Z 2a. 24–26 °C (75–78 °F). Subdued light. Water peat-filtered, very clean, free of infusorians	Live and dried food	I/18

No.	Scientific name	Popular name	Distribution	Length cm	Characteristics	Sex differences
25	*Hyphessobrycon flammeus*	Flame tetra	Area around Rio de Janeiro	4 (1.5 in)	Active, sometimes rather aggressive. Suitable for a community tank	♂ more slender, more brightly coloured, the black edges of anal and ventral fins more pronounced
26	*Hyphessobrycon georgettae*	Strawberry tetra	Northern South America	3 (1.1 in)	Peaceful, delicate, not suitable for boisterous tank mates	♂ brighter red to brownish red. ♀ considerably stouter at spawning time
27	*Hyphessobrycon griemi*	Griem's tetra	Brazil	3.0–3.5 (1.1– 1.3 in)	Peaceful and suitable for community tank	♂ somewhat smaller and more intensely coloured
28	*Hyphessobrycon herbertaxelrodi*	Black neon	Amazon region	3.5 (1.3 in)	Peaceful, sociable, suitable for community tank	♂ more slender with bluish-white fin tips
29	*Hyphessobrycon heterorhabdus*	Flag tetra	Amazon and northern South America	3.5–4.0 (1.3– 1.5 in)	Active, peaceful shoaling fish suitable for a community tank	♂ more slender
30	*Hyphessobrycon ornatus*	Ornate tetra	Northern South America	5–6 (2– 2.4 in)	Active, peaceful, playful fish, suitable for a community tank	♂ more slender, slightly larger, and more brightly coloured. Dorsal and anal fins larger and drawn out to a point
31	*Hyphessobrycon pulchripinnis*	Lemon tetra	Brazil, Para region	4 (1.5 in)	Active, peaceful	♂ more slender and bright yellow at spawning time
32	*Hyphessobrycon scholzei*	Black-line tetra	Amazon, Para region	5 (1.9 in)	Active, peaceful, suitable for a community tank	♂ more slender and decorative
33	*Lamprocheirodon axelrodi*	Cardinal tetra	Tropical South America, region of Rio Negro	3.5–4.0 (1.3– 1.5 in)	Peaceful shoaling fish, swimming mostly in the middle water	Little difference. ♂ more slender, ♀ becoming stouter

Maintenance	Breeding	Diet	Page/Figure
TS II/III. Pg. 7. Shelter places among plants. 20–30 °C (68–86 °F). At lower temperatures and in light that is too bright the fish become paler. Clean, clear water, but hardness not critical	Z 1. 23–25 °C (73–77 °F). May be quite productive. Rearing not difficult	Live and dried food	I/5
TS II. Pg. 7, with clumps of feathery plants. Soft water. Warmth-loving: 25–30 °C (77–86 °F)	Z 2a. TS III. 28 °C (82 °F). Substrate covered with peat. Water up to 3 °dH, peat-filtered. Clump of feathery plant to provide shelter	Live and dried food	187/5
TS II/III. Pg. 7. 22–26 °C (71–78 °F), if less fish become paler and sluggish, as they do in too bright light. Use dark substrate	Z 1. As for *H. flammeus*	Live and dried food	187/14
TS II/III. Pg. 6. 22–25 °C (71–77 °F). Water not too soft, light not too bright, dark substrate	Z 2a. 24–26 °C (75–78 °F). Breeding held to be rather difficult	Live and dried food	187/4
TS II/III. Pg. 6/7. 23–25 °C (73–77 °F). Soft water. Tank not too brightly lit	Z 2a. Not easy. Hardness about 3 °dH, slightly acid, peat filtration	Live and dried food	I/17
TS III. Pg. 6/7. 23–26 °C (73–78 °F). Water hardness not very critical. Shady places and dark substrate enhance well-being	Z 2a. 24–26 °C (75–78 °F). Best bred in an old-established tank. Soft water, but has bred in up to 10 °dH. Breeding fish allowed to find own mates, as not all individuals are compatible. May be quite productive. Rearing not difficult	Live and dried food	I/4
TS II/III. Pg. 7. 22–24 °C (71–75 °F)	Z 2a. Breeding held to be difficult, some pairs will not spawn together. 24–26 °C (75–78 °F), up to 5 °dH. Not very productive. Fry sensitive	Live and dried food	I/11
TS II/III. Pg. 7. Shelter among plants and enough swimming space. 20–23 °C (68–73 °F). Clear, clean water, hardness not critical	Z 1. 23–26 °C (73–78 °F). Fairly productive. Rearing not difficult	Live and dried food	187/6
TS II/III. Pg. 6. Subdued light, floating plants to give shade. Hardness not critical, except for breeding (not over 5 °dH). 22–24 °C (71–75 °F)	Z 2a. 24–25 °C (75–77 °F). 3 °dH. Breeding rather more difficult and less productive than in *Paracheirodon innesi*	Fine live and dried food	186/3

No.	Scientific name	Popular name	Distribution	Length cm	Characteristics	Sex differences
34	*Metynnis hypsauchen* (formerly *M. schreitmulleri*)	Schreitmuller's metynnis	Amazon region	15 (6 in)	Active, always some-what shy shoaling fish. Occasionally aggressive towards other fish	Front of anal fin convex in ♂, straight in ♀. Anal also more brightly coloured in ♂
35	*Moenkhausia pittieri*	Diamond tetra	Venezuela (Lake Valencia)	6 (2.4 in)	Very active swim-mer. Good for a community tank	♂ larger with more elongated fins
36	*Moenkhausia sanctae-filomenae*	Red-eye tetra	Rio Para-guay	6–7 (2.4–2.7 in)	Peaceful, not very active shoaling fish. Good for commu-nity tank	♂ smaller and more slender
37	*Nannostomus eques*	Tube-mouthed pencilfish	Guyana, Rio Negro, central Amazon	5 (1.9 in)	Peaceful, sociable, appearing stiff when swimming. May be active in a large tank	♂ more brightly coloured. Red on anal fin is brighter. In both sexes day and night coloratios differ
38	*Nannostomus beckfordi aripirangensis*	Golden pencilfish	Amazon, Aripiranga island	4 (1.5 in)	Peaceful, playful, best kept with other pencilfish	♂ more slender, a more intense red. Ventral fins with a bluish border
39	*Nannostomus bifasciatus*	Two-banded pencilfish	River Suri-nam	6 (2.4 in)	As for preceding species	♂ less colourful. Red on caudal fin intense
40	*Nannostomus marginatus*	Dwarf pencilfish	Guyana, Amazon region	3.5 (1.3 in)	As for No. 38	May be difficult to distinguish. ♂ rather more slender, red on fins more intense
41	*Nannostomus trifasciatus*	Three-banded pencilfish	Guyana, Rio Negro, Amazon region	6 (2.4 in)	As for No. 38	♂ more slender, with row of red spots in the golden band along the side
42	*Nematobrycon palmeri*	Emperor tetra	Colombia	5.5 (2.1 in)	♂♂ aggressive to-wards one another, otherwise very suit-able for community tank	♂ with elongated rays in distal and caudal fins. Anal fin with a more distinct border

Maintenance	Breeding	Diet	Page/Figure
TS V. Pg. 12. Tough plants not easily eaten, or no plants. Plenty of swimming space, also hiding-places among roots and rocks. 24–27 °C (75–80 °F)	Spawns best as a shoal in a large tank. 25 °C (77 °F). Water not too hard. The few relatively large eggs hatch in about 4 days. Fry free-swimming 5 days later, take brine shrimp immediately. Fast-growing	Live and dried food and plant matter	III/7
TS III/IV. Pg. 7. Plant clumps to provide hiding-places, and sufficient swimming space. 24 °C (75 °F)	Z 1. TS IV. 24–26 °C (75–78 °F). After vigorous driving spawns above and among the plants. Very productive, up to 400 eggs. Fry at first remain hidden. Sensitive to temperature fluctuations	Live and dried food	II/10
TS III. Pg. 7. Likes to rest among the plants. 20–26 °C (68–78 °F)	Z 1. 22–24 °C (71–75 °F). Fry like to remain near the bottom and are somewhat sensitive to bright light. Fast-growing	Live and dried food	186/16
TS III/IV. Pg. 7. Surface partly covered with floating fern. 23–25 °C (73–77 °F)	Z 4. Requires care. Eggs laid on leaf undersides, usually fall to the bottom, where difficult to see. Hatch in 24–30 hours, fry free-swimming in 5 days, take brine shrimp immediately	Small live and dried food. Will not feed from substrate	II/13
TS II/III. Pg. 7. 22–25 °C (71–77 °F). Dark substrate, peat filtration, subdued lighting. Water hardness not critical except for breeding	Z 4. Relatively easy with clear, clean water up to 12 °dH. 23–25 °C (73–77 °F). Up to 200 offspring	Small live and dried food	II/7
As for preceding species	Z 4. Bad egg-eater. Water up to 8 °dH. Not very productive	Live and dried food	187/10
As for No. 38	Z 4. 24 °C (75 °F), up to 8 °dH. Bad egg-eater. Not productive, 40 offspring is a good result. Slow-growing	Live and dried food	II/6
As for No. 38	Z 4. As for No. 40, but more productive, although only breeds sporadically	Live and dried food	II/8
As for *Hemigrammus* species	As for *Nannostomus* species. Not very productive	Live and dried food	

No.	Scientific name	Popular name	Distribu-tion	Length cm	Characteristics	Sex differences
43	*Neolebias ansorgei*	African redfin	West Africa	4 (1.5 in)	Peaceful, but some-what shy and deli-cate. Best kept as a pair	♂ more slender, more brightly coloured
44	*Paracheirodon innesi*	Neon tetra	Amazon upper reaches, in shady waters	3.5 (1.3 in)	Active, peaceful shoaling fish, keep-ing near the bottom. Excellent for com-munity tank	♂ more slender
45	*Petitella georgiae*	False rummy-nose	Peru, Rio Huallaga	6 (2.4 in)	Active, peaceful shoaling fish	♂ more slender, with brighter coloration
46	*Phago loricatus*	Striped pike characin	Niger region	15 (6 in)	Pike-like predatory fish	Unknown
47	*Phenaco-grammus interruptus*	Congo tetra	Congo region (Zaire)	♂ 8 (3 in) ♀ 6 (2.4 in)	Active, peaceful shoaling fish, excel-lent for community tank with larger tetras	♂ larger, more brightly coloured, with larger, some-what elongated fins
48	*Pristella riddlei*	X-ray fish	Amazon, Guyana, Venezuela	4 (1.5 in)	Active, peaceful, very suitable for community tank	♂ smaller and more slender
49	*Pygocentrus piraya*	Piranha	Widely dis-tributed in tropical South America	15 (6 in) or more	Predatory, with powerful, dangerous dentition. Suitable for large public aquarium tanks	♂ becomes blackish with age, ♀ reddish to bright red
50	*Thayeria boehlkei*	Boelke's penguin fish	Amazon region	6–7 (2.4–2.75 in)	Peaceful, active in community tank, where best kept in a shoal. Single indi-viduals become timid	♂ more slender, ♀ considerably stouter, particularly at spawning time

Maintenance	Breeding	Diet	Page/Figure
TS II/III. Pg. 7, dense clumps of feathery plants. 24–26 °C (75–78 °F). Water clean, clear, not too hard	Z 2a. 26 °C (78 °F), up to 10 °dH. All-glass tank with sand and marble-sized gravel and subdued light. Spawns over several days, total about 200 eggs, which hatch in 36–40 hours. Fry free-swimming on 5th day. Feed initially on *Paramecium,* a few days later on brine shrimp. Very small fry stay near bottom	Small live food. Dried food evidently not much liked	188/6
TS II/III. Pg. 6 or 7. Subdued lighting. Dark substrate and background. Peat filtration. 20–23 °C (68–73 °F)	Z 2a. 21–22 °C (69–71 °F), up to 5 °dH, preferably less. Breeding not very easy. Use only young individuals just mature. Spawn is light-sensitive. Fry free-swimming after 5–6 days, when light can return to normal	Live and dried food	I/8
As for No. 22, with which it is constantly confused	Difficult, but occasionally successful. Best put together as a pair. Soft water, up to 5 °C (41 °F), pH c. 7	Live and dried food	I/13
TS IV. Pg. 7. 25 °C (77 °F). Roots, plants and rocks forming hiding-places	Breeding unknown. In the wild it feeds almost exclusively on chunks of flesh bitten from larger, peaceful fish	Large live food, small fish, large insect larvae	188/7
TS IV/V. Pg. 7. Requires adequate space for swimming, but rest among the plants. 23–25 °C (73–77 °F). Water peat-filtered, not too hard	Z 2b. TS V. 23–25 °C (73–77 °F), not higher. Productive, up to 500 relatively large eggs. Fry not difficult to rear	Live and dried food. For breeding, offer insects and their larvae. Likes to feed at the surface	187/12
TS III. Pg. 7, with scattered dense vegetation, leaving sufficient space for swimming. 23–24 °C (73–75 °F)	Z 1. 24 °C (75 °F). Fry are very small. Feed initially on *Paramecium* and rotifers, later with fine live and dried food	Live an dried food	I/10
TS VI. Pg. 7 with tough plants. Only small individuals suitable for the home aquarium. Take care when feeding acclimatized fish	Breed successfully in several public aquaria, but scarcely possible in the home aquarium	Meat, fish	187/2
TS III/IV. Pg. 7, with plant clumps to provide hiding-places, leaving sufficient space for swimming. Some floating plants to provide shade. Water not too hard (up to 10 °dH)	Z 2a. TS IV. 25–27 °C (77–80 °F). Fresh, preferably soft water. Very numerous eggs hatch in 12–15 hours. Fry free-swimming in 4 days, and light-sensitive. Feed initially on *Paramecium* and rotifers, quite soon on brine shrimp	Live and dried food	II/9

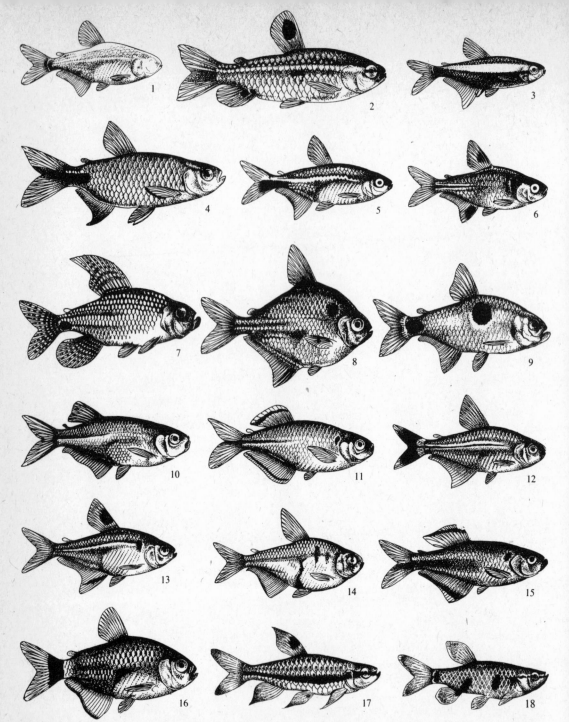

1 *Astyanax mexicanus (Anoptichthys jordani)*, blind cave characin (6) 2 *Arnoldichthys spilopterus*, red-eyed characin (5) 3 *Lamprocheirodon axelrodi*, cardinal tetra (33) 4 *Alestes longipinnis*, long-finned characin (2) 5 *Hemigrammus hyanuary*, green neon (17) 6 *Creagrutus beni*, gold-striped characin (–) 7 *Crenuchus spilurus*, sailfin characin (–) 8 *Poptella orbicularis*, disc tetra (–) 9 *Exodon paradoxus*, buck-toothed tetra (–) 10 *Gephyrocharax atracaudatus*, platinum tetra (–) 11 *Glandulocauda inaequalis*, chirping tetra (–) 12 *Hemigrammus marginatus*, black-tailed tetra (18) 13 *Hemigrammus unilineatus*, one-line tetra (–) 14 *Hyphessobrycon griemi*, Griem's tetra (27) 15 *Mimagoniates microlepis*, blue tetra (–) 16 *Moenkhausia sanctaefilomenae*, red-eye tetra (36) 17 *Copella metae*, black-banded pyrrhulina (–) 18 *Pyrrhulina vittata*, striped vittata (–)

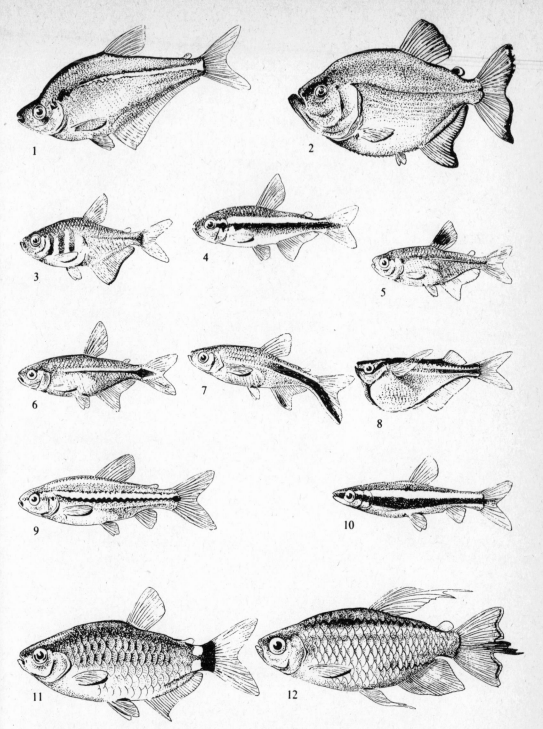

1 *Charax gibbosus*, hump-backed headstander (–) 2 *Pygocentrus piraya*, piranha (49) 3 *Hyphessobrycon bifasciatus*, yellow tetra (23) 4 *Hyphessobrycon herbertaxelrodi*, black neon (28) 5 *Hyphessobrycon georgettae*, strawberry tetra (26) 6 *Hyphessobrycon scholzei*, black-line tetra (32) 7 *Thayeria sanctaemariae*, St Maria penguin fish (–) 8 *Carnegiella marthae*, black-winged hatchetfish (7) 9 *Nannaethiops tritaeniatus*, three-striped African characin (–) 10 *Nannostomus bifasciatus*, two-banded pencilfish (39) 11 *Moenkhausia oligolepis*, glass tetra (–) 12 *Phenacogrammus interruptus*, Congo tetra (47)

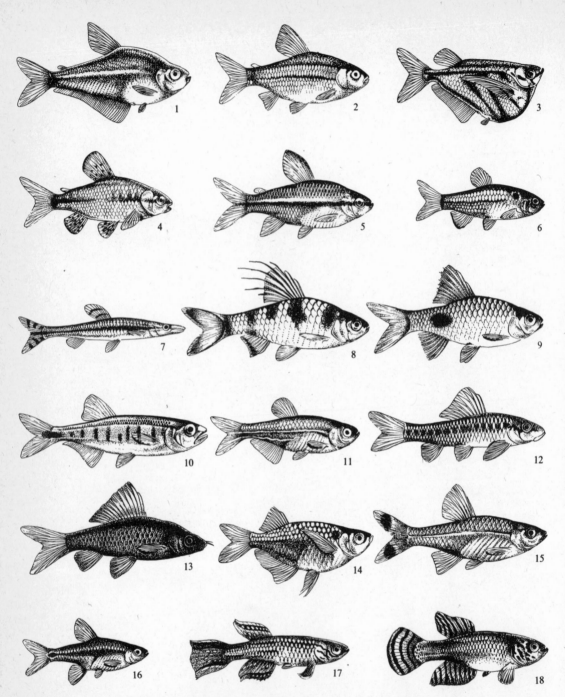

1 *Roeboides guatemalensis*, Guatemala glass characin (–) 2 *Curimatopsis saladensis*, green-banded characin (–) 3 *Carnegiella strigata*, marbled hatchetfish (8) 4 *Characidium rachovi*, Rachov's ground tetra (–) 5 *Nannaethiops unitaeniatus*, African one-striped characin (–) 6 *Neolebias ansorgei*, African redfin (43) 7 *Phago loricatus*, striped pike characin (46) 8 *Barbus arulius*, arulius barb (51) 9 *Barbus filamentosus*, filament barb (54) 10 *Barilius christyi*, golden-mouth (–) 11 *Brachydanio kerri*, blue danio (70) 12 *Gyrinocheilus aymonieri*, algae-eater (77) 13 *Labeo bicolor*, red-tailed labeo (78) 14 *Laubuca laubuca*, Indian glass barb (–) 15 *Rasbora trilineata*, scissors-tail (81) 16 *Rasbora urophthalma*, spot-tail rasbora (82) 17 *Roloffia calabarica*, blue lyretail panchax (133) 18 *Cynopoecilus ladigesi*, Ladiges' cynopoecilus (110)

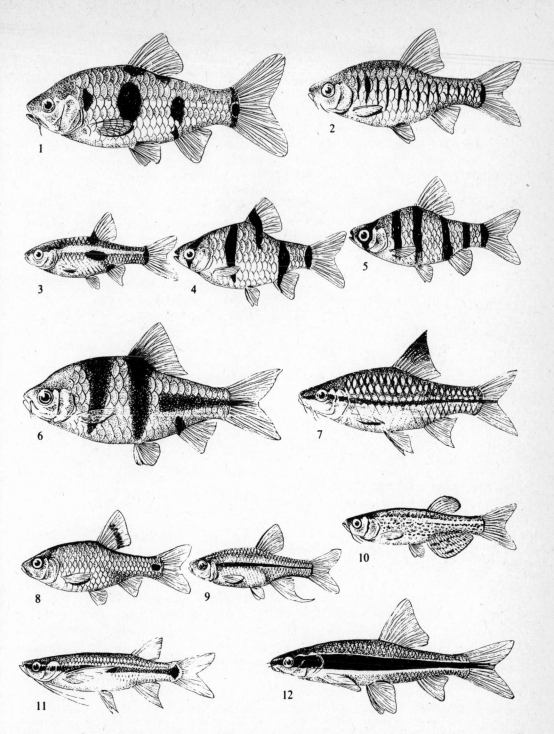

1 *Barbus dunckeri*, Duncker's barb (–) 2 *Barbus fasciolatus*, African banded barb (–) 3 *Barbus gelius*, golden dwarf barb (55) 4 *Barbus partipentazona*, banded barb (–) 5 *Barbus hexazona*, six-banded barb (–) 6 *Barbus lateristriga*, spanner barb (57) 7 *Barbus holotaenia*, African longstripe (–) 8 *Barbus vittatus*, striped barb (–) 9 *Barbus woehlerti*, sickle barb (–) 10 *Brachydanio frankei*, leopard danio (69) 11 *Esomus danrica*, flying barb (76) 12 *Epalzeorhynchus siamensis*, Siamese flying fox (75)

Barbs (Cyprinidae)

This is a family with numerous species distributed in Europe, Asia, Africa and North America. There are no native barbs in South America, where their place is taken by the characins. They are also absent from Australia and the Australasian islands, except for a few that have been introduced for commercial reasons.

The family is of considerable economic importance as several species are valued as a source of human food. Some of these are bred artificially and have almost become domesticated animals. The common carp of Europe can scarcely be found in the wild now. The larger species only have limited use in the aquarium, except as young specimens.

The aquarist is, of course, interested primarily in the smaller members of the family. Many of the species from south-east Asia are very suitable for the home aquarium on account of their small size, attractive coloration, undemanding habits and readiness to breed. To a lesser extent, small barbs from Europe, Africa and North America are also of interest to the aquarist.

The important genus *Barbus* was founded scientifically on the common barbel of Europe which is still known as *Barbus barbus*. Over the years several attempts have been made to split up the genus *Barbus* into genera such as *Puntius*, *Capoeta* and *Barbodes*. These are no longer accepted and the original generic name has been restored.

The barbs have an elongated, longish or broadly ovate body, covered with cycloid scales of various sizes; in some of the smaller species the scales are relatively large. The fins are not usually enlarged. Occasionally the fin rays extend beyond the edge of the fin itself. The mouth may be protrusible and in certain cases the edges of the jaws carry one or more pairs of barbels, but in some species these may be entirely absent. In contrast to the closely related characins, the barbs have no true teeth, but one to two rows of horny pharyngeal teeth. The form of the pharyngeal teeth can be used to separate the genera and species.

Barbs live in various types of water, but almost always in fresh waters. Many like more or less fast-flowing water, others are found in lakes, ponds, ditches and swamps. Some are able to survive in unfavourable conditions, whereas others are sensitive to the composition of the water. No generalization can be made about the living requirements of barbs, which is understandable in view of the wide distribution of the family. Some species live directly below the water surface, some in open water, others close to the bottom or in among dense vegetation. Those which live close to the bottom detect their food with the help of the barbels or the sensitive lips or they may burrow in search of it. This characteristic must be borne in mind when setting up the aquarium tank, as the burrowing activities may cause cloudiness of the water unless countermeasures are taken. The substrate can be covered with a layer of clean, washed gravel as this will prevent the burrowing fish from reaching the lower, loamy layers. Alternatively, a top layer of boiled peat will allow the fish to burrow without causing cloudiness of the water. In addition, the dark peat layer usually enhances the fishes colours. Species from streams would prefer a sandy or stony substrate.

Aquarium tanks with burrowing fish should never have any plants with feathery leaves, such as *Cabomba*, *Limnophila* or *Myriophyllum*, as detritus particles settle on the leaf filaments and the plants die. Some cyprinids require plant food and so attack the leaves and particularly the shoot tips of submerse plants. In such cases it is best to use only tough-leaved plants.

The cyprinids are mostly active fish which live in shoals, so the vegetation should not be too dense. Such species should be accommodated in long tanks which leave sufficient space for swimming. For surface-living species the space beneath the water surface should be quite free. Floating plants should not be used, or if they are, they should be restricted to the corners of the tank where they will provide hiding-places for the fish. However, this advice does not apply to all species. Many small barbs like dense vegetation, into which they can retreat to rest.

In general, the barbs are undemanding aquarium fish, and only a few species require special water conditions, particularly when they are to be bred. Their food requirements are also not difficult to fulfil, and they will take all kinds of live and dried food, as well as soft plant matter, algae and even organic detritus. Temperature requirements depend upon their original habitat, and details are given in the tables.

Breeding is generally quite easy. Most species spawn at random, releasing their sexual products into the open water or among vegetation, after a period of active driving. Apart from the European bitterling and one or two others, brood protection is not found. Some barbs have a tendency to hybridize, even in the wild, producing variations in form and colour.

Z 5: Barbs without special water requirements which spawn at random or produce adhesive eggs

For such species breeding is generally not difficult. Mating is preceded by a period of driving, sometimes lasting for hours, during which sham matings may occur. In true mating the partners come close together, with the male sometimes curling his body round the female. Each spawning, which may extend over a period of hours, consists of a series of individual matings during which some of the eggs and sperm are released. In every case fertilization occurs immediately. The number of eggs produced varies according to the species, size and age of the breeding pair.

The fish can be put together as a pair or two to one (two males, one female) or even in a group, with more males than females. Many barbs, but not all, like bright light, such as morning sunshine, for spawning. The size of the tank depends upon the expected produc-tivity of the fish. It could be an all-glass tank with a volume of only 15 litres (3·3 gals) or a tank holding 100 litres (22 gals) or more. The tank and the relevant equipment must be carefully cleaned. In general, there is no need for a substrate.

Most barbs are notorious spawn robbers, so the tank bottom should be fitted with a grating or covered with a layer of marble-sized stones. Some species like fine-leaved plants or a mop of green plastic filaments anchored to the bottom with glass rods. Those that spawn above or among the plants may like to have a few plants that grow erect.

The eggs are often non-adhesive and merely sink to the bottom. Those that are sticky will adhere to the plants and can be shaken loose as soon as the parent fish have been removed from the tank. Depending upon the temperature the eggs hatch in twenty to seventy hours, in some species more. The newly-hatched fry then hang for some days from the plants or from the tank glass. They are free-swimming after five to six days. In certain cases they can then be fed on *Paramecium* and rotifers, later on brine shrimps and microworms. It is not unusual for the fry to take brine shrimp nauplii immediately. Powdered dried food, available on the market, is very useful for rearing the fry. Large broods can be divided up among several tanks.

Group Z 5 consists of table numbers 51, 55, 57, 59, 61, 62, 64, 65, 68, 74, 76 and 83.

Z 6: Barbs with special water requirements which spawn at random or produce adhesive eggs

In general, the advice given under Z 2a and Z 2b (Characidae, p. 154) will also apply here. However, breeding may be difficult, the species concerned requiring very soft water with a pH below 7. The eggs and fry may be sensitive to attacks by bacteria and infusorians (see 'Hints on the breeding of aquarium fishes'). In other respects the advice given under Z 5 should be followed.

Group Z 6 consists of table numbers 56, 60, 66, 79 and 82.

Z 7: Goldfish and goldfish varieties

Goldfish are generally bred in open-air hatcheries, while the varieties, such as veiltail, telescope eye etc., are bred in the aquarium. This requires large tanks, particularly when there are large numbers of offspring which have to be sorted according to form and coloration. In general, the breeding of goldfish varieties is best left to the professional breeder who has large numbers of tanks at his disposal. In the end even large broods will only yield very small numbers of first-class specimens, so it is not surprising that these are correspondingly expensive.

No.	Scientific name	Popular name	Distribution	Length cm	Characteristics	Sex differences
51	*Barbus arulius*	Arulius barb	South-east India	12 (4.7 in)	Peaceful, active, sociable, good for community tank with larger barbs	♂ larger, more colourful, the dorsal fin rays extending beyond the edge
52	*Barbus conchonius*	Rosy barb	Northern India in flowing waters	8 (3 in)	Peaceful, active shoaling fish, good for a community tank with fish not requiring a high temperature	♂ somewhat smaller, bright red at spawning time, dorsal fin with black tip. ♀ stouter
53	*Barbus everetti*	Clown barb	Malaysia, Borneo, in flowing waters	10 (3.9 in)	Peaceful, active, likes to burrow. Suitable for community tank with larger barbs	♂ more slender, usually also rather more colourful
54	*Barbus filamentosus*	Filament barb	Southern India and Sri Lanka	12 (4.7 in)	Relatively peaceful shoaling fish, does well with other larger barbs	♂ more brightly coloured. In old individuals the dorsal fin rays extend beyond the fin edge
55	*Barbus gelius*	Golden dwarf barb	India, Bengal, Assam	♂ 4 (1.5 in) ♀ 4.5 (1.7 in)	Active, peaceful, burrows a little. Good with others that are not too active	♂ more slender
56	*Barbus hulstaerti*	Butterfly barb	Lower Congo	3.5–4 (1.3–1.5 in)	Active, peaceful, delicate fish best kept with members of its own species	♂ somewhat larger (?), with larger shoulder marking and black edge to dorsal fin
57	*Barbus lateristriga*	Spanner barb	Malaya, Indonesia	20 (7.8 in)	Active, peaceful fish, likely to burrow. Good with other large barbs	♂ more intensely coloured, with dorsal fin dark red at the base

Maintenance	Breeding	Diet	Page/Figure
TS IV/V. Pg. 2, with sufficient swimming space. 24–26 °C (75–78 °F), minimum 20 °C (68 °F)	Z 5. Spawns after vigorous driving among plants. Very productive. Transparent eggs hatch in 36 hours, fry free-swimming after 6 days	Live and dried food	188/8
TS II/IV. Pg. 1 a, with some dense clumps. MT 12–15 °C (53–59 °F), but full colours only at 20 °C (68 °F) or more. Clear, clean water and bright light	Z 5. Not difficult. Water depth 15 cm (6 in). Spawns after driving in vegetation or open water. Very productive. Attractive mutant forms often produced	Live and dried food	V/3
TS IV/V. Pg. 2. Needs shady places and plenty of swimming space. 24 °C (75 °F). Frequent water changes	Z 5. Very productive, spawning among vegetation in subdued light. Fry require new fresh water from time to time. Fast-growing and sexually mature at 2 years. 27 °C (80 °F)	Largish live and dried food	IV/6
TS IV/V. Pg. 2. 24 °C (75 °F), but down to 20 °C (68 °F) in winter. Sufficient swimming space	Z 5. 24 °C (75 °F). Large tank. Spawns among vegetation. Rearing of fry not difficult. Half-grown individuals have transverse stripes and are therefore quite different from the parents	Live and dried food with some plant matter	188/9
TS II/III. Pg. 3. 18–24 °C (64–75 °F). MT 16 °C (60 °F). Old established tank with peat substrate. Partial renewal of water from time to time	Z 5. 23 °C (73 °F). Spawns in bright light, preferably in morning sun. Eggs attached to underside of broad leaves, but many go mouldy if temperature too high. Fry not difficult to rear. In the aquarium this species degenerates after several generations	Small live and dried food, plant matter, including algae	189/3
TS II/III. Pg. 3, with dense clumps. Dark substrate and roots for shelter. Soft, peat-filtered water, up to 3 °dH. 20–23 °C (68–73 °F), MT 18 °C (64 °F)	Said to breed best in fully furnished tanks, but can be bred in a separate tank, as Z 6. Fry very small, feed at first on *Paramecium,* and after few days on brine shrimp	Fine live and dried food	
TS IV/V. Pg. 2. 24–25 °C (75–77 °F). Sufficient space. Frequent water changes, as metabolism is active	Z 5. 24–26 °C (75–78 °F). Large spawning tank. Fry take brine shrimp immediately and must be sorted out regularly	Live and dried food, plant matter	189/6

193

No.	Scientific name	Popular name	Distribution	Length cm	Characteristics	Sex differences
58	*Barbus nigrofasciatus*	Black ruby	Sri Lanka, in shady mountain streams	6.5 (2.5 in)	Active, peaceful, sociable	♂ more colourful, and when excited the front of body becomes deep purplish-red, the rear velvety black
59	*Barbus oligolepis*	Island barb	Indonesia	5 (1.9 in)	Peaceful, sociable	♂ more slender, the dorsal and anal fins with black edge
60	*Barbus pentazona*	Five-banded barb	Borneo	5 (1.9 in)	Active, sociable, playful and good for a community tank	♂ rather smaller and more slender, the red on the fins more intense
61	*Barbus semifasciolatus*	Green barb	South China	10 (3.9 in)	Active, peaceful fish which digs. Good for community tank	♂ smaller and more slender, the belly orange at spawning time
62	*Barbus 'schuberti'* (selected form of *B. semifasciolatus*)	Golden barb	Not known	7 (2.7 in)	Active, peaceful, good for a community tank	♂ more slender, often also rather smaller
63	*Barbus tetrazona*	Sumatra barb	Sumatra	5 (1.9 in)	Active, playful, sometimes quarrelsome. Good for community tank	♂ more slender, the red on the fins more intense
64	*Barbus ticto stoliczkae*	Stoliczka's barb	India, Sri Lanka	8 (3 in)	Active, peaceful shoaling fish, good for a community tank	♂ more slender, dorsal fins red with black spots
65	*Barbus ticto* (subspecies)	Two-spot barb (Odessa form)	Not known	8 (3 in)	Peaceful shoaling fish for the community tank	♂ more slender, with spotted fins and broad blood-red longitudinal band
66	*Barbus titteya*	Cherry barb	Sri Lanka	5.5 (2.1 in)	Active, peaceful, keeping apart from other species. ♂♂ somewhat quarrelsome at spawning time	♂ more slender, bright red when excited

Maintenance	Breeding	Diet	Page/Figure
TS III/IV. Pg. 3. 22–24 °C (71–75 °F), MT 20 °C (68 °F). Likes bright and shady places. Becomes colourless in very bright light. Dark substrate with roots	Z 5. Rather productive. After spawning the ♂ evidently needs a few weeks rest. Rearing of fry not difficult	Live and dried food, plant matter	V/6
TS II/III. Pg. 3. 23–24 °C (73–75 °F), MT 18 °C (64 °F). Peat substrate. Mature water	Z 5. 24–27 °C (75–80 °F). Spawns in all-glass tanks, the eggs attached to plants. Latter should be removed to separate rearing tank at frequent intervals	Live and dried food, plant matter	V/3
TS II/IV. Pg. 3, with floating plants for shade. 22–25 °C (71–77 °F), MT 20 °C (68 °F). Dark substrate and soft, peat-filtered water	Z 6. 24–26 °C (75–78 °F). Spawns in dense vegetation, sometimes over several hours. Fry not difficult to rear. ♂ must rest 2–3 weeks between each spawning	Live and dried food, with some plant food (algae)	
TS III/IV. Pg. 2, with plant clumps to hide in. 20–24 °C (68–75 °F), MT 17 °C (62 °F). Clear, oxygen-rich water	Z 5. Breeding easy, as for No. 52	Live and dried food, plant matter	IV/7
As for No. 61	As for No. 61	Live and dried food	IV/16
TS II/IV. Pg. 3, with some dense vegetation and floating plants. 22–24 °C (71–75 °F), MT 20 °C (68 °F). Water not too hard. Dark substrate	Z 6. 24–26 °C (75–78 °F). Water not above 10 °dH, preferably less. Spawns among plants	Live and dried food	IV/17
As for No. 52, but at slightly higher temperature, 23–26 °C (73–78 °F)	As for No. 52, 23–25 °C (73–77 °F)	Live and dried food	
As for No. 52	As for No. 52	Live and dried food	
TS II/III. Pg 3. Well-planted, old-established tank with subdued light (use floating plants). 23–25 °C (73–77 °F) MT 20 °C (68 °F)	Z 6. Not very easy. The few eggs laid individually, attached to plants. Fry hide away. Not very productive, 60 offspring being a good result	Live and dried food	IV/8

No.	Scientific name	Popular name	Distribu-tion	Length cm	Characteristics	Sex differences
67	*Carassius auratus*	Goldfish	First devel-oped in China from a silver form	20 (7.8 in)	Peaceful. All gold-fish races like to bur-row	At spawning time ♂ has nuptial tuber-cles, at other times sexes only distin-guishable by form of anus
68	*Brachydanio albolineatus*	Pearl danio	Burma, Malaya, Sumatra	6 (2.4 in)	Active, peaceful shoaling fish, good for a community tank with other fast-swimming fish	♂ more slender, rather more brightly coloured
69	*Brachydanio frankei*	Leopard danio	Not yet known	5 (1.9 in)	As for No. 68	♂ more slender
70	*Brachydanio kerri*	Blue danio	Islands in Gulf of Bengal	6 (2.4 in)	As for No. 68	♂ more slender
71	*Brachydanio nigrofasciatus*	Spotted danio	Burma	4 (1.5 in)	As for No. 68	♂ more slender, dots finer
72	*Brachydanio rerio*	Zebra danio	India	5 (1.9 in)	As for No. 68. A very active fish	♂ more slender, with areas between the longitudinal blue bands golden, but silvery in ♀
73	*Danio aequipinnatus* (formerly *D. malabaricus*)	Giant danio	West coast of India	10 (3.9 in)	Peaceful, actively swimming fish, good for a tank with other fast-swimming fish	♂ more slender, with orange bases to ventral, dorsal and anal fins
74	*Danio devario*	Bengal danio	Northern India	6 (2.4 in)	Active, peaceful, not so fast as No. 73	♂ more slender, more colourful
75	*Epalzeo-rhynchus siamensis*	Siamese flying fox	Thailand, Malaya	14 (5.5 in)	Active, peaceful bottom-living fish. Single individuals good in community tanks. Eats algae	None known
76	*Esomus danrica*	Flying barb	India, Sri Lanka, south-east Asia	8 (3 in)	Active, peaceful, surface-living, apt to jump	♂ smaller and more slender, caudal spot red, but brownish in ♀

Maintenance	Breeding	Diet	Page/Figure
TS V/VI. Pg. 11 a. Clear, oxygen-rich, filtered water and clean gravel substrate. 10–21 °C (50–69 °F), MT 6 °C (42 °F). Selected forms require more warmth	Z 7. 18–22 °C (64–71 °F). Large breeding tanks and several sorting tanks. Eggs laid at random after active driving, hatch in 5–7 days. Fry easy to rear	Omnivorous. Large amounts of live and dried food	V/7
TS II/IV. Pg. 3. Plenty of swimming space. Clear, oxygen-rich water. Likes sunlight. 20–23 °C (68–73 °F), MT 18 °C (64 °F). Substrate of round gravel	Z 5. 23–25 °C (73–77 °F). Very productive. Spawns among fine-leaved plants. Put 2 ♂ with one ♀. Eggs hatch in about 3 days and fry free-swimming a week later. Feed on *Paramecium,* rotifers and powdered dried food	Live and dried food	IV/3
As for No. 68	As for No. 68	Live and dried food	189/10
As for No. 68, but a little warmer, about 24 °C (75 °F)	As for No. 68	Live and dried food	189/11
As for No. 68, but a little warmer, 24–25 °C (75–77 °F)	As for No. 68. Not very productive, e.g. 100 young	Live and dried food	IV/4
As for No. 68, but not so warm, 20–23 °C (68–73 °F), MT 18 °C (64 °F)	As for No. 68	Live and dried food	IV/2
TS V. Pg. 3. Long tank with well-fitting lid. 23–25 °C (73–77 °F), MT 20 °C (68 °F)	Z 5. As for No. 68. Very productive, up to 1,000 fry or more, so tank must be large. 24–26 °C (75–78 °F)	Live and dried food	IV/11
TS IV. Pg. 3. As for No. 68. 21–24 °C (69–75 °F)	Z 5. 24–26 °C (75–78 °F). As for No. 68. Not so productive as No. 73	Live and dried food	IV/1
TS III/V. Pg. 2–3. 22–28 °C (71–82 °F). Likes to hide among roots and plants	Not yet bred in the aquarium	Live and dried food, algae	187/12
TS IV. Pg. 3. Long spacious tank, well-fitting lid. 22–24 °C (71–75 °F)	Z 5. 26–28 °C (78–82 °F). Likes plenty of light, prefers to spawn in morning sun. Very productive, up to 600 eggs, which hatch in 48 hours. Fry free-swimming 6 days later	Live and dried food	189/11

No.	Scientific name	Popular name	Distribu-tion	Length cm	Characteristics	Sex differences
77	*Gyrinocheilus aymonieri*	Algae-eater	Thailand	15 (6 in)	Active, becoming rather robust with age and disturbing other fish. Young individuals good consumers of algae and suitable for a community tank	None known
78	*Labeo bicolor*	Red-tailed labeo	Thailand	15 (6 in)	Tends to be aggressive towards others of its species. Use single individuals in a community tank	None known
79	*Rasbora heteromorpha*	Harlequin fish	South-east Asia	4 (1.5 in)	Active, tolerant and good for a tank with small, delicate fish	♂ more slender, with black marking extending down to ventral fin base
80	*Rasbora maculata*	Spotted rasbora	South-east Asia	2.5 (1 in)	Active and suitable for a community tank with other fish dwarfs	♂ smaller, more slender, more intensely coloured
81	*Rasbora trilineata*	Scissors-tail	Malaya, Indonesia	10 (3.9 in)	Large, active species, suitable for a community tank with larger, fast-swimming fish. Enjoys occasional rests among the plants	♂ more slender
82	*Rasbora urophthalma*	Spot-tail rasbora	Sumatra	2.5 (1 in)	Attractive small fish, good for a community tank with other fish dwarfs	♂ more slender, more colourful
83	*Tanichthys albonubes*	White Cloud Mountain minnow	South China	3.5 (1.3 in)	Active, peaceful shoaling fish, good for a tank with other fish that do not need a high temperature. Not a bad egg-eater	♂ more slender, more colourful

Maintenance	Breeding	Diet	Page/Figure
TS III/IV. Pg. 3. 25 °C (77 °F). Dense plant clumps, rocks and roots to provide hiding-places. Clear oxygen-rich water	Not yet bred in the aquarium	Live and dried food, plant matter, algae	188/12
TS IV/V. Pg. 2, densely planted. Rather subdued light. 22 °C (71 °F). Clear, soft peat-filtered water	Only bred a few times	Live and dried food	188/13
TS II/III. Pg. 3 or 6, particularly with *Cryptocoryne*. Soft, peat-filtered water. Dark substrate. 22–23 °C (71–73 °F)	Z 6. 25–28 °C (77–82 °F). Soft water, not exceeding 6 °dH. Subdued light. Eggs laid on underside of broad leaves, hatch in about 24 hours, fry fed initially on brine shrimp. Not all pairs compatible, so allow them to select their own mates. Do not use for breeding until 1 year old	Live and dried food	IV/10
TS I/II. Pg. 3 or 6, dense planting, especially with *Cryptocoryne,* a few floating plants to give shade. Dark substrate, soft water. 25–27 °C (77–80 °F), MT 22 °C (71 °F)	Z 6. Soft, peat-filtered water, not over 5 °dH, preferably less. 25–30 °C (77–86 °F). Water depth 10 cm (3.9 in), darken lower half of breeding tank. Feed fry initially on *Paramecium*. Not very productive, up to 40 eggs	Live and dried food	IV/9
TS IV. Pg. 3. Plenty of swimming space. 21–25 °C (69–77 °F), MT 18 °C (64 °F)	Z 5. Water hardness less than 12 °dH. 24–26 °C (75–78 °F)	Live and dried food	188/15
As for No. 80	As for No. 80, but even less productive	Live and dried food	188/16
TS II/III. Pg. 11. 18–22 °C (64–71 °F), MT 15 °C (59 °F)	Z 5. 20–22 °C (68–71 °F). Spawns among fine-leaved plants, the ♂ encircling the ♀. Rear fry on very fine live and dried food. Breeding the veiltail mutant is more difficult.	Live and dried food	V/4

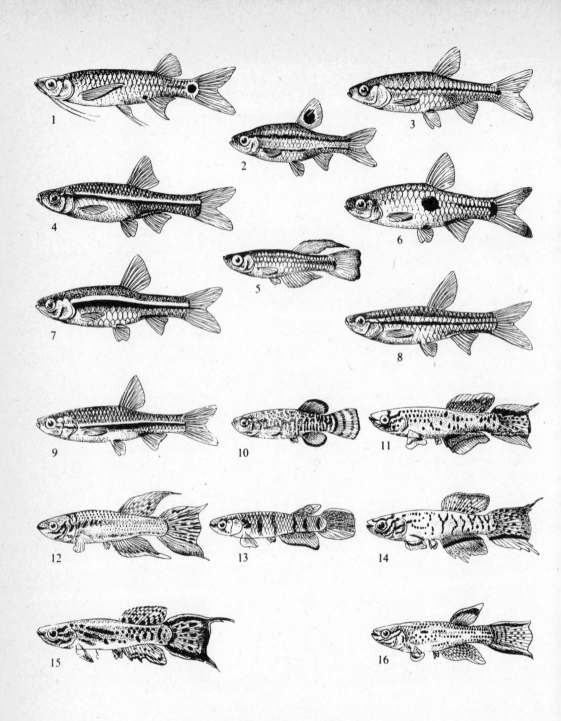

1 *Esomus malayensis*, Malayan flying barb (–) 2 *Rasbora dorsiocellata*, eye-spot rasbora (–) 3 *Rasbora daniconius*, slender rasbora (–)
4 *Rasbora leptosoma*, golden-lined rasbora (–) 5 *Aplocheilichthys myersi*, Myers' micropanchax (–) 6 *Rasbora elegans*, elegant rasbora
(–) 7 *Rasbora meinkeni*, Meinken's rasbora (–) 8 *Rasbora pauciperforata*, red-striped rasbora (–) 9 *Rasbora taenia*, gold-striped rasbora
(–) 10 *Aphanius iberus*, Spanish toothcarp (–) 11 *Aphyosemion gardneri*, Gardner's panchax (91) 12 *Aphyosemion bivittatum* ' *splendopleu-ris* ', red lyretail (–) 13 *Roloffia petersi*. Peters' aphyosemion (–) 14 *Aphyosemion filamentosum*, plumed lyretail (90) 15 *Aphyosemion ar-noldi*, Arnold's aphyosemion (–) 16 *Aphyosemion gardneri* ' *nigerianum* ', Gardner's panchax (91)

Egg-laying toothcarps
(Cyprinodontidae)

According to the most recent investigations the Cyprinodontidae are regarded as a family within the sub-order Cyprinodontoidea, which also includes the livebearing toothcarps (family Poeciliidae) and a few other families.

The egg-laying toothcarps have a very wide distribution, with representatives in almost all parts of the world. The greatest numbers of species are found in the tropics and subtropics, but not so many in the temperate zone. Species occur in North America, where they extend furthest north, and there are a few European species, in Spain.

These toothcarps are primarily freshwater fish, although a few species can be found in brackish waters and even in the sea, where they live close to the coasts. Some toothcarp species have a remarkable ability to adapt to changing water conditions.

The systematic division of the family is somewhat problematical. The situation is particularly difficult in the case of the West African toothcarps (*Aphyosemion, Roloffia* and others), in which the relationships are not at all clear. Many members of these genera previously regarded as species must now be considered only as subspecies or as colour variants.

The egg-laying toothcarps are essentially small fish, the largest species not exceeding 12–15 cm (4·7–6 in) in length. In some the body form is pike-like and elongated, with only slight lateral compression. The back is flat and the dorsal and anal fins positioned far to the rear. The large mouth almost always faces upwards, which generally indicates that the fish lives close to the surface. However, some species spawn near the bottom. Many of these toothcarps live in shallow water. In addition to the pike-like type there are others with a more or less tall, squat body and more pronounced lateral compression.

The scales are relatively large, and in some species the lateral line is lacking. It is replaced by a marked concentration of surface nerves on certain parts of the body, particularly the head. Barbels are never present. The upper jaw is not moveable, or scarcely so, but the lower jaw is more or less protrusible. The jaws and other parts are provided with teeth. The fins are generally well developed, and in the males they are frequently enlarged, with protruding fin rays. External sex differences are usually well marked. The females of certain species are very similar and frequently difficult to distinguish. In some cases this leads to unforeseen hybridization. In members of the South American genus *Cynolebias* the number of rays in the dorsal and anal fins varies according to the sex.

Egg-laying toothcarps are found in large numbers in small bodies of water, in streams flowing into rivers, in backwaters, lagoons, swamps and flooded areas. They are of no commercial importance, except in the aquarium trade. They are, however, sometimes useful as consumers of mosquito larvae. Some species live in shoals, some in smaller groups and others are solitary. In streams they swim against the current or remain among the surface vegetation where they catch insects that land on the water. Some species may be intolerant and aggressive, while a few species are aggressive predators. However, most species feed on invertebrate animals. The squat species also consume algae. Many species of *Rivulus* are amphibious, lying out on floating plants and moving to swampy places, even out of the water, where they catch their food.

These toothcarps show several remarkable breeding habits. In general, active brood protection does not occur, although the American flagfish *(Jordanella floridae)* practises a form of brood protection. On the other hand, some care is taken at spawning time, when the eggs are laid in the substrate, on plant roots, in soft algal growths or close to the surface among the roots of floating plants. Many species spawn over long periods, laying batches of a few eggs at daily intervals. The breeding of the so-called seasonal fish is particularly interesting. In these the eggs are embedded in the mud, where they lie for weeks or months before they develop and eventually hatch. This is an adaptation to the regular alternation of wet and dry periods.

The maintenance of egg-laying toothcarps in the aquarium is not particularly difficult, although some species require a certain amount of care. The short life span can be combatted by avoiding high temperatures and excessively rich food. Some of these toothcarps are not suitable for an ordinary community tank. They are either intolerant and aggressive or they may retire into a quiet corner.

In the wild most toothcarps feed on insects and their larvae, partly also on fish spawn and algae. In captivity they also prefer live food. Some species readily take dried food but others refuse or ignore it.

Certain of the smaller species are perfectly content in a small tank, but others require more space. In general, those from tropical rain-forests require shallow water, dense vegetation, hiding-places among tree roots and subdued light. Others like sunlight or at least bright light, which may possibly be filtered through floating plants. The temperature varies according to the species and the original location.

In some species, breeding presents no difficulties, but in others it may be somewhat complicated, requiring a certain amount of knowledge and experience. Breeding has been known to take place quite successfully in a fully furnished tank, but in many cases it will be necessary to set up special breeding tanks. The following are a few special hints on breeding (referred to in the 'Breeding' column of the tables by their Z number).

Z 8: Toothcarps living close to the surface and spawning among plants

Many of these species can be bred in a fully furnished aquarium if large numbers of offspring are not required.

For planned breeding the tank should have a volume of 30–80 litres (6·5–17·5 gals), depending upon the size of the fish. Reflection from the glass bottom of the tank may be a source of irritation, so the bottom can be covered with a layer of boiled activated charcoal, or a sheet of black paper can be pasted onto the outside of the tank bottom. Any kind of clean water can be used, but mains water should be allowed to stand for one day. The degree of hardness is often of little importance, but the water temperature should be 24–28 °C (75–82 °F). The spawning substrate may be clumps of fine-leaved plants reaching to below the water surface, floating plants with tufted roots or synthetic fibre. The breeding fish, eggs and fry are very tolerant of temperature fluctuations.

The breeding fish should be kept separate and well fed before being put together. One male to one female can be used, or one male to two females if the former drives vigorously. Spawning takes place among the plants. At each separate mating the female may produce a single egg, more rarely two or three. A spawning period may extend over a period of two weeks or more. During this time the breeding pair remain in the spawning tank until the female has exhausted her supply of eggs, in most cases a total of 150–300. Over this period the pair should be fed on rinsed water-fleas or whiteworms, in order so far as possible to prevent them eating their own eggs. At the end of the spawning period the parent fish should be removed and kept separately so that in due course they will be ready to spawn again.

The eggs must then be removed from the water plants either by using a pipette with an appropriate orifice or by cutting off pieces of plant with attached eggs. It is more convenient to use a mop of synthetic fibre, which can be transferred daily into the rearing tank and replaced by a new mop.

The eggs hatch after ten to fourteen days, and the fry collect near the water surface. They can be fed immediately on very tiny live food, including brine shrimp nauplii. At intervals the fry should be sorted according to size to prevent the larger from attacking the smaller.

Group Z 8 consists of table numbers 99–104, 113–117, 125, 126 and 129–131.

Z 9a: Toothcarps (*Aphyosemion* and others) that spawn among plants

The species belonging to this group lay their eggs on plants or roots near the surface, in the middle water layers or on the bottom, or they do so on synthetic fibre.

Planned breeding can be carried out in small tanks, preferably all-glass, with a substrate of boiled activated charcoal or peat; alternatively a sheet of black paper can be pasted to the outside of the bottom, in which case there is no need for a substrate. The water used for breeding must be soft, preferably 3–6 °dH, but never exceeding 8 °dH. If such a water is not available from the mains it is quite feasible to use rain water filtered through activated charcoal or a mixture of mains water with distilled or fully de-ionized water. Clumps of fine-leaved plants, floating ferns or mops of synthetic fibre can be used as a spawning substrate. After it has been filled the tank should be left standing for a few days and the water should then be completely clear. The temperature must be 20–22 °C (68–71 °F).

The breeding fish should be kept separate and well fed before being put together, usually one male with one female. For spawning they move to the plants or the synthetic fibre and come close alongside one another. The male folds his dorsal and anal fins around the female's body, in such a way that the released eggs are at first caught in his anal fin. These toothcarps spawn over a period of one to three weeks, the female producing about thirty eggs per day. These are removed every evening either by pipette or by snipping off a piece of plant with eggs attached, and transferred to a rearing tank or dish filled with water from the spawning tank to a depth of 2 cm (0·8 in). The water can be disinfected with a weak solution of trypaflavin or other commercial preparation that inhibits bacteria and infusorians. The eggs must not be kept in the dark, nor should they receive too much light. Mouldy eggs should be removed every day. The breeding pair should be fed during the spawning period on rinsed water-fleas and whiteworms.

The development period varies, and more detailed information on this will be found in the tables. The fry remain in the egg cases until they are capable of swimming. They do not always manage to break out on their own. In such cases experienced breeders recommend that some powdered dried food should be strewn over the surface of the water in the dish. The idea is that this will encourage the multiplication of infusorians which attack and weaken the egg cases so that the fry are then able to break out. A lens is useful to watch the stages of egg development.

The newly hatched fry are collected with a teaspoon and transferred to the rearing tank with the same type of water at the same temperature. They are voracious, and will immediately take brine shrimp nauplii and other tiny live food. From time to time the fry can be sorted according to size to prevent cannibalism.

Group Z 9a consists of table numbers 84–95 and 97–100.

Z 9b: Toothcarps (*Aphyosemion* and others) that spawn in the substrate

The reproductive habits of the toothcarps in this group form a kind of transition to that of the seasonal fish described in group Z 10. Like the latter, they bury their eggs in the substrate, but these do not suffer a period of semi-desiccation. In principle, their breeding behaviour is similar to that of the fish just described that spawn among plants. Everything described under Z 9a on breeding tanks, water composition, temperature and mating behaviour also applies here. The only difference is that the eggs are laid within the substrate and they have a resting period.

These substrate-spawning toothcarps will spawn in a normal aquarium if conditions are reasonably suitable for them. However, planned breeding is more suitable if a good productive result is wanted.

A spawning period extends over several weeks, with a few eggs being laid every day in the substrate, which should be peat or activated charcoal as described for group Z 9 a. At each mating the fish press themselves against the bottom. After the eggs have been released and fertilized the male beats his caudal fin and this stirs up some of the substrate, which covers the eggs.

The advantage of boiled peat as a substrate is that it is sterile. There is no need to remove the eggs from the peat at the end of the spawning period. Instead they and the peat can be transferred to a shallow plastic refrigerator box which is then filled with water from the spawning tank to a depth of 1–2 cm (0·4–0·8 in). If the substrate is activated charcoal the eggs have to be carefully removed to a separate shallow dish, but this is a tricky job as they are easily damaged. Whichever method is used, the dishes must be kept in the dark at a constant temperature, and any mouldy eggs should be removed as a daily routine. From time to time the developmental stage reached by the eggs can be checked with a magnifying lens. The water in the dishes can be treated with a weak solution of trypaflavin or other bacteriostatic preparation. The eggs hatch after some weeks or months, and the fry (see Z 9 a) are caught up and transferred into a rearing tank. It should be remembered that the eggs will have been laid at different dates and will therefore hatch at different intervals.

When fed on brine shrimp nauplii and other tiny live food the fry will grow very rapidly and will be mature at three to four months. They should not, however, be put to breed until they are six months old.

Group Z 9 b contains table numbers 90–92, 96 and 135.

Z 10: Seasonal fishes
This term is applied to those toothcarps that live in waters that periodically dry up. The

No.	Scientific name	Popular name	Distribution	Length cm	Characteristics	Sex differences
84	*Aphyosemion australe*	Lyretail	West Africa, around Gabon	6 (2.4 in)	Active, rather peaceful, good for community tank with other tolerant fish	♂ much more colourful, the elongated fin tips white. ♀ drab.
85	*Aphyosemion bivittatum*	Red lyretail	West Africa, Cameroon to Niger	6 (2.4 in)	Active and peaceful, good for a community tank	♂ more colourful, with elongated fins. ♀ drab with longitudinal bands
86	*Aphyosemion bualanum*	African swamp killie	West Africa, Cameroon	5 (1.9 in)	Peaceful, like No. 84	♂ much more colourful. ♀ drab
87	*Aphyosemion calliurum* (= *vexillifer*)	Red-chinned aphyosemion	Tropical West Africa	6.5 (2.5 in)	Active, peaceful, good for a community tank	♂ more colourful, fin tips elongated. ♀ drab
88	*Aphyosemion christii* (also marketed as *A. cognatum* and *A. schoutedeni*)	Schouteden's aphyosemion	Lower Congo	5 (1.9 in)	Active, peaceful, good for a community tank with other peaceful fish	♂ more colourful, fins slightly pointed. ♀ drab with rounded fins

fish themselves do not survive the dry period. It is only the eggs, buried in the mud before the waters dry up, that survive a resting period in the dried mud. When the rains return the eggs hatch within a few hours. In the course of a few months the fry develop into mature fish which spawn before the onset of the next dry season, when they themselves die. They are, therefore, extraordinarily short-lived and in practice only survive for a single season. It is only in the aquarium, at relatively low temperatures and with moderate feeding, that they live longer than twelve months.

With short breaks between the individual spawning periods they mate during more or less the whole of their mature life. A single spawning period lasts for one to three weeks. For planned breeding proceed as given under group Z 9b, with one male and one female and a substrate of peat. The water must not be soft (up to 10 °dH). Before they are put together the breeding fish should be kept apart and fed copiously. They must also be fed on carefully washed water-fleas and whiteworms during the actual spawning period.

At the end of each period the breeding fish should be removed and the water drawn off. The wet peat is then transferred to a covered plastic container and stored in the dark at a temperature of 20–23 °C (68–73 °F). The eggs can lie for a long time in the damp peat, the actual period depending upon the species and various other conditions. Hatching takes place when the peat is flooded with water at the same temperature; this frequently happens within a few hours. The fry are then removed, using a teaspoon, and transferred to a rearing tank. On no account should this process be speeded up. The longer the eggs are allowed to rest in the peat, the greater the number of fry hatching at the same time. They are easy to rear and grow very rapidly.

Group Z 10 contains table numbers 118, 123, 124, 127 and 128.

Maintenance	Breeding	Diet	Page/Figure
TS I/III. Pg. 4, densely planted, not too much light. Peat substrate with roots. 20–24 °C (68–75 °F), sensitive to higher temperatures	Z 9a. The eggs hatch in 14–24 days	Live food, with dried food only as a supplement	VI/14
TS I/III. Pg. 4. 22–24 °C (71–75 °F). As for No. 84. Addition of a little salt is sometimes recommended	Z 9a. The eggs hatch in 14–21 days. Spawns in the open water	Live food, with dried only as a supplement	VI/3 and 8
TS I/III. Pg. 4. As for No. 84	Z 9a. As for No. 84	Live food, with dried only as a supplement	
TS II/III. Pg. 4. 22–24 °C (71–75 °F). As for No. 84	Z 9a. Spawns near the surface. Eggs hatch in 14–21 days	Live and dried food	VI/15
TS II/III. Pg. 4. 22–24 °C (71–75 °F). As for No. 84	Z 9a. Spawns near the surface. Eggs hatch in 14–21 days. Relatively productive	Live food, with dried only as a supplement	214/2

No.	Scientific name	Popular name	Distribu-tion	Length cm	Characteristics	Sex differences
89	*Aphyosemion exiguum*		West Africa, Cameroon and Gabon	5 (1.9 in)	Peaceful, rather shy in bright light, other-wise as for No. 84	♂ more colourful, ♀ with orange bor-der to dorsal and anal fins
90	*Aphyosemion filamentosum*	Plumed lyretail	West Africa, Togo	5.5 (2.1 in)	Active, peaceful	♂ more colourful. Caudal and anal fins much elongated, the edges fringe-like
91	*Aphyosemion gardneri* (= *nigerianum*)	Gardner's panchax	Cameroon	6 (2.4 in)	Not very peaceful	♂ somewhat more colourful. Differ-ences less marked than in other species
92	*Aphyosemion gulare* (= *beauforti*)	Yellow gularis	Liberia, Cameroon	8 (3 in)	Predatory and intol-erant	♂ more colourful
93	*Aphyosemion labarrei*	Labarre's aphyosemion	Congo	5 (1.9 in)	Active, peaceful	♂ intense blue. ♀ uniform brown, with few dark spots
94	*Aphyosemion mirabile*		Cameroon, with several local forms	6 (2.4 in)	♂ sometimes very aggressive	♂ intense blue, with red pattern. ♀ brownish
95	*Aphyosemion scheeli* (= *A. 'burundi'*)	Scheel's aphyosemion	West Africa, Ni-ger delta	6 (2.4 in)	♂ sometimes very aggressive	♂ blue with orange fin edges. ♀ grey-brown
96	*Aphyosemion sjoestedti* (formerly marketed as *A. coeruleum*)	Blue gularis	Niger delta to Cameroon	12 (4.7 in)	Robust predator, the largest in the genus	♂ more colourful, fins larger, 3-pointed caudal fin
97	*Aphyosemion striatum* (sometimes as *A. lujae*)	Red-striped aphyosemion	Gabon	6 (2.4 in)	Peaceful, sociable	♂ intense blue-green, with rows of red dots. ♀ drab
98	*Aphyosemion walkeri* (= *A. spurelli*)	Walker's killifish	Ghana and Ivory Coast	6 (2.4 in)	♂ sometimes very aggressive	♂ metallic green with red fin edges. ♀ grey-brown with irregular dots

Maintenance	Breeding	Diet	Page/Figure
TS I/III. Pg. 4. As for No. 84	Z 9a. As for No. 84	Live food, with dried only as a supplement	
TS II/III. Pg. 4. 22–24 °C (71–75 °F). As for No. 84	Z 9b. May be difficult. Eggs hatch in 28–42 days	Live food	200/14
TS II/III. Pg. 4. 21–24 °C (69–75 °F). As for No. 84	Z 9b. Eggs hatch in 21–42 days	Live food	200/11 and 16
TS III/IV. Pg. 4. 20–24 °C (68–75 °F), best at 22 °C (71 °F). Water can have salt (60 g to 50 litres/20 oz to 11 gals) but not absolutely necessary. Otherwise as for No. 84	Z 9b. 20–23 °C (68–73 °F). Eggs hatch in 42–70 days	Live insect larvae, earthworms, small fish	VI/2
TS I/III. Pg. 4. 18–22 °C (64–71 °F), not higher. Clear, oxygen-rich water, otherwise as No. 84	Z 9a. 20–22 °C (68–71 °F). Eggs hatch in 14–18 days	Live food, with dried only as a supplement	
TS III. Pg. 4. 20–24 °C (68–75 °F). As for No. 84	Z 9a. 20–25 °C (68–77 °F). Eggs hatch in 18–21 days	Live food, with dried only as a supplement	
TS I/III. Pg. 4. 20–24 °C (68–75 °F). As for No. 84	Z 9a. 20–25 °C (68–77 °F). As for No. 84	Live food, with dried only as a supplement	
TS III/IV. Pg. 4. 20–24 °C (68–75 °F), MT 16 °C (60 °F). As for No. 84. Possibly 60 g salt to 50 litres (20 oz to 11 gals) water	Z 9b. Eggs hatch in 42–70 days. Sort out fry to prevent cannibalism	Insect larvae, small fish, dried food	VI/1
TS I/III. Pg. 4. As for No. 84. 20–24 °C (68–75 °F)	Z 9a. 20–25 °C (68–77 °F). As for No. 84	Live food, with dried only as a supplement	
TS I/III. Pg. 4. 20–24 °C (68–75 °F). As for No. 84	Z 9a. 20–25 °C (68–77 °F). As for No. 84	Live food, with dried only as a supplement	

No.	Scientific name	Popular name	Distribution	Length cm	Characteristics	Sex differences
99	*Aplocheilichthys macrophthalmus*	Lamp-eye panchax	West Africa, Nigeria	3.5 (1.3 in)	Peaceful, shoaling, surface-living. Likes to jump	♂ more colourful, dorsal and anal fins drawn out to a point
100	*Aplocheilichthys pumilus*	Pygmy lamp-eye	East African lakes	5.5 (2.1 in)	Peaceful, shoaling, surface-living. Likes to jump	♂ more slender, more colourful
101	*Aplocheilus blocki*	Green panchax	India (Madras)	5 (1.9 in)	Peaceful, rather delicate and not to be kept with other fish that are too robust. Good jumper	♂ more colourful, dorsal and anal fins pointed
102	*Aplocheilus dayi*	Ceylon killifish	South India and Sri Lanka	7 (2.7 in)	Peaceful, often shy surface-living fish	♂ more colourful, dorsal and anal fins pointed
103	*Aplocheilus lineatus*	Panchax lineatus	India and Sri Lanka	10 (3.9 in)	Active, predatory, surface-living, only to be kept with larger fish	♂ more colourful, somewhat larger. ♀ with cross bars on rear of body
104	*Aplocheilus panchax*	Blue panchax	India, Sri Lanka	8 (3 in)	Somewhat predatory, surface-living, but tolerates fish of the same size	♂ more colourful
105	*Austrofundulus dolichopterus*	Sicklefin killie	Venezuela	5 (1.9 in)	♂♂ quarrel, otherwise peaceful. Best kept in a tank without other species	♂ with much elongated dorsal and anal fins, colours more intense
106	*Austrofundulus transilis*	Venezuelan killifish	Venezuela to north Guyana	7 (2.7 in)	♂♂ very aggressive. Do not keep with other species	♂ intense metallic blue, ♀ grey with few dots on fins
107	*Cynolebias belotti*	Argentine pearlfish	La Plata region	♂ 7 (2.7 in) ♀ 5 (1.9 in)	Active, but very aggressive. Do not keep with other species. Adults always ready to spawn	♂ blue with paler markings, ♀ brownish. Fin ray numbers differ
108	*Cynolebias nigripinnis*	Dwarf Argentine pearlfish	Rio Parana	♂ 5 (1.9 in) ♀ 4 (1.5 in)	Attractive, active, not always very peaceful	♂ dark blue, ♀ yellow-brown

Maintenance	Breeding	Diet	Page/Figure
TS I/II. Pg. 4, with dense clumps. Floating plants to cover part of surface. Prefers soft water, but can be kept, sometimes even bred, up to 15 °dH. 20–30 °C (68–73 °F). Tank with well-fitted lid. Very short-lived	Z 8. Spawns in normal aquarium or in separate all-glass tank, over period of about 2 weeks. Eggs visible in ripe ♀♀, laid on plants individually, hatch in 7–14 days. 24–25 °C (75–77 °F). Transfer newly hatched fry to separate rearing tank. Sensitive to infusorians and to fatty layer on water surface	Live and dried food	VI/9
TS I/II. Pg. 4. As for No. 99	As for No. 99	Live and dried food	
TS III. Pg. 4. 23–26 °C (73–78 °F). Floating plants to cover part of surface. Well-fitting lid	Z 8. 23–28 °C (73–82 °F). Not very productive. Fry rather delicate	Live and dried food	VI/16
TS III/IV. Pg. 4. As for No. 101	Z 8. 23–28 °C (73–82 °F). As for No. 101	Live and dried food	
TS III/IV. Pg. 4. As for No. 101	Z 8. 23–28 °C (73–82 °F). Very large fry are easy to rear in a spacious tank with dense vegetation	Insects and their larvae, fish, dried food	VI/7
TS III/VI. Pg. 4. As for No. 101	Z 8. As for No. 103	Insects, midge larvae, small fish, dried food	VI/6
TS I/III. 18–24 °C (64–75 °F). Soft, peaty water. As for No. 84	Z 10. Peat substrate. Eggs lie in damp peat for 4–6 months. Fry grow rapidly, can breed at 10 weeks	Live food, particularly midge larvae	
TS III. 18–24 °C (64–75 °F). Can be kept in medium-hard water, otherwise as No. 84	Z 10. Peat or sand substrate. Eggs lie dormant 6 months. Otherwise as No. 105	Live food	
TS III. Pg. 4. Peat or fine sand substrate. Likes sun and temperature fluctuating 20–25 °C (68–77 °F)	Z 10. Very attractive courtship. Spawns over period of 8–10 days. Young can breed at 70–90 days. Rearing not difficult with brine shrimp	Abundant live food, dried only as a supplement	VII/1
TS III. As No. 107	As No. 107	Abundant live food, dried only as a supplement	216/1

No.	Scientific name	Popular name	Distribution	Length cm	Characteristics	Sex differences
109	*Cynolebias whitei*	White's pearlfish	Brazil	♂ 8 (3 in) ♀ 5 (1.9 in)	Peaceful with other fish. In a species tank ♂ fights for territory	♂ dark brown with greenish-blue iridescent dots. ♀ yellow-brown
110	*Cynopeocilus ladigesi*	Ladiges' cynopeocilus	Area around Rio de Janeiro	♂ 4.5 (1.7 in) ♀ 3.5 (1.3 in)	Peaceful, suitable for community tank with smaller toothcarps	♂ more intensely coloured with banded fins, ♀ brownish, drab
111	*Cyprinodon macularius*	Desert pupfish	California	♂ 5 (1.9 in) ♀ 4 (1.5 in)	Usually very aggressive, so keep only in a species tank	♂ grey-blue to steel-blue, ♀ brownish-grey
112	*Cyprinodon variegatus*	Sheepshead minnow	Atlantic coasts of N. and C. America	♂ 8 (3 in) ♀ 6 (2.4 in)	Keep only in a species tank	♂ very intensely coloured, ♀ yellow with numerous cross bars
113	*Epiplatys annulatus*	Rocket panchax	West Africa: Liberia, Guinea	4 (1.5 in)	Peaceful, surface-living, good for community tank	♂ more colourful, ♀ paler
114	*Epiplatys chevalieri*	Chevalier's epiplatys	Congo middle reaches and estuary	♂ 8 (3 in) ♀ 6 (2.4 in)	Active, not always peaceful	♂ more colourful, ♀ with dark longitudinal bands
115	*Epiplatys dageti monroviae* (formerly *E. chaperi*)	Panchax chaperi	West Africa: Ghana, Liberia	6 (2.4 in)	Peaceful, surface-living, good for a community tank	♂ more colourful, throat red. ♀ with colourless fins
116	*Epiplatys fasciolatus*	Banded epiplatys	West Africa. Also several local races in upper Nile	8 (3 in)	Predatory, surface-living, to be kept with others of same size	♂ more colourful, dorsal and anal fins pointed
117	*Epiplatys sexfasciatus*	Six-banded epiplatys	West Africa, Liberia to lower Congo	11 (4.3 in)	Predatory, to be kept with others of same size, but not too active	♂ more colourful, dorsal and anal fins pointed. ♀ rather smaller and drab

Maintenance	Breeding	Diet	Page/Figure
TS III. As No. 107	As No. 107	Abundant live food, dried only as a supplement	
TS II. As No. 107	Z 10. As No. 107. Unlike the 2 preceding species, does not burrow when mating. Young can breed at 8 weeks	Live and dried food	188/18
TS I/III. 20–30 °C (68–86 °F). Otherwise as No. 125. Even tolerates very hard water	Z 8. Eggs laid on plants, hatch in 10–14 days	Live and dried food, plant matter	
TS I/III. Not above 23 °C (73 °F). Otherwise as No. 125	Z 8. Eggs laid on plants, hatch in 8–12 days	Live and dried food, plant matter	
TS II/III. Pg. 4, floating plants, but not too dense as fish become rather shy. 23–24 °C (73–75 °F). Water up to 10 °dH	Soft, slightly acid water, 24 °C (75 °F). Spawns on bottom, also below surface. Eggs hatch in 10–14 days. Rear very small fry on *Paramecium*, then brine shrimp	Live and dried food	216/5
TS III/IV. Pg. 4. 23–24 °C (73–75 °F), not over 15 °dH. Otherwise as No. 115	Z 8. 24 °C (75 °F). Spawning period lasts about 2 weeks. Parents attack eggs and young. Breeding regarded as rather difficult	Abundant live food	VII/8
TS II/III. Pg. 4. Floating plants on part of surface. 21–23 °C (69–73 °F), MT 16 °C (60 °F)	Z 8. 24 –26 °C. Spawns on floating plants (*Riccia*, water fern roots.) May be fairly productive, 200–300 eggs in a spawning period, which hatch in 8–10 days. Fry fast-growing. Sort out to prevent cannibalism	Live and dried food	VII/3
TS III/IV. Pg. 4. As for No. 115. Give 1 teaspoon salt to 5 litres water for newly imported fish. 21–24 °C (69–75 °F)	Z 8. 24–25 °C (75–77 °F). Eggs sensitive to sunlight. Spawning period lasts 2–3 weeks. Fry grow fast, must be sorted out	Abundant live food, possibly dried food	216/3
TS III/IV. Pg. 4, densely planted. Likes light. 21–24 °C (69–75 °F)	Z 8. Not very productive. Eggs hatch in about 14 days. Fry take brine shrimp immediately	Abundant live food, with dried as supplement	216/7

No.	Scientific name	Popular name	Distribution	Length cm	Characteristics	Sex differences
118	*Fundulosoma thierryi* (also erroneously as *Aphyosemion walkeri*)		West Africa, Ghana	♂ 4 (1.5 in) ♀ 3 (1.1 in)	Peaceful, bottom-living fish. May quarrel among themselves	♂ colourful, ♀ yellow-brown
119	*Fundulus chrysotus* (there is a chequered mutant form)	Golden ear	South-eastern United States, in brackish waters	7 (2.7 in)	Relatively peaceful, but aggressive at spawning time. Sociable, but not to be kept with smaller fish	♂ more colourful, ♀ considerably less so
120	*Garmanella pulchra*	Mexican killifish	Mexico, Yucatan peninsula	4 (1.5 in)	Peaceful, but quarrelsome among themselves. Keep in a species tank	♂ with orange to blood-red fins, ♀ yellow-brown
121	*Jordanella floridae*	American flagfish	Florida to Yucatan	6 (2.4 in)	Peaceful, but ♂ may be aggressive at spawning time	♂ more colourful, ♀ with dark spot on dorsal fin and chessboard pattern on flanks
122	*Lucania* (formerly *Chriopeops*) *goodei*	Bluefin top minnow	Florida	6 (2.4 in)	As No. 121	♂ with red caudal fin, ♀ paler without blue coloration
123	*Nothobranchius palmquisti*	Palmquist's nothobranchius	East Africa	♂ 8 (3 in) ♀ 7 (2.7 in)	Very short-lived, not suitable for community tank. Kept as a pair they spawn ceaselessly	♂ brightly coloured. The uniformly coloured ♀♀ of all species of the genus are very similar and easily confused
124	*Nothobranchius rachovi*	Rachov's nothobranchius	East Africa	7 (2.7 in)	As No. 123	As No. 123
125	*Pachypanchax playfairi*	Playfair's panchax	East Africa, Madagascar, Seychelles	10 (3.9 in)	Quarrelsome, not good for community tank	♂ more colourful, ♀ stouter

Maintenance	Breeding	Diet	Page/Figure
TS I/II. Pg. 4. Otherwise as No. 107	Z 10. Eggs rest about 8 weeks. Fry very small	Live and dried food	
TS III/IV. Pg. 4. 23–25 °C (73–77 °F), MT 20 °C (68 °F). Water depth not too high. Lives near bottom and in middle water layers	24–27 °C (75–80 °F). Sexes 1/1. Spawns in algae, fine-leaved plants, or plastic mop. Eggs must be transferred to rearing dish to avoid being eaten by parents. Hatch in 9–10 days at 25 °C (77 °F). Not difficult to rear	Live and occasionally dried food	216/8
TS II/IV. Pg. 4. Otherwise as No. 125	Z 8. 24–28 °C (75–82 °F). White eggs, laid among plants hatch in 10–14 days	Live and dried food	
TS I/III. Pg. 4 or 11, densely planted. Likes algae and plenty of light. 20–21 °C (68–69 °F). Soft sand substrate	Sexes 1/1. 22–25 °C (71–77 °F). Water depth 15–20 cm (6–8 in), hardness not critical. After vigorous driving, spawns on or among plants, laying 30–120 eggs over 8–10 day period. ♂ practises a loose form of brood protection. In large tank ♀ can remain, otherwise remove her. Eggs hatch in 6–9 days, and ♂ is then removed. Fry grow fast, taking brine shrimp immediately, and need some plant food	Live and dried food, plant matter	VI/10
As No. 121	Spawns among plants, preferably near the surface. Parents attack spawn. Eggs hatch in 10–14 days	Live and dried food	
TS II/III. Pg. 4. Peat substrate. 20–23 °C (68–73 °F), higher temperature reduces life span	Z 10. Eggs should preferably be given a resting period in damp peat, but will hatch in water. At 20–23 °C (68–73 °F) eggs hatch in 8–10 weeks	Abundant live food	
As No. 123	As No. 123. Resting period about 7 months	Abundant live food	VI/11
TS III/IV. Pg. 4, with floating plants. 23–25 °C (73–77 °F), MT 20 °C (68 °F). Provide hiding-places. Water composition not critical, but new imports should have 1 teaspoon salt per 10 litres water	Z 8. Sexes 1/1. Spawns among plants, particularly floating plant roots. 150–300 eggs laid over period of about 14 days. At 25 °C (77 °F) eggs hatch in about 14 days	Abundant live food	VI/4

No.	Scientific name	Popular name	Distribu-tion	Length cm	Characteristics	Sex differences
126	*Procatopus gracilis*	Nigerian lamp-eye	West Africa, Nigeria	6 (2.4 in)	Shoaling fish, for a species tank	♂ iridescent, ♀ yellow-brown
127	*Pterolebias longipinnis*	Featherfin panchax	Lower Amazon	♂ 9 (3.5 in) ♀ 6 (2.4 in)	Active, rather intol-erant	♂ with much en-larged fins
128	*Pterolebias peruensis*	Peruvian panchax	Peru and upper Amazon	♂ 9 (3.5 in) ♀ 6 (2.4 in)	Can be kept with similar species but best kept separately	♂ with elongated fins
129	*Rivulus cylindraceus*	Cuban rivulus	Cuba	♂ 5 (1.9 in) ♀ 5.5 (2.1 in)	Peaceful, surface-living, good for a community tank	♂ more colourful, ♀ with a pale-bor-dered eye-spot on the caudal peduncle
130	*Rivulus holmiae*	Golden-tailed rivulus	Guyana	10 (3.9 in)	To be kept only with large species	♂ intense blue, cau-dal fin with yellow border. ♀ with black border to caudal fin, no eye-spot
131	*Rivulus milesi*	Yellowtail panchax	Colombia and south-ern Central America	8 (3 in)	Sometimes preda-tory. To be kept only with large species	♂ with black-bordered tail, belly golden to reddish, ♀ marbled
132	*Roloffia bertholdi*	Berthold's panchax	West Africa, Sierra Leone	5 (1.9 in)	As No. 84, but very shy	♂ blue with red pattern, ♀ yellow-brown, no spots on the caudal peduncle
133	*Roloffia calabarica*	Blue lyretail panchax	West Africa, Liberia	6 (2.4 in)	As No. 84	♂ blue, ♀ grey with dark marbling
134	*Roloffia geryi*	Gery's panchax	Guinea and Sierra Leone	5 (1.9 in)	As No. 84	♂ blue, ♀ with dark zigzag band
135	*Roloffia occidentalis* (formerly marketed as *Aphyosemion sjoestedti*)	Red aphyosemion	Guinea to Cameroon, Niger delta	8 (3 in)	Not very peaceful	♂ more colourful

Maintenance	Breeding	Diet	Page/Figure
TS I/III. Pg. 4. Otherwise as No. 99	Z 8. As No. 99	Live and dried food	
TS III/IV. Pg. 4. 21–23 °C (69–73 °F), not higher. Soft, slightly acid water	Z 10. When spawning, over period of 2–3 weeks, the pair burrow in the substrate. Eggs hatch in 8–10 weeks	Abundant live food, insect larvae, small earthworms	216/11
As No. 127	As No. 127, but there are populations whose eggs hatch without a resting period	Live food, as No. 127	
TS III. Pg. 4, with densely planted areas and floating plants on which they like to lie. The air above the surface must therefore be warm. Good tank lid. 23–25 °C (73–77 °F), MT 18 °C (64 °F)	Z 8. Sexes 1/1. 25–26 °C (77–78 °F). Water depth 20 cm (8 in). Spawns after strenuous driving beneath the surface. Eggs laid among *Riccia* and floating plant roots, hatch in 10–12 days. Easy to rear. Sort out fry	Abundant live food, some dried food	VII/2
TS III/IV. As No. 129. Good tank lid, as excellent jumper	Z 8. As No. 129	Abundant live and dried food	216/13
TS III/IV. As No. 129	Z 8. As No. 129	Abundant live and dried food	252/2
TS I/III. As for *Aphyosemion* species	Z 9a. Eggs hatch in 18–24 days	Live food, with dried food as a supplement	
TS I/III. As for No. 84	Z 9a. Eggs hatch in 18–24 days	Live food, with dried as a supplement	188/17
TS I/III. As No. 84	Eggs rest in peat 4–6 weeks, or hatch in water 18–24 days	Live food, with dried as supplement	
TS III/IV. Pg. 4. 20–23 °C (68–73 °F). As for No. 84	Z 9b. 20–23 °C (68–73 °F). Eggs usually hatch after resting period of 12–20 weeks	Abundant live food (insect larvae, earthworms, small fish)	

1 *Cynolebias nigripinnis*, dwarf Argentine pearlfish (108) 2 *Aphyosemion schoutedeni*, Schouteden's aphyosemion (88) 3 *Epiplatys fasciolatus*, banded epiplatys (116) 4 *Epiplatys macrostigma*, large-spotted epiplatys (–) 5 *Epiplatys annulatus*, rocket panchax (113) 6 *Epiplatys ornatus*, emerald epiplatys (–) 7 *Epiplatys sexfasciatus*, six-barred epiplatys (117) 8 *Fundulus chrysotus*, golden ear (119) 9 *Oryzias javanicus*, Java medaka (–) 10 *Pachypanchax homalonotus*, green panchax (–) 11 *Pterolebias longipinnis*, featherfin panchax (127) 12 *Rivulus ocellatus*, ocellated rivulus (–) 13 *Rivulus holmiae*, golden-tailed rivulus (130) 14 *Rivulus strigatus*, herringbone rivulus (–) 15 *Brachyrhaphis episcopi*, bishop (–) 16 *Gambusia affinis holbrooki*, eastern mosquitofish (137) 17 *Poecilia (Micropoecilia) branneri*, Branner's livebearer (–) 18 *Jenynsia lineata*, one-sided livebearer (–)

Livebearing toothcarps
(Poeciliidae)

This is the second large family of toothcarps within the sub-order Cyprinodontoidea, and resembles the egg-laying toothcarps in many anatomical characteristics. However, the live-bearers differ in their method of reproduction, and particularly in the males' possession of a copulatory organ. The Poeciliidae contain a large number of species that have become extremely popular within the aquarium world. There are a few other families of livebearing toothcarps which are closely related to the Poeciliidae, but they are only of limited interest to the aquarist.

The Poeciliidae are restricted to South and Central America and the southern United States, where they are widely distributed and found in all kinds of waters. A few species live temporarily in brackish water, or even enter the sea. They occur in such large numbers that they have acquired the popular name 'millions fish'. They play an important role in the control of mosquito larvae, and for this reason certain species have been introduced into some tropical regions with problems of malaria and other fevers. Certain areas, for example the Panama Canal zone, have been opened up to human settlement in this way.

The livebearing Poeciliidae are more accurately described as ovoviviparous, that is, the females carry eggs that are ready to hatch immediately. The development is practically restricted to the body cavity of the female, the young developing within the egg case from which they escape when the eggs leave the female's body. There are a few species in closely related families in which the embryos are nourished within the maternal body cavity.

Most species in the family Poeciliidae are peaceful. The exceptions are the pike-top minnow, *Belonesox belizanus* – an outright predator – and the somewhat aggressive species of *Gambusia*. Their tolerant behaviour makes most livebearers ideal fish for a community tank. Naturally, this does not mean that rival males do not fight, and since this may involve damage to the fins, valuable species, such as the tall-finned mollies, should be kept only as a pair in a community tank. Many members of the family are ideal for the beginner aquarist. They are undemanding, and on account of their small size, can be quite happy living in a small or very small tank. They are, however, sociable fish, which are seen at their best in a community tank with sufficient space for swimming.

Their temperature requirements vary, depending upon their original distribution. Some livebearers are completely undemanding in this respect, while others require a certain amount of heat. In any case they should not be kept at temperatures below 18–20 °C (64–68 °F).

With a few exceptions they do not have any special dietary requirements. They will take any kind of food produced commercially for tropical fish, particularly dried foods, but these should be varied in composition. Breeders like to feed dried foods and brine shrimp nauplii because with these two foods there is no danger of infection by disease vectors. Many species also require a supplement of plant food, and are therefore valuable as consumers of algae.

In most cases breeding is not difficult, except perhaps when some of the numerous colour and form varieties are involved. The members of some genera are very variable. They tend to produce mutations which will often hybridize with one another.

The males are almost always smaller than the females. As they become sexually mature the anal fin is modified to form a moveable copulatory organ, the gonopodium. This is inserted into the female's genital opening to fertilize the eggs. A single mating is sufficient for several broods. Mated females are soon recognizable as such by their stout body, and in many cases by a dark spot at the rear of the belly, which is known as the pregnancy spot. The young are born in their egg case, from which they escape during birth or immediately afterwards. They swim immediately to the surface, where they fill the swimbladder with air. They may also avoid attack by adults when the water surface is covered with floating plants. The number of offspring produced at a time varies from one to two hundred, according to the size and age of the female.

Livebearing toothcarps can be bred in a community tank, provided the vegetation is sufficient to protect the young from the attacks of adult fish. A system of planned breeding will, however, be necessary if a large brood is desired.

Z 11: General hints on breeding
For planned breeding the size of the tank will somewhat depend upon the number of offspring expected. The members of some genera, such as the mollies, will require a large tank if the young are to develop properly. In general, the water should not be too soft, with a hardness not less than 8–10 °dH. Some species come from brackish water areas where the composition fluctuates. It would then be advisable to add one level teaspoonful of cooking salt to 10 litres (2 gals) of tank water. In the case of the mollies the addition of 10 per cent of sea water is recommended; this can be made up from commercially available salt mixtures.

Pregnant females can be transferred from the holding tank to a smaller tank with some dense vegetation. If the females are allowed to give birth in the holding tank the side facing the light must be densely planted and the surface covered with floating ferns. Whichever method is used, the newly born young congregate at the surface, usually at places where the floating fern leaves lie partially submerged. This allows the young to be caught in a spoon and transferred to a rearing tank. For some species the female can be put into a special spawning tank which is suspended inside the holding tank. The young escape through a narrow slit and immediately rise to the surface. This method protects the young from the attacks of the female, and is particularly necessary in the case of predatory forms, such as *Belonesox* and species of *Gambusia*.

The rearing tank must be sufficiently large. The young will not develop properly if they are too crowded. They generally consume large amounts of food so that their excretory products soon accumulate, and these too inhibit the growth of the young. If it is not possi-

No.	Scientific name	Popular name	Distribution	Length cm	Characteristics	Sex differences
136	*Belonesox belizanus*	Pike top minnow	Southern Mexico to Honduras	♂ 12 (4.7 in) ♀ 20 (7.8 in)	Pike-like predator. Initially somewhat shy. ♀ very aggressive	♂ smaller, ♀ larger and stouter
137	*Gambusia affinis affinis*	Mosquitofish	Florida, Texas, north Mexico	♂ 3.5 (1.3 in) ♀ 8 (3 in)	Quarrelsome, best kept without other species. Introduced in many areas to control mosquitoes	♂ may have black chequer pattern, ♀ rarely so
138	*Girardinus metallicus*	Girardinus	Cuba, Costa Rica	♂ 5 (1.9 in) ♀ 9 (3.5 in)	Active fish, good for a community tank	♂ more colourful, with more pattern

ble to avoid overcrowding it will be necessary to remove one fifth of the tank water, preferably every second day, and replace it with water at the same temperature and having the same composition.

Rearing the young is not difficult. They eat very tiny live food, showing a preference for brine shrimp nauplii, and also powdered dried food. Special types of dried food, available commercially, have a composition designed for the requirements of young fish. Most species need some plant food when young and also as adults. This may be algae or also dried food with a plant basis. For breeding and rearing the temperature should be 22–25 °C (71–77 °F).

Many livebearing toothcarps hybridize with one another. Such species should not, therefore, be kept together. Thus, species in the genus *Poecilia* will hybridize, and so will species of *Xiphophorus*. Occasionally there may be hybridization between members of different genera. Naturally the selected varieties of a species also hybridize, and this results in the disappearance of the desired characteristics. Females that have mated with males of other varieties are no longer useful for further breeding, because a single mating is sufficient for several broods.

Z 11a: Breeding races and varieties

The selected races now offered for sale are produced from mutations or from the hybridization of various forms. Sometimes they are so fixed genetically that they will produce offspring which resemble the parents, provided the female has not been mated with the wrong male. To keep the races pure the aquarist must either only keep fish of the same pure strain together, or he must keep males and females separate. They are then only put together for breeding purposes. In some species the genetics are relatively uncomplicated. The most difficult task is presented by the extraordinarily variable guppy *Poecilia (Lebistes) reticulata*. Guppy breeding is hard work, which demands all the skill of the breeder and a knowledge of the specialist literature. Guppy breeders are organized in clubs and associations in many countries, and these even operate on an international level.

Some selected forms of the swordtail are shown in the black-and-white illustrations on p. 224.

Maintenance	Breeding	Diet	Page/Figure
TS IV/V. Pg. 5, densely planted. 20–30 °C (68–86 °F). No special water requirements, except possibly the addition of a little salt	Z 11. A spawning box is necessary for good results. ♀ produces 20–200 young, each 25 mm (0.9 in) long which immediately take live food and grow fast	Live food: insect larvae, earthworms, particularly small fish	VIII/3
TS II/III. Pg. 5, densely planted to give hiding-places	Z 11. 22 °C (71 °F). Spawning box necessary. Breeding not always easy. ♀♀ should not be too young. Up to 80 young born after 4–5 weeks	Live food preferred, dried food, algae	216/16
TS II/III. Pg. 5. 22–25 °C (71–77 °F). Likes clear water that is not too old	Z 11. 24–26 °C (75–78 °F). Gestation about 4–6 weeks, up to 100 very small young	Live and dried food, plant matter	VII/12

No.	Scientific name	Popular name	Distribution	Length cm	Characteristics	Sex differences
139	*Heterandria formosa*	Least killifish	South Carolina to Florida	♂ 2 (0.8 in) ♀ 3 (1.1 in)	Peaceful, not very shy, best kept in a species tank	No colour differences
140	*Poecilia (Lebistes) reticulata*	Guppy	Trinidad and parts of South America, north of Amazon	♂ 2.5 (1.9 in) ♀ 5 (1.9 in) (wild forms)	Peaceful, very active, good for community tank	♂ more colourful, very variable, ♀ occasionally with a coloured caudal fin
141	*Poecilia (Limia) melanogaster*	Black-bellied limia	Jamaica, Haiti	♂ 4 (1.5 in) ♀ 6.5 (2.5 in)	Peaceful, sometimes very active	♂ more intensely coloured, ♀ with striking large spot on abdomen
142	*Poecilia (Limia) nigrofasciata*	Black-barred limia	Haiti	♂ 4.5 (1.7 in) ♀ 7 (2.7 in)	Peaceful, sociable fish	♂ more intensely coloured, becomes high-backed with age
143	*Poecilia (Limia) vittata*	Cuban limia	Cuba, Haiti	♂ 6 (2.4 in) ♀ 10 (3.9 in)	Peaceful, active, sociable fish	♂ more intensely coloured, dorsal and caudal fins yellow with a dark pattern
144	*Poecilia (Mollienesia) latipinna*	Sailfin molly	Virginia to Mexico, often in sea or brackish water	♂ 9 (3.5 in) ♀ 11 (4.3 in)	Peaceful, very active. ♂♂ may quarrel among themselves, so keep as a pair	♂ more colourful, with taller dorsal fin, which can be erected like a sail
145	*Poecilia (Mollienesia) sphenops*	Pointed-mouth molly	Texas to Venezuela	♂ 4–7 (1.5–2.7 in) ♀ 6–10 (2.4–3.9 in)	Active, peaceful fish, very variable in coloration and size	♂ generally more colourful
146	*Poecilia (Mollienesia) velifera*	Mexican sailfin molly	Coastal areas of Yucatan	15 (6 in)	Very active, fairly peaceful. ♂♂ tend to quarrel with each other	♂ more active, with very large sail-like dorsal fin

(There are also chequered, completely black and albinotic forms of this species.)

Maintenance	Breeding	Diet	Page/Figure
TS I/II. Pg. 4, with densely planted areas. Good lighting or sunshine. 20–24 °C (68–75 °F), MT 18 °C (64 °F)	Z 11. Chases its own young, hence dense planting, including floating plants *(Riccia)*. Over period of 14 days produces 1–2 young per day	Tiny live and dried food, algae	VII/13
TS I/IV. Pg. 5. 20–22 °C (68–71 °F), MT 18 °C (64 °F), up to 28 °C (82 °F) for certain selected forms	Z 11 and 11 a. Not difficult. Gestation 4–6 weeks, up to 100 young or more. Special requirements for certain races	Live and dried food, algae	VIII/4
TS II/III. Pg. 5. 22–26 °C (71–78 °F). Requires more swimming space than the other limias	Z 11. 26 °C (78 °F). Gestation 4–6 weeks, 20–50 young, which grow rapidly	Live and dried food, plant matter	VII/7
TS III. Pg. 5. Bright lighting or sun (encourages algae). 24–28 °C (75–82 °F), MT 20 °C (68 °F)	Z 11. 26–28 °C (78–82 °F). Gestation 4–5 weeks, 20–50 rather large young	Live and dried food, plant matter (algae)	224/2
TS III/IV. Pg. 5. Bright lighting or sun. Add 10 % salt water. 24–26 °C (75–78 °F), MT 20 °C (68 °F)	Z 11. 24–26 °C (75–78 °F). Gestation 4–5 weeks, 20–50 young, not chased if parents are well fed	Live and dried food, plant matter (algae)	VII/6
TS IV/V. Pg. 5. 20–24 °C (68–75 °F), not higher. 5–10 % added salt water may do good, but plants will suffer. Must have hiding-places (roots, rocks)	Z 11. 20–24 °C (68–75 °F). Very large tank. Lower temperatures stimulate sexual maturity. Gestation 8–10 weeks, up to 80 young, which require plenty of food	Live and dried food, particularly plant food	
TS II/IV. Pg. 5. 22–26 °C (71–78 °F). Sensitive to temperature fluctuations and infusorians. Shuffling movements when unwell. Black forms require plenty of warmth. The original form likes a little salt in the water	Original form: 24–26 °C (75–78 °F). Z 11. Large tank, plenty of algae and plant food, sunlight. Gestation 4–8 weeks, 100 offspring or more. Black molly: 25–28 °C (77–82 °F). For breeding do not use fish that are too young. Gestation 6–10 weeks. Frequently not all the young are deep black	Live and dried food, algae, plant matter	
TS IV/V. Pg. 5. No plants if much sea water or salt is added. Decorate with rocks, roots, to provide shelter. 25–28 °C (77–82 °F), if possible not less. Sensitive to water pollution. Likes plenty of light and algal films	Z 11. Very large tank. 25–30 °C (77–86 °F). Only use ♂♂ with large dorsal fin, at least 1½ years old. ♀ must still be virgin. Gestation 8 weeks, 30–100 young or more. Rear with brine shrimp, unicellular algae, powdered food containing much plant matter	Abundant live and dried food, algae, plant matter	VII/10

No.	Scientific name	Popular name	Distribu-tion	Length cm	Characteristics	Sex differences
147	*Phallichthys amates*	Merry widow	Guatemala, Costa Rica, Honduras	♂ 3.5 (1.3 in) ♀ 6 (2.4 in)	Not very active, rather shy. Only keep with peaceful species	No significant colour differences
148	*Phalloceros caudimaculatus*	Caudo	From Rio to La Plata region	♂ 3 (1.1 in) ♀ 5 (1.9 in)	Peaceful, active fish that lasts well. Not often sold nowadays	♂ with dark-edged dorsal fin

(A chequered form has been marketed as *P.c. reticulatus* and a chequered form with bright golden-yellow ground coloration has been erroneously known as 'golden gambusia'.)

No.	Scientific name	Popular name	Distribu-tion	Length cm	Characteristics	Sex differences
149	*Xiphophorus helleri*	Swordtail	Mexico, Honduras, Guatemala	♂ 7 (2.7 in) without sword, ♀ 10 (3.9 in)	Active, but not always completely peaceful. In particu-lar old ♂♂ quarrel with one another	♂ rather more colourful. Lower caudal fin lobe elongated to form the 'sword'
150	*Xiphophorus maculatus*	Platy	S. Mexico, Guatemala, Honduras	♂ 3.5 (1.3 in) ♀ 6 (2.4 in)	Peaceful, sociable fish, suitable for a community tank	Sexes scarcely distinguishable in coloration
151	*Xiphophorus montezumae*	Montezuma helleri	Mexico	♂ 4.5 (1.7 in) ♀ 6 (2.4 in)	Peaceful, sociable, but also rather shy	♂ rather more in-tensely coloured, with larger dorsal fin
152	*Xiphophorus variatus*	Variatus platy	Mexico	♂ 4 (1.5 in) ♀ 6 (2.4 in)	Peaceful, sociable fish, suitable for a community tank	♂ more colourful. ♀ resembles ♀ of No. 149

(The following species is only described here because it is livebearing. It is not related to the tooth-carps, but belongs to the half-beak family [Hemirhamphidae].)

No.	Scientific name	Popular name	Distribu-tion	Length cm	Characteristics	Sex differences
153	*Dermogenys pusillus*	Half-beak	Thailand, Malaya, In-donesia, in fresh and brackish water	♂ 7 (2.7 in) ♀ 9 (3.5 in)	Peaceful, active, rather timid, sur-face-living fish. Not very suitable for a community tank	Difference in the form of the anal fin. ♂ rather more colourful

Maintenance	Breeding	Diet	Page/Figure
TS I/II. Pg. 5. 20–25 °C (68–77 °F). Likes dense vegetation	Z 11. 22–26 °C (71–78 °F). Gestation 4–6 weeks. 10–50 young, do not grow very fast	Live and dried food	VII/11
TS I/II. Pg. 5, with some dense vegetation. Can be kept at room temperature, 18–22 °C (64–71 °F), MT 15 °C (59 °F). The chequered forms require rather more warmth	Z 11. Gestation 4–5 weeks, 20–80 young. The chequered forms may be rather delicate. Many young die after birth	Live and dried food	VII/5
TS III/IV. Pg. 5, with some dense vegetation to provide hiding-places. 22–26 °C (71–78 °F). Requires plenty of swimming space	Z 11. Large tanks for breeding. Gestation 4–6 weeks. Up to 150 young or more. Numerous selected forms give standard designations and valued for exhibition purposes	Live and dried food, algae, plant matter	224/7 VIII/7
TS II/III. Pg. 5. 20–25 °C (68–77 °F)	Z 11. Gestation 4–5 weeks, 20–100 young. Selected forms, see No. 149	Live and dried food, algae, plant matter	224/8 VIII/6
TS II/III. Pg. 5. 20–25 °C (68–77 °F)	Z 11. Gestation 4–5 weeks. Young grow rapidly	Live and dried food, algae, plant matter	224/4
TS II/III. Pg. 5. 22–26 °C (71–78 °F). Likes light and algal growth	Z 11. 24–26 °C (75–78 °F). Gestation 4–5 weeks, 20–100 young, sometimes more. Selected forms, see No. 149	Live and dried food, algae, plant matter	224/9 VIII/5
TS III/IV. Pg. 5. 25–30 °C (77–86 °F) or even more. Clean, clear water. For new imports one teaspoonful salt should be added to 5 litres (1.1 gals) of water. Cover part of the surface with floating ferns	Z 11. TS III. 28–32 °C (82–89 °F) Densely planted, particularly also with floating plants such as *Riccia*. Lower the water level. Gestation 4–6 weeks, 10–40 young, whose survival depends on how the parents have been fed	Live food, e.g. wingless fruitflies, newly hatched labyrinth fish. Only feeds at the surface	252/3

223

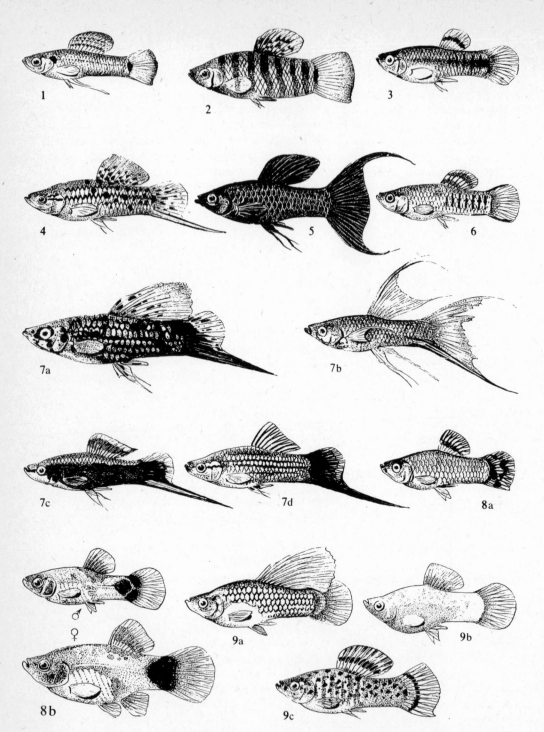

1 *Heterandria (Pseudoxiphophorus) bimaculata*, pseudo-helleri (–) 2 *Poecilia (Limia) nigrofasciata*, black-barred limia (142) 3 *Poecilia (Limia) caudofasciata*, blue poecilia (–) 4 *Xiphophorus montezumae*, Montezuma helleri (151) 5 *Poecilia (Mollienesia) latipinna*, lyretail form of sailfin molly (144) 6 *Poecilia (Poecilia) vivipara*, one-spot livebearer (–) 7a–d *Xiphophorus helleri*, swordtail, selected forms (149) 8a–b *Xiphophorus maculatus*, platy, selected forms (150) 9a–c *Xiphophorus variatus*, Variatus platy, selected forms (152)

Labyrinth fishes (Anabantoidea)

These fish comprise a sub-order within the order Perciformes. The sub-order includes the family Luciocephalidae and the labyrinth fish which, according to the latest scientific work, are classified in a number of separate families. These are the climbing perches (Anabantidae), the true labyrinth fish (Belontiidae), the kissing gouramis (Helostomatidae) and finally the larger gouramis (Osphronemidae).

The term labyrinth fish refers to the auxiliary respiratory organ situated in the upper part of the gill cavity. This organ supplements the oxygen-collecting activities of the gills, which are not always very efficient. The fish rises to the surface and fills the labyrinth organ with atmospheric air. As a rule this aerial respiration is even used when gill respiration should be sufficient. Certain species are so tied to aerial respiration that they will die, by drowning, if they are denied access to the surface.

The snakeheads (family Ophicephalidae) are included in the table although they are no longer regarded as part of the Anabantoidea. They live in shallow, very warm and often muddy waters. In times of drought, when their own waters dry up, they survive by burrowing in the mud or by migrating overland until they reach the next water source. The body is elongated, and the dorsal and anal fins are also elongated, with only soft rays. The head and body are covered with large scales.

The snakeheads are nocturnal predators. They like an aquarium tank with a dark substrate, dense vegetation and hiding-places among a tangle of roots. The reproductive habits are of interest, for the young are tended by the parents for a long time, but breeding is scarcely likely to take place in the home aquarium. The family is distributed in southern Asia and Africa.

The family Luciocephalidae has only a single species in the Malay Archipelago. It has a pike-like form and habits. The large head, with a deeply cleft, protrusible mouth, is particularly striking. The dorsal and anal fins are positioned far back, and the ventral fins are much elongated. The fish lies in wait for prey in the subdued light under river banks. The reproduction method is not known but it may possibly involve mouthbrooding.

The numerous species of labyrinth fish are distributed in the tropics and subtropics of eastern and south-east Asia. A few species occur in tropical Africa. The body may be squat or more or less elongated. The lips may be swollen, while the head and body are covered with scales which in certain cases even extend on to the fins. Some species are moderately laterally compressed, others very much so. The dorsal and anal fins are divided into a spiny and a soft-rayed part. The soft rays are frequently much elongated, and the caudal fin may also have elongated rays. The ventral fins are positioned beneath the pectoral fins and in some species are elongated or even drawn out into long filaments the length of the body. The anus is situated in the front part of the body, but the body cavity with the swimbladder may reach back almost to the caudal fin.

Labyrinth fish live in many different types of water, but mainly in shallow ponds and ditches, the backwaters of rivers, flooded areas and paddy-fields. Some species also live in streams and other flowing waters. In general, they prefer places with rich vegetation rather than the open water.

The diet consists of all kinds of invertebrates, and many species require a supplement of plant matter, particularly algae. In the aquarium they also eat dried food. The gourami *(Osphronemus goramy)* and the kissing gourami *(Helostoma temmincki)* reach a size which makes them a source of human food.

In general, the composition of the water is not critical. Only a few species require soft, slightly acid water. In their home water these fish are able to survive in unfavourable conditions, even in waters poor in oxygen, because of the ability to use atmospheric air. One species, the true climbing perch *(Anabas testudineus)*, can survive when its home waters dry up completely, by migrating overland and searching for more favourable water conditions.

During spawning the male encircles the female's body and the eggs are laid below the surface and float free, owing to their content of oil. Certain species spawn beneath leaves or in cavities, while a few are mouthbrooders.

The vast majority of the species build a nest of air bubbles at the surface; this structure sometimes incorporates algae and parts of the vegetation. The nest is vigorously maintained and enlarged by the male. After an attractive courtship the fish spawn beneath the nest in the manner already described. The eggs usually rise on their own into the nest. If any sink to the bottom they are retrieved by the male, sometimes also with help from the female, and placed in among the air bubbles of the nest. The aquarium tank must be vibration-free, because the bubble nest can easily fall apart. The female should be removed after spawning. The male guards the eggs and the fry while they are still not free-swimming. He continues to add new air bubbles to the bottom of the nest so that the eggs become more deeply embedded. As soon as the young start

No.	Scientific name	Popular name	Distribution	Length cm	Characteristics	Sex differences
154	*Anabas testudineus*	Climbing perch	South-east Asia, widely distributed	up to 25 (9.8 in)	Shy, aggressive, nocturnal, likes to jump	♂ with slightly pointed dorsal and anal fins
155	*Belontia signata*	Combtail	Sri Lanka	13 (5.1 in)	Robust, somewhat intolerant, likes to live hidden	♂ rather larger, the dorsal and anal fins pointed
156	*Betta picta*	Javan betta	Java, Sumatra	5 (1.9 in)	Peaceful	Few differences. Fins slightly pointed in ♂
157	*Betta splendens*	Fighting fish	Malaya, Thailand, Cambodia, Vietnam	7 (2.7 in)	Individuals of the same size are generally peaceful, but ♂♂ fight one another. Not very suitable for a community tank	♂ more colourful, fins larger, particularly in the selected forms, which have sail-like fins

to swim free the male should also be removed from the tank.

For the first few days the very small fry require infusorians and tiny algae, but they will soon take small live food, such as brine shrimp nauplii, and powdered dried food. The temperature should be kept constant. In general, the hardness of the water is not critical, but if it is this is mentioned in the table. The breeding tank need not be very large unless the parent fish are likely to produce a large number of offspring, which happens in certain species. It is best to reduce the depth of the water to 10 cm (4 in), at the most 15 cm (6 in). During the first thirty days of the rearing period some very gentle aeration is recommended while the fry are developing their labyrinth organs. The young fish increase in size at varying rates so from time to time they should be sorted and placed in different size groups.

Labyrinth fish will produce perfectly adequate broods in a fully furnished aquarium tank, and a system of planned breeding is only necessary when large numbers of offspring are required.

Maintenance	Breeding	Diet	Page/Figure
TS IV/V. Pg. 12, only tough plants in pots. Rocks, roots for hiding. 20–30 °C (68–86 °F), MT 12 °C (53 °F). Provide a good tank lid	Sexes 1/1. 25–28 °C (77–82 °F). Spawns beneath the roots of floating plants. Eggs collect together at the surface. Brood not protected	Abundant live food (mosquito larvae, insects, *Tubifex*, small fish), plant matter	
TS IV/V. Pg. 1. 25 °C (77 °F). Not too much light, floating plants give half shade. Rocks, roots for hiding. Likes to jump, so provide good tank lid	Sexes 1/1. 28 °C (82 °F). Water depth 20 cm (10 in). ♂ drives very vigorously, so ♀ needs safe places to hide. Often does not build a bubble nest, but spawns below the surface where the eggs float free	Abundant live and dried food	234/1
TS III. Pg. 1. 20–25 °C (68–77 °F), MT 17 °C (62 °F). Tolerates temperature fluctuations	Sexes 1/1. 25–30 °C (77–86 °F). Mouthbrooder. Spawns near the bottom. Eggs taken up into throat sac of ♂. Fry released after 9 days. From then on rear like other labyrinth fish	Live and dried food	
TS II/III. Pg. 1, with densely planted areas and floating plants. Roots to give shelter. Peat substrate. 26–30 °C (78–86 °F). Does not like temperature fluctuations	Sexes 1/1. Up to 30 °C (86 °F). Builds a relatively small bubble nest. Selected forms require several tanks for rearing, separation of the sexes and selection of the best individuals. For the full development of the fins the finest ♂♂ are kept in small all-glass tanks	Live and dried food	X/4 and 6

No.	Scientific name	Popular name	Distribu-tion	Length cm	Characteristics	Sex differences
158	*Colisa chuna*	Honey gourami	N.E. India, Bangladesh	6 (2.4 in)	A peaceful fish, though ♂ somewhat aggressive at spawning time. Best kept as a pair, as not happy in too lively company	♂ considerably more colourful, particularly when excited, dorsal fin slightly pointed
159	*Colisa fasciata*	Banded gourami	Bengal, Assam, Burma	♂ 10 (3.9 in) ♀ 8 (3 in)	Sometimes rather shy. At spawning ♂ becomes aggressive	♂ more colourful, dorsal fin slightly pointed
160	*Colisa labiosa*	Thick-lipped gourami	S.E. Asia, Burma	♂ 6–8 (2.4–3 in) ♀ 5–6 (1.9–2.4 in)	Peaceful, rather shy, particularly when kept only as a pair	♂ more colourful, lips more swollen, dorsal fin slightly pointed
161	*Colisa lalia*	Dwarf gourami	Bengal, Assam	6 (2.4 in)	In general, peaceful. Rather shy when kept as a pair. ♂ aggressive at spawning time	♂ considerably more colourful, dorsal fin slightly pointed
162	*Ctenopoma fasciolatum*	Banded climbing perch	Central Africa, Congo region	8 (3 in)	Not very peaceful. ♂ particularly is very aggressive at spawning time	♂ more colourful, the dorsal fins pointed. ♀ somewhat smaller
163	*Ctenopoma oxyrhynchus*	Sharp-nosed ctenopoma	Congo region	10 (3.9 in)	Relatively peaceful, rather shy and likes places to hide	♂ dorsal and anal fins pointed
164	*Helostoma temmincki*	Kissing gourami	Thailand, Malaya, Indonesia	up to 30 (11.8 in)	Peaceful, grows large, but is still a very popular aquarium fish	Seen from above the ♀ is considerably stouter than the ♂

(There is a pale yellowish or whit-ish selected form of this species.)

Maintenance	Breeding	Diet	Page/Figure
TS II/III. Pg. 1, densely planted. 25–28 °C (77–82 °F). Peat substrate, sunlight and algae. Roots for hiding	Sexes 1/1. 28–30 °C (82–86 °F). Builds a bubble nest, but not always very carefully	Live and dried food	234/5
TS IV. Pg. 1 with areas of dense vegetation, and floating plants. Likes bright light and algae. 25–28 °C (77–82 °F), but not very sensitive to temperature fluctuations	Sexes 1/1. Builds a very large, often untidy nest. 28 °C (82 °F). Shallow water. Very productive in large tanks	Live and dried food	IX/3
TS III/IV. Pg. 1, with densely planted areas, floating plants. 25–28 °C (77–82 °F), but more or less can be tolerated	As for No. 159. A zealous bubble nest builder	Live and dried food	IX/2
TS II/III. Pg. 1, with densely planted areas and floating plants. Provide *Riccia* for nest building. Likes bright light (sun) and algae. 25–30 °C (77–86 °F)	Sexes 1/1. Builds a firm bubble nest incorporating algae and parts of plants. 28–32 °C (82–89 °F)	Live and dried food	IX/1
TS III/IV. Pg. 1. 22–25 °C (71–77 °F), MT 18 °C (64 °F). Peat substrate, light not too bright. Roots for hiding	Sexes 1/1. Small bubble nest, somewhat fleetingly built. ♀ does not turn on her back during spawning	Prefers live food. Also eats small fish	IX/9
TS IV. Pg. 1. 28–30 °C (82–86 °F)	Sexes 1/1. The eggs are released below the water surface where they float free. No brood protection	Prefers live food. Likes to feed on the bottom	234/2
TS V/VI. Pg. 1, but only use tough plants as these fish are avid plant-eaters. Likes bright light and algae	Sexes 1/1. 26–30 °C (78–86 °F). Very large tanks needed as the fish are extraordinarily productive. Eggs laid below the surface. Mating is very stormy, with little encircling. Eggs, lighter than water, collect at the surface or remain hanging on the plants. No brood protection. Eggs hatch in 2 days and fry swim free 5–6 days later. They need plenty of tiny live food and powdered dried food with a base of plant matter	Live and dried food, plant matter, all in large amounts	X/5

229

No.	Scientific name	Popular name	Distribution	Length cm	Characteristics	Sex differences
165	*Luciocephalus pulcher*	Pike-head	Malaya, parts of Indonesia	18 (7 in)	Predatory fish that waits for prey among dense vegetation	Differences in the structure of the anal fin
166	*Macropodus opercularis*	Paradise fish	South China, Vietnam	8 (3 in)	An interesting, but not very tolerant fish. ♂ aggressive at spawning time. Best kept as a pair, not very suitable for a community tank	♂ more colourful, dorsal and anal fins with long, pointed tips. ♀ smaller
167	*Macropodus opercularis concolor*	Black paradise fish	probably south China	8 (3 in)	As No. 166	As No. 166
168	*Ophicephalus striatus* (This snake-head serves as a representative of several related species in S. Asia and Africa.)	Striped snake-head	India	100 (39 in)	Mainly nocturnal predator, particularly suitable for a public aquarium	Unknown
169	*Pseudosphromenus cupanus cupanus*	Spike-tailed paradise fish	India, Sri Lanka	5.5 (2.1 in)	Peaceful, good for a community tank	♂ rather more colourful, with pointed dorsal and anal fins
170	*Pseudosphromenus cupanus dayi*	Brown spike-tailed paradise fish	India, S.E. Asia, parts of Indonesia	6 (2.4 in)	As No. 169	♂ more colourful at spawning time, otherwise few differences. Central caudal fin rays elongated
171	*Sphaerichthys osphromenoides*	Chocolate gourami	Malaya, Sumatra	5 (1.9 in)	Peaceful, rather shy, delicate fish, requiring special attention	Few differences in coloration
172	*Trichogaster leeri*	Pearl gourami	Thailand, Malaya, Sumatra, Borneo	12 (4.7 in)	In general peaceful, but ♂ rather aggressive at spawning time. Good for a community tank with peaceful fish	♂ more colourful, fins generally larger, breast and belly becoming orange when the fish is excited. ♀ smaller

Maintenance	Breeding	Diet	Page/Figure
TS IV. Pg. 1, densely planted. Floating plants. Roots for hiding. 24 °C (75 °F). Brisk aeration, or even better to provide moving water, which the fish like	Breeding unknown, may be a mouth-brooder	Abundant live food (insect larvae, fish)	252/7
TS III/IV. Pg. 1, with densely planted areas. Roots and floating plants for shelter. Water not too deep. Tank with a good lid, as the fish jump. 20–30 °C (68–86 °F), MT 15 °C (59 °F)	Sexes 1/1. Builds a large, solid bubble nest. Needs a large breeding tank, as very productive. ♀ must not be too small as the ♂ may be very aggressive	Live and dried food	IX/5
As No. 166	As No. 166	Live and dried food	
TS IV. Only tough plants in pots, otherwise decorate with roots and rocks. 25–30 °C (77–86 °F). Young individuals of the various species are interesting to keep	Scarcely feasible for the home aquarium. Eggs and fry guarded and tended by both parents	Abundant live food (insects and their larvae, fish)	252/5
TS II/III. Pg. 1, densely planted. Floating plants. Roots for hiding. Likes sunlight and algae. 20–24 °C (68–75 °F), MT 15 °C (59 °F)	Sexes 1/1. Builds a small brownish bubble nest, but also spawns in cavities among roots. May be fairly productive	Live and dried food	IX/6
TS II/III. Pg. 1, densely planted. Floating plants. Roots for hiding. Peat substrate. 20–28 °C (68–82 °F)	Sexes 1/1. Builds a small bubble nest beneath floating plants, but also spawns in small cavities, with only a few air bubbles collected on the roof. May be fairly productive. 26–28 °C (78–82 °F)		
TS III/IV. Pg. 1, densely planted. 24–30 °C (75–86 °F). Soft, peat-filtered water, not over 15 cm (6 in) deep. Peat substrate and roots to give hiding-places	Breeding seldom achieved. Sexes 1/1. 26–28 °C (78–82 °F). Eggs are laid in a cohesive bunch and incubated in the mouth of the ♀. Usually not more than 40 young, which are no longer tended after leaving the mouth	Live food (midge larvae, wingless fruit flies), dried food (?)	IX/7
TS IV/V. Pg. 1, densely planted. Floating plants. Likes sunlight and algae. Water not too deep.	Sexes 1/1. 30 °C (86 °F). Builds a large, flat bubble nest. The breeding tank must be very spacious, as large pairs in particular are very productive	Live and dried food	X/3

No.	Scientific name	Popular name	Distribution	Length cm	Characteristics	Sex differences
173	*Trichogaster microlepis*	Moonlight gourami	Thailand	12 (4.7 in)	As No. 172	♂ with orange-red ventral fin filaments. ♀ somewhat smaller
174	*Trichogaster pectoralis*	Snake-skin gourami	S.E. Asia	13 (5.1 in) or more	As No. 172	♂ with orange ventral fin filaments and larger dorsal fin. ♀ somewhat smaller
175	*Trichogaster trichopterus*	Three-spot gourami	India, S.E. Asia	12 (4.7 in)	Generally peaceful, but ♂ rather aggressive at spawning time. Suitable for keeping with similar species	♂ with larger, pointed dorsal fin
176	*Trichopsis pumilus*	Pygmy gourami	Thailand, Malaya, Vietnam	3.5 (1.3 in)	Peaceful and not shy, in spite of its delicate nature. When excited, produces audible sounds	♂ rather more colourful, with slightly pointed fins
177	*Trichopsis vittatus*	Croaking gourami	Burma, Thailand, Sumatra	6 (2.4 in)	As No. 176	♂ with very pointed fins, the filaments elongated

Maintenance	Breeding	Diet	Page/Figure
As No. 172	Builds a large, tall bubble nest, incorporating plant fragments. If the latter are absent (e.g. *Riccia*) the tank plants will be attacked and damaged. Very productive	Live and dried food, plant matter	234/3
As No. 172	As No. 172. Very productive	Abundant live and dried food	234/4
As No. 172, but not requiring so much warmth	As No. 172. Also very productive. Several attractive selected forms (blue, marbled or Cosby, silver and golden filaments)	Live and dried food	X/2
TS I/III. Pg. 1, densely planted. Floating plants. Water not too deep. 25–28 °C (77–82 °F)	Sexes 1/1. 30 °C (86 °F), with as little temperature fluctuation as possible as the very small young are sensitive to this. Builds a bubble nest, but sometimes not very efficiently. Not very productive	Live and dried food	252/6
TS II/III. Pg. 1. As No. 176	As No. 176. Builds a flimsy bubble nest. Up to 150 young	Live and dried food	IX/4

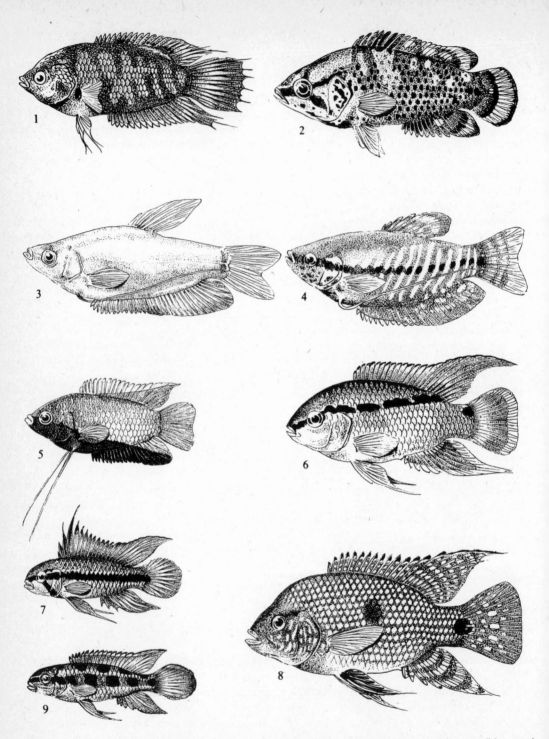

1 *Belontia signata*, combtail (155)   2 *Ctenopoma oxyrhynchus*, sharp-nosed ctenopoma (163)   3 *Trichogaster microlepis*, moonlight gourami (173)   4 *Trichogaster pectoralis*, snake-skin gourami (174)   5 *Colisa chuna*, honey gourami (158)   6 *Aequidens itanyi*, green acara (179)   7 *Apistogramma trifasciatum*, blue apistogramma (187)   8 *Geophagus gymnogenys*, dark geophagus (–)   9 *Crenicara maculata*, chess-board cichlid (–)

Cichlids (Cichlidae)

This family is part of the sub-order Percoidea in the order Perciformes. Cichlid species have typical perch-like characteristics, even though these are not always immediately obvious. These include the division of the dorsal and anal fins into front spiny and rear soft-rayed parts. In males the soft-rayed parts are usually more markedly pointed than in the females. As a rule the large ventral fins are positioned below the pectoral fins, which may also be very large. The general body form varies from torpedo-shaped, pike-like types to the circular profiles of the discus fish.

Many cichlids are large and powerfully built. The head is relatively massive and the forehead, particularly in older males, is bulging and often has a marked depression above the eyes, which are themselves very large and striking. It is understandable that such fish must be kept in a large tank, particularly when they are to be bred. Many aquarists who do not have such large aquarium tanks are therefore inclined to take more interest in the smaller cichlid species, which have been increasingly imported in recent years. Apart from the true dwarf cichlids of the genera *Apistogramma* and *Nannacara,* these include the brightly coloured species of *Pelvicachromis* from Africa and the remarkable cichlids from the East African lakes. Small and dwarf cichlids can be regarded as those in which the length of the male does not exceed 8 cm (3·15 in).

The family has many species, with the main area of distribution lying in tropical Africa, from Niger and Congo in the west to the Nile and Lake Victoria in the east, as well as several lakes in the rift valley of eastern Africa. There are also several species in Central and South America, but only two in Asia, of which one can almost be regarded as a marine fish. In general, cichlids are essentially freshwater fish, with a few species occasionally entering brackish waters.

Large cichlids prefer deep, standing or slow-flowing waters, often with vegetation near the banks of lakes, lagoons and bays. The smaller species are usually found in more restricted waters, such as forest and savannah streams, ditches and ponds. Some species are adapted for life in particular environmental conditions. Thus, the East African lakes have their own endemic cichlid species. In some fast-flowing waters there are species which can scarcely be recognized as members of the family, and there are even cichlids in subterranean waters and in lakes with warm water. Outside the periods of spawning many cichlids live in quite large communities, which move about searching for food. Sometimes these groups are formed into 'schools' according to age. At spawning time the pairs leave the group and take up breeding territories. Some species live more or less the whole time in defined territories.

Most cichlids are not predators in the true sense of the word. The smaller species feed on invertebrates. Some also require plant food. So long as they are not fully grown the large cichlids also feed on invertebrates. They will take practically anything that appears in front of their mouth, such as worms, mosquito and other insect larvae, water insects, snails, amphibian larvae and small fish. Older individuals tend to become more and more predatory and to hunt actively for food. There are some cichlids with peculiar feeding habits, such as the algal browsers of Lake Malawi and those in the same habitat that feed on fish scales and eyes.

In captivity most cichlids take everything offered, not only live food but also dried foods, as flakes, tablets or freeze-dried. Naturally they will also accept frozen foods, suitably thawed.

The coloration of cichlids is often brilliant, or at least striking. Particularly characteristic are the iridescent spots and streaks on the gill covers, flanks and fins. Coloration and pattern may change completely in response to the environment, or to emotional stimuli, certain colour patterns being associated with clearly defined forms of behaviour. Thus the victor in a fight wears a pattern differing from that of the vanquished. The individual phases in the reproductive cycle, too, are usually marked by characteristic colour patterns.

As a rule the sexes differ from one another in coloration, the males being, usually but not always, more intensely coloured. This is particularly so when they have the more active role in breeding, but the situation is completely reversed when the females play the leading role. Sometimes the coloration of the sexes is so different that they appear to belong to different species, but there are also species in which external sex differences are scarcely perceptible, and in extreme cases the sexes are only distinguishable at spawning time, from the differing shape of the genital papillae.

In the aquarium, breeding is usually quite easy, unless prevented by intolerant behaviour. Some partners are not compatible, and this applies as much to the dwarf cichlids as to the large species. The best method is to rear a group of young individuals together, so that they can choose their own partners. On the other hand, when the breeding pair has to be selected from adults the result may be successful, but there may also be serious quarrels that can lead to the death of the weaker partner. A peaceful bond may depend upon the female being ready to spawn, because the male often sees an unripe female as a rival rather than a partner. It is then best to separate the two fish by a sheet of glass until the female is really ready to spawn. In any case the weaker partner should always be introduced to the breeding tank a few days before the stronger.

As already mentioned, many cichlids establish a territory during the breeding period, in which they raise their brood. In a normal home aquarium the available space is usually not large enough for the requirements of the territory, and this leads to quarrels over the territorial boundaries. This certainly happens with the large cichlids, but also with smaller species when they are kept in a tank that is too restricted. Some cichlids destroy the tank plants, not because they are seeking food but because they are making strenuous efforts to

clean the spawning site and rid it of unwanted plants. In general the dwarf and smaller species do not molest well-rooted plants, provided the tank arrangement is sufficiently diverse.

In most cases cichlids will breed in a fully established aquarium tank. The following hints are intended to supplement the information given in the tables. Sometimes it may be necessary to remove eggs or fry from parents which are not tending them properly. In such cases the following procedure should be carried out.

The spawning underlay (rock, root, plant leaves) should be carefully transferred, if possible with some water, into an all-glass tank. This should then be filled with water from the spawning tank. The spawning underlay must be placed in the same position as it had in the spawning tank. Very light aeration close to the spawn will help to keep the water gently moving. To prevent the eggs becoming mouldy, the water can be dosed with a commercial preparation that inhibits bacteria and infusorians. Any eggs that do become mouldy must be removed with a pipette. The disinfectant is removed by filtration through activated charcoal shortly before the fry start to swim free. As soon as the fry have been feeding for a few days they can be transferred to a rearing tank, with water at the same temperature.

Z 12a: Actively burrowing cichlids that spawn on the substrate
These are generally large fish that require correspondingly spacious aquarium tanks. They burrow relentlessly, and re-arrange the tank to suit their own requirements, so the substrate should consist only of very clean, washed coarse sand or gravel. Hiding-places are essential, and these can be made from roots and rocks, sometimes even reeds. Rocks should be positioned firmly on the tank bottom, and if they are arranged to form caves they must be fixed so that they cannot topple over. As soon as the rocks have been suitably arranged, a deep layer of gravel can be spread around them.

Plants rooted in the bottom can be dispensed with but tough water plants in pots with coarse gravel to prevent them being dug up can be incorporated in the rockwork. Floating plants are also quite suitable and some aquarists allow the aerial roots of *Monstera* to grow down into the tank. These quickly produce dense tufts which also have the advantage of removing much of the dissolved organic waste from the water.

For planned breeding a compatible pair is placed in a tank, and quite soon these parent fish will start to prepare for spawning. With spread fins the male swims around the female and approaches her with a bobbing movement. The fish gently bite one another, swim round in circles and rub flanks. After some searching in which both sexes take part, a spawning site is chosen and carefully cleaned. This may be a rock, a root or other firm underlay, sometimes even the aquarium glass. Numerous pits are dug (some of which are not used) and a great deal of energy is expended. Plants may be dug up and leaves broken off. The eggs laid on the spawning site are tended by both parents in turn, and there is often division of labour, with the male guarding the whole territory while the female tends the spawn and fry. Mouldy eggs are picked out and the water is kept moving by beats of the pectoral fins. The number of eggs varies according to the species, age and size of the female; it may be from 300 to 1,000, or even more. The number is always less than would be produced by a species that spawns at random and does not protect the brood. The newly hatched fry are first moved into the pits where they are guarded, and as soon as they are free-swimming they follow the parents around. The fry instinctively keep in a little group and react to certain signs made by the parents. They are easy to rear as they will immediately take brine shrimp and other small live and dried foods. When the parent fish start preparations for a new brood, possibly after a few weeks, they or the fry should be removed from the tank. There is no point in the home aquarist raising large numbers of young cichlids, as these will only be difficult to dispose of.

Group Z 12a contains table numbers 179–193, 190, 191, 193–195 and 197.

Z 12b: Less actively burrowing cichlids that spawn in the substrate

This group contains large, small and very small fish. The volume of water in the tank will depend upon the size of the fish and the number of offspring expected, but it should not be too small. As the fish do not burrow very actively and thus do not disturb the vegetation, the tank can be planted in the normal way. Hiding-places needed by the fish are provided by rocks, roots and other decorative materials such as half coconut shells or reeds. The substrate can be of sand that is not too coarse. It is sufficient to have a top layer, a few centimetres thick, of carefully washed sand, while the lower layer need only be briefly rinsed. At the worst the fish will only dig a few shallow pits.

With certain reservations the species included in this group are far less aggressive than those in group Z 12a. However, during the periods of spawning both sexes become somewhat aggressive towards other members of their own species and towards other fish. At this time even dwarf cichlids become very quarrelsome. For instance, the brood-protecting females of *Nannacara anomala* will even attack larger fish and worry their male partners to death. In the dwarf cichlids and in certain West African species the female is the more active partner. In general their reproductive behaviour is more or less the same as in the large cichlids. This also applies to angelfish *(Pterophyllum)* which, like the discus fish, spawn on leaves. The latter produce a skin secretion which wholly or partly serves to nourish the fry during their first weeks.

Generally speaking, the larger cichlids have no special requirements as regards the composition of the water, but there are a few species in this group which need soft, perhaps even slightly acid water. In many species the number of offspring is not very large.

Group Z 12b contains the following table numbers 178, 180, 183–187, 192, 196, 198–200, 210–213, 217–223, 232, 235–237.

Z 13: Burrowing and non-burrowing mouthbrooding cichlids

For mouthbrooding cichlids the tank should be set up as described for group Z 12b. Only those species that burrow very actively should be accommodated as recommended for group Z 12a. The substrate should consist of sand or gravel that is not too coarse, because the mouthbrooders dig pits in which spawning takes place.

In African mouthbrooders a certain ritual has been developed. The male first digs a shallow depression in the sand. He then entices the female there. After spawning the eggs are either fertilized immediately and then taken into the female's mouth, or they are taken up first and fertilization takes place somewhat later. In the latter case the anal fin of the male concerned has so-called egg spots, also known

No.	Scientific name	Popular name	Distribution	Length cm	Characteristics	Sex differences
178	*Aequidens curviceps*	Flag cichlid	Amazon region	♂ 7 (2.7 in) ♀ 6 (2.4 in)	Peaceful fish, scarcely digs	♂ more colourful, dorsal and anal fins pointed
179	*Aequidens itanyi*	Green acara	Northern South America	14 (5.5 in)	Relatively peaceful, scarcely digs	♂ with pointed dorsal and anal fins
180	*Aequidens maronii*	Keyhole cichlid	Surinam, Guyana	♂ 10 (3.9 in) ♀ 8 (3 in)	One of the most tolerant cichlids, does not dig or attack the plants	Old ♂♂ have elongated fin tips
181	*Aequidens portalegrensis*	Port acara	Brazil, Paraguay, Bolivia	15 (6 in)	Rather intolerant, likes to dig, but there are individual differences	♂ more colourful, fin tips more elongated
182	*Aequidens pulcher*	Blue acara	Colombia, Rio Magdalena, Panama	15 (6 in)	Relatively peaceful, does not dig much	♂ more colourful, fins rather more elongated. ♀ often with transverse bars
183	*Apistogramma agassizi*	Agassiz's dwarf cichlid	Central Amazon, Rio Paraguay	♂ 8 (3 in) ♀ 5 (1.9 in)	Peaceful, does not dig, but ♂ rather aggressive at spawning time	Sexes very different in coloration. When protecting brood ♀ is yellow
184	*Apistogramma ortmanni*	Ortmann's dwarf cichlid	Northern South America and central Amazon	♂ 7 (2.7 in) ♀ 5 (1.9 in)	Peaceful, likes to hide	Sexes very different in coloration. ♀ at spawning time is bright yellow

238

as egg dummies. The female is attracted to these and snaps at them. At the same moment the male releases sperm, which is drawn into the female's mouth, where it fertilizes the eggs. The eggs and fry remain for ten to twenty-five days in the mouth of the female, who may or may not feed during this period. The fry are released when they are completely free-swimming. They then feed immediately on tiny food such as brine shrimp nauplii. At night or when in danger, the fry will still seek shelter in the mother's mouth.

After spawning the male should be removed from the tank, or if this is not possible the female should be taken out. This requires great care, and a net should not be used, as the female may release the eggs from her mouth. It is best to take her up as gently as possible in a glass vessel. In very spacious tanks with numerous hiding-places the breeding pair can be left together.

Group Z 13 contains the following table numbers: 189, 201–205, 209, 214–216, 226–231, 233, 238, 239.

Maintenance	Breeding	Diet	Page/ Figure
TS III/IV. Pg. 8. 23–25 °C (73–77 °F). Frequent partial water changes	Z 12b. Sexes 1/1. 26–28 °C (78–82 °F). TS IV. Some pairs are bad at tending the brood	Live and dried food	XIV/1
TS IV/V. Pg. 10. Frequent partial water changes. 22–25 °C (71–77 °F), MT 16 °C (60 °F)	Z 12a or 12b. TS V. Fairly productive	Abundant live and dried food	234/6
TS IV/V. Pg. 8 or 9. 23–26 °C (73–78 °F), MT 20 °C (68 °F)	Z 12b. May be difficult, not all pairs are compatible. 24–26 °C (75–78 °F). Young tended for a long time	Abundant live and dried food	XIV/4
TS IV/V. Pg. 10. 22–26 °C (71–78 °F), MT 16 °C (60 °F)	Z 12a or b. Can sometimes be bred in a fully planted tank, if the plants are well rooted	Abundant live and dried food	252/8
TS IV/V. Pg. 10. Plants in pots, covered with stones. 23–26 °C (73–78 °F), MT 16 °C (60 °F)	Z 12a. 25–26 °C (77–78 °F). Fairly productive	Abundant live and dried food	XIII/4
TS III/IV. Pg. 8, with roots, rocks, caves. 23–26 °C (73–78 °F), MT 20 °C (68 °F). Water up to 10 °dH. May be sensitive to chemicals in the water	Z 12b. Eggs attached to roof of a cave. ♀ tends spawn and fry, latter up to 3 weeks. 200 young. Remove ♂. Not all individuals tend the brood	Live and dried food	XI/7
TS II/III. Pg. 8. As No. 183. 23–26 °C (73–78 °F), not below 22 °C (71 °F)	Z 12b. 27–30 °C (80–86 °F). As No. 183	Live and dried food	

No.	Scientific name	Popular name	Distribution	Length cm	Characteristics	Sex differences
185	*Apistogramma ramirezi*	Ramirez's dwarf cichlid	Orinoco region, may be more widely distributed	♂ 6 (2.4 in) ♀ 5 (1.9 in)	Peaceful, active, playful	Sexes with similar coloration. ♂ with elongated 1st fin rays
186	*Apistogramma reitzigi*	Yellow dwarf cichlid	Region of central Rio Paraguay	♂ 6 (2.4 in) ♀ 4 (1.5 in)	Peaceful, undemanding	Sexes very different in coloration. ♂ with tall dorsal fin, ♀ bright yellow at spawning time
187	*Apistogramma trifasciatum*	Blue apistogramma	Amazon region	♂ 5 (1.9 in) ♀ 4 (1.5 in)	Temperamental, not very peaceful at spawning time	♂ with elongated front fin rays. ♀ yellowish at spawning time
188	*Astronotus ocellatus*	Oscar	Amazon region	30 (11.8 in)	Robust digger, becoming predatory with age	Little difference, except shape of genital papilla
189	*Aulonocara nyassae*	African peacock	Lake Malawi	15 (6 in)	Keep in groups, also with other Malawi mouthbrooders	♂ with blue, green, red iridescence. ♀ grey-brown with stripe pattern
190	*Cichlasoma cyanoguttatum*	Rio Grande perch	N. Mexico, southern U.S.A.	25 (9.8 in)	Boisterous, likes to dig	♂ more colourful, bulging forehead develops with age. ♀ more squat
191	*Cichlasoma facetum*	Chanchito	S. Brazil, Uruguay, Argentina	25 (9.8 in)	Boisterous, likes to dig	Only small differences. ♂ rather more colourful, the fins slightly pointed
192	*Cichlasoma festivum*	Festivum	Guyana south to La Plata region	♂ 15 (6 in) ♀ 12 (4.7 in)	Peaceful, does not dig. Good for a tank with *Pterophyllum*	Difficult to tell apart. ♂ with blue-green throat, dorsal and anal fins pointed. ♀ more squat
193	*Cichlasoma meeki*	Firemouth cichlid	Guatemala, Yucatan	♂ 15 (6 in) ♀ 10 (3.9 in)	Relatively peaceful, except at spawning time. Some like to dig	♂ more colourful, dorsal fin pointed
194	*Cichlasoma nigrofasciatum*	Zebra cichlid	Guatemala	♂ 15 (6 in) ♀ 10 (3.9 in)	Relatively peaceful, except at spawning time	Only small differences. ♂ rather more colourful, dorsal fin may be more pointed

Maintenance	Breeding	Diet	Page/Figure
TS III. Pg. 8. 22–26 °C (71–78 °F). Clear water up to 12 °dH	Z 12b. 25–30 °C (77–86 °F), not above 8 °dH. Spawns on rocks or in pits. Both parents protect brood. Fry take brine shrimp immediately, but are sensitive and grow slowly	Live and dried food	XI/5
TS II/III. Pg. 8. Roots and rocks for shelter. 21–25 °C (69–77 °F). No special water requirements	Z 12b. Eggs attached to roof of a cave, tended by ♀ alone. ♂ can be removed after spawning	Live and dried food	XIII/3
TS III. Pg. 8. 22–24 °C (71–75 °F). Water composition not critical	Z 12b. 23–24 °C (73–75 °F), not higher. As No. 183	Live and dried food	234/7
TS V. Rocks and roots, no plants. 22–26 °C (71–78 °F), MT 16 °C (60 °F)	Z 12a. 26–28 °C (78–82 °F). Very productive. Young with colours differing from those of adults	Abundant live and dried food, fish	XIV/9
TS V. Can be planted. Roots and flat stones for shelter. 24–26 °C (75–78 °F), MT 20 °C (68 °F)	Z 13. Mouthbrooder. 20–50 fry released from parent's mouth after 22 days incubation	Abundant live and dried food	
TS V. Rocks and roots, no plants. 22–26 °C (71–78 °F), MT 18 °C (64 °F)	Z 12a. 24–25 °C (75–77 °F). Very productive	Abundant live and dried food	260/3
TS V. Rocks and roots, no plants. 17–23 °C (62–73 °F), MT 12 °C (53 °F)	Z 12a. 21–24 °C (69–75 °F). Very productive	Abundant live and dried food	XI/1
TS V/VI. Pg. 9. Hiding-places, good light, 25 °C (77 °F). No soft plants as the species eats the fresh shoots	Z 12b. 25–28 °C (77–82 °F). Large tank with *Echinodorus* plant on which up to 400 eggs are laid. Fry hang by filaments from plant. Both parents tend the brood	Live and dried food, plant matter	XII/1
TS IV/V. Pg. 10. Plants in pots, covered with stones. 22–24 °C (71–75 °F)	Z 12a. 24–26 °C (75–78 °F). Fairly productive. Young grow fast	Abundant live and dried food	XIII/1
TS IV/V. Pg. 10. 20–24 °C (68–75 °F), MT 16 °C (60 °F). Not all dig vigorously. Plants in pots, covered with stones	Z 12a. 22–26 °C (71–78 °F). Parents usually tend the brood very assiduously	Abundant live and dried food	252/9

No.	Scientific name	Popular name	Distribu-tion	Length cm	Characteristics	Sex differences
195	*Cichlasoma octofasciatum* (formerly *C. biocellatum*)	Jack Dempsey	Guatemala, Costa Rica, Amazon region	20 (7.8 in)	Boisterous, likes to dig	♂ more colourful, ♀ more yellowish with dark transverse bars
196	*Cichlasoma severum*	Banded cichlid	Northern South America	20 (7.8 in)	Peaceful, but aggressive at spawning time. Digs actively	♂ more colourful, with more pronounced red dot pattern
197	*Cichlasoma spilurum*		Central America	12 (4.7 in)	Relatively peaceful, digs only a little and respects the plants	♂ more colourful
198	*Crenicara filamentosa*	Chessboard cichlid	Central Amazon	♂ 10 (3.9 in) ♀ 6 (2.4 in)	Peaceful, does not dig	♂ with elongated dorsal, caudal and anal fins. ♀ with deep red ventral fins
199	*Crenicichla lepidota*	Pike cichlid	Eastern tropical South America	Up to 20 (7.8 in)	Predatory, with pike-like habits. Lurks among roots, plants for prey	♂ rather more colourful, the dorsal and anal fins slightly pointed. Otherwise few differences
200	*Etroplus maculatus*	Orange chromide	India, Sri Lanka	8 (3 in)	Peaceful, non-digging. Only attacks the plants when the diet is deficient in plant matter	♂ a beautiful golden-yellow, ♀ always paler and somewhat smaller
201	*Geophagus balzani*		Southern South America, Paraguay	15 (6 in)	Peaceful, but continually burrowing in the substrate so only use tough plants	♂ with a large forehead bump and blue-green dots on anal and ventral fins
202	*Geophagus jurupari*	Earth-eater	Amazon region	Over 20 (7.8 in)	Peaceful, but sometimes digs very actively	Forehead bump more developed in ♂
203	*Geophagus steindachneri* (= *G. hondae*)		South America, exact location unknown	Up to 15 (6 in)	Peaceful, but sometimes very aggressive towards its own kind	♂ with a red forehead bump
204	*Geophagus surinamensis*	Surinam earth-eater	Northern South America, Guyana	Over 20 (7.8 in)	Peaceful, but aggressive at spawning time	♂ larger, no reliable colour differences

Maintenance	Breeding	Diet	Page/Figure
TS V. Rocks and roots, no plants. 22–24 °C (71–75 °F)	Z 12a. 25–28 °C (77–82 °F). Very productive. Very aggressive at spawning time	Abundant live and dried food	XIV/5
TS V. Rocks and roots, no plants. 24–28 °C (75–82 °F), MT 21 °C (69 °F)	Z 12a. 25–28 °C (77–82 °F). May be very productive.	Abundant live and dried food	XI/2
TS IV/V. Pg. 10. 22–24 °C (71–75 °F), MT 15 °C (59 °F)	Z 12b. 26 °C (78 °F). Likes to spawn in plant shade, but prefers caves	Abundant live and dried food	
TS III/IV. Pg. 8, densely planted. Roots, rock for shelter. 23–26 °C (73–78 °F). Sensitive to water pollution	Z 12b. 26 °C (78 °F). Sexes 1/1, ♀ being more active. Spawns in caves (flowerpots, coconut shells). ♀ only tends the brood	Live and possibly dried food	
TS V. Pg. 9. 24–27 °C (75–80 °F), MT 21 °C (69 °F). Some dense planting. Rocks, roots essential for shelter. A good tank lid as the fish likes to jump. Separate off immature ♀♀ with a glass pane	Z 12b. 26–28 °C (78–82 °F). Sexes 1/1. Very large breeding tank. Spawns on rocks, ♂ tends brood alone, so remove ♀. Very productive	Only abundant live food, including fish	XII/2
TS IV/V. Pg. 12. 22–25 °C (71–77 °F). Hiding-places. Frequent partial water changes. Also small amount of salt or alternation of fresh and weak brackish water	Z 12b. 25–30 °C (77–86 °F). Productive, up to 300 young, tended by both parents. Add 5% sea water, otherwise young are very sensitive	Live and dried food	XI/6
TS IV/V. 25–30 °C (77–86 °F), MT 20 °C (68 °F). Plants will be dug up unless well anchored	Z 12a. 25–30 °C (77–86 °F). Spawns on flat rocks, guarded by ♀ alone, who keeps young in her mouth for 10 days after hatching. Very productive	Abundant live and dried food	
As No. 201	As No. 201	Abundant live and dried food	
TS IV, plants not attacked. Chews its way through the substrate. 20–26 °C (68–78 °F)	As No. 201. Eggs often taken up by ♀ just after being laid and then released after 10–15 days	Abundant live and dried food	
TS V, plants not attacked. 25–30 °C (77–86 °F)	As No. 201	Abundant live and dried food	

No.	Scientific name	Popular name	Distribution	Length cm	Characteristics	Sex differences
205	*Haplochromis burtoni*	Burton's mouthbrooder	Lake Chad and upper Nile	♂ 10 (3.9 in) ♀ 8 (3 in)	Rather robust, mouth-brooding fish. At spawning time ♂ very aggressive towards	♂ with egg dummies on the anal fin, which play important role in the fertilization of the eggs in the mouth of ♀
206	*Hemichromis bimaculatus*	Jewel cichlid	Senegal to Congo and Nile, also Sahara oases	15 (6 in)	Quarrelsome, actively digging fish	Difficult to distinguish except by form of genital papilla. ♂ often more colourful
207	*Hemichromis fasciatus*	Banded jewelfish	Senegal to Congo	15 (6 in)	One of the most boisterous cichlids. Digs actively	Few differences. ♂ rather more slender
208	*Herotilapia multispinosa*	Rainbow cichlid	Central America	12 (4.7 in)	Peaceful, vegetarian. Does not dig much	♂ larger, with pointed dorsal and anal fins
209	*Iodotropheus sprengerae* (formerly *Melanochromis brevis*)	Red-brown mouthbrooder	Lake Malawi	♂ 12 (4.7 in) ♀ 8 (3 in)	As for No. 228	♂ usually with 2 yellow spots (egg dummies) on anal fin
210	*Julidochromis marlieri*	Marlier's julie	Lake Tanganyika	7–10 (2.7– 3.9 in)	Peaceful as pairs, but quarrelsome territorially	Not certain. Allow pairs to form naturally
211	*Julidochromis ornatus*	Golden julie	Lake Tanganyika	7–10 (2.7– 3.9 in)	As No. 210	As No. 210
212	*Julidochromis regani*	Regan's julie	Lake Tanganyika	7–10 (2.7– 3.9 in)	As No. 210	As No. 210
213	*Julidochromis transcriptus*	Black-and-white julie	Lake Tanganyika	7–10 (2.7– 3.9 in)	As No. 210	As No. 210
214	*Labeotropheus fuelleborni*	Fuelleborn's cichlid	Lake Malawi	♂ 15 (6 in) ♀ 12 (4.7 in)	Aggressive in a small tank. Best kept, several together, in a rocky tank with plenty of hiding-places	Widely differing coloration. ♂ with spots (egg dummies) on the anal fin

Maintenance	Breeding	Diet	Page/Figure
TS IV/V. Pg. 10. 25 °C (77 °F). Not particularly sensitive to temperature fluctuation. Sand substrate, rocks, roots for shelter	Z 13. 25 °C (77 °F). As for No. 226. Eggs fertilized in the mouth of ♀	Live and dried food	260/1
TS IV/V. 20–24 °C (68–75 °F). Clean, washed sand, no plants. Rocks and roots for shelter are essential	Z 12a. 26 °C (78 °F). Most pairs tend the brood well, when compatible. Very productive	Abundant live and dried food	XIV/7
TS IV/V. 22–24 °C (71–75 °F). Numerous hiding-places are essential	Z 12a. 25–28 °C (77–82 °F). Difficult to make up a pair owing to intransigence of the fish, but may be very productive	Abundant live and dried food	252/10
TS IV/V. 22–26 °C (71–78 °F). Only tough-leaved plants. Several hiding-places are essential	Z 12a. 25–28 °C (77–82 °F). Allow pairs to form naturally. Very productive	Live food and plant matter	
As No. 228	As No. 228	Abundant live and dried food	
TS III/IV. 22–24 °C (71–75 °F). No soft water. Plants not damaged. Small caves under flat stones used as territories	Spawns in the caves. Often several broods of different ages grow up together. Only becomes aggressive at sexual maturity and with territorial demands	Live and dried food	
As No. 210	As No. 210	Live and dried food	
As No. 210	As No. 210	Live and dried food	
As No. 210	As No. 210	Live and dried food	
As No. 228	As No. 228	Live and dried food	260/2

No.	Scientific name	Popular name	Distribution	Length cm	Characteristics	Sex differences
215	*Labeotropheus trewavasae*	Trewavas's cichlid	Lake Malawi	♂ 15 (6 in) ♀ 12 (4.7 in)	As No. 214	♂ with blue body and red fins. ♀ have differing coloration according to the population
216	*Labidochromis vellicans*		Lake Malawi	♂ 15 (6 in) ♀ 12 (4.7 in)	As No. 214	♂ with egg dummies on the anal fin
217	*Lamprologus brichardi*	Princess of Burundi	Lake Tanganyika	♂ 10 (3.9 in) ♀ 8 (3 in)	Peaceful, but quarrel among themselves	Very uncertain. Allow pairs to form naturally
218	*Lamprologus congolensis*	Congo lamprologus	Congo lower reaches	♂ 15 (6 in) ♀ 7 (2.7 in)	♂ very quarrelsome, solitary, establishes a territory	♂ with shiny golden scales
219	*Lamprologus elongatus*		Lake Tanganyika	Over 15 (6 in)	Very predatory. Only keep with others when young	♂ larger. Insignificant colour differences
220	*Nannacara anomala*	Golden-eyed dwarf cichlid	Northern South America	♂ 7 (2.7 in) ♀ 4 (1.5 in)	Peaceful outside the breeding period, when ♀ becomes very aggressive, particularly towards the ♂	Sexes with completely different coloration. ♀ dark at spawning time
221	*Nanochromis nudiceps*	Blue Congo dwarf cichlid	Congo region	7 (2.7 in)	Very territorial fish. Territories are keenly guarded	♀ rather more colourful, with striking emerald-green belly
222	*'Pelmatochromis' thomasi*	Thomasi cichlid	Tropical West Africa	♂ 8 (3 in) ♀ 6 (2.4 in)	Relatively peaceful. Does not dig or attack the plants	No great colour differences. Dorsal fin of ♂ somewhat pointed
223	*Pelvicachromis pulcher*	Kribensis	West Africa, Niger region	9 (3.5 in)	In general, peaceful and does not dig	♂ rather smaller and more intensely coloured

Maintenance	Breeding	Diet	Page/Figure
As No. 228	As No. 228	Live and dried food	
As No. 228	As No. 228	Live and dried food	
TS IV. 22–26 °C (71–78 °F). No soft water. Plants not damaged. Let fish form defined territories	Spawns in small caves. Young tended by ♀ about 3 days after hatching. Several broods of different ages grow up together, without the older young becoming aggressive	Abundant live food	
Tank with large area and shallow water. 24–28 °C (75–82 °F). Provide several territorial sites, even for only 1 pair	Spawns under flat stones. Brood protection almost exclusively by ♀	Abundant live and dried food	
TS V, 24–28 °C (75–82 °F), the territories to form with dense vegetation	Spawns on flat rocks, about 400 eggs hatch in 3 days, take first food after 5 more days	Abundant live food, including fish	
TS III. Pg. 9, with some densely planted areas. Hiding-places. 23–25 °C (73–77 °F)	Z 12b. 24–26 °C (75–78 °F). ♀ protects brood alone, and is then very aggressive towards ♂, which should be removed immediately after spawning. Careful brood protection. Young not difficult to rear	Live and dried food	XI/4
TS IV. Pg. 8, densely planted. Numerous hiding-places (roots, plants, coconut shells, flowerpots etc.). 24 °C (75 °F). Soft, peat-filtered water enhances the coloration	Z 12b. Sexes 1/1. Before spawning, several small pits are dug in the sand of a cave. The eggs are attached to the roof of a cave, and hatch in about 1 week. Fry take brine shrimp immediately. 24–28 °C (75–82 °F). Brood tended by the more active ♀	Live and dried food, algae, plant matter	253/12
TS IV. Pg. 8, with some densely planted areas. Roots, rocks, plants for hiding-places. 22–26 °C (71–78 °F). No special water requirements	Z 12b. Not particularly difficult. Spawns on rocks or other firm objects. Up to 500 young, not difficult to rear	Live and dried food	260/6
As for No. 221	Z 12b. Sexes 1/1. 25–28 °C (77–82 °F). As No. 221	Live and dried food	XII/4

No.	Scientific name	Popular name	Distribution	Length cm	Characteristics	Sex differences
224	*Pelvicachromis subocellatus*		Congo region	10 (3.9 in)	As No. 223	♂ inconspicuous, ♀ colourful. Scales around the belly marking are silvery to shiny golden-red
225	*Pelvicachromis taeniatus*	Striped pelvicachromis	Nigeria, Ghana	♂ 8 (3 in) ♀ 6 (2.4 in)	As No. 223	♂ with a different pattern, particularly on the caudal fin, and with pointed dorsal and anal fins. ♀ sometimes more colourful
226	*Pseudocrenilabrus multicolor*	Egyptian mouthbrooder	Nile region	7 (2.7 in)	Relatively peaceful outside the breeding season. ♂ very aggressive towards ♀ at spawning time	♂ more brightly coloured. Throat sac more prominent in the ♀
227	*Pseudocrenilabrus philander*		South and central Africa, in several local forms	8 (3 in)	As No. 226	♂ with red tip to anal fin
228	*Pseudotropheus auratus*	Malawi golden cichlid	Lake Malawi	♂ 12 (4.7 in) ♀ 8 (3 in)	Temperamental, sometimes intolerant. Best kept as a group in a spacious tank with several hiding-places	♂ with spots (egg dummies) on anal fin, generally blue. ♀ golden-yellow. Subordinate ♂♂ coloured as ♀
229	*Pseudotropheus elongatus*	Slender pseudotropheus	Lake Malawi	♂ 12 (4.7 in) ♀ 10 (3.9 in)	As No. 228	♂ more grey-blue, ♀ brownish
230	*Pseudotropheus tropheops*		Lake Malawi, several populations	13 (5.1 in)	As No. 228	♂ darker, ♀ yellow to orange-red

Maintenance	Breeding	Diet	Page/Figure
As No. 221	As No. 221	Live and dried food	
As No. 221	Z 12b. 25–28 °C (77–82 °F). As No. 221	Live and dried food	
TS III. Pg. 8, densely planted. 20–23 °C (68–73 °F). Numerous hiding-places (rocks, roots). Clean sand substrate	Z 13. 24–26 °C (75–78 °F). ♂ makes shallow depressions in the sand. At spawning the fish 'creep' round one another in circles, as the eggs are fertilized and taken into the mouth of the ♀. During the incubation period the ♀ does not feed. Young leave mouth of ♀ after about 11 days. There may be 30–100 young, which for a further week retreat to mouth of ♀ at night or when in danger, until this is no longer spacious enough. Young take brine shrimp immediately. ♂ must be removed from the tank after spawning	Live and dried food	XI/3
As No. 226	As No. 226	Live and dried food	
TS V. Pg. 8. 24 °C (75 °F). No soft water. Numerous hiding-places (rocks, roots) are essential	Z 13. The relatively few eggs are incubated in the mouth of the ♀, which continues to feed at this time. The young leave the mouth after about 4 weeks, but are still kept together for a further 2 weeks. Easy to rear	Live and dried food, plant matter	260/7
As no. 228	As No. 228	Live and dried food, plant matter	
As No. 228	As No. 228	Live and dried food, plant matter	

No.	Scientific name	Popular name	Distribu-tion	Length cm	Characteristics	Sex differences
231	*Pseudotropheus zebra*	Malawi blue cichlid	Lake Mala-wi, several populations	12 (4.7 in)	As No. 228	♂ blue to brilliant whitish blue, ♀ grey-blue, or spotted or orange-red

(All species of *Pseudotropheus* are best kept as one ♂ with several ♀♀, as a ♂ ready to spawn tends to concentrate his aggression on a single ♀ which may be seriously damaged.)

No.	Scientific name	Popular name	Distribu-tion	Length cm	Characteristics	Sex differences
232	*Pterophyllum scalare*	Angelfish	Amazon region	15 long (6 in) 25 tall (9.8 in)	May be rather ag-gressive during the breeding period. Should not be kept with much smaller fish. Best kept to-gether with *Cichla-soma festivum* and other large peaceful fish	Only distinguishable with certainty by the form of the genital papilla at spawning time. ♂ usually has a distinctly convex forehead, while that of ♀ is almost straight

(Selected forms include: black scalare, marbled, golden, smoky, silver, moon, ghost, veiltail and others.)

No.	Scientific name	Popular name	Distribu-tion	Length cm	Characteristics	Sex differences
233	*Sarotherodon mossambicus* (formerly *Tilapia*)	Mozambique mouthbrooder	Southern Africa	25 (9.8 in)	Boisterous. Digs actively	♂ in the breeding period deep black with white breast and throat
234	*Steatocranus casuarius*	African blockhead	Middle Congo rapids	10 (3.9 in)	Relatively peaceful bottom-living and cave-dwelling fish, best kept only with members of its own species	♂ somewhat larger, the frontal bulge be-coming larger with age
235	*Symphysodon aequifasciata axelrodi*	Brown discus	Middle Amazon	20 (7.8 in)	Peaceful and sensi-tive to disturbances. A selective feeder. May also be suscep-tible to certain dis-eases	Difficult to distin-guish, and with cer-tainty only by the form of the genital papilla at spawning time

(The genus contains several brightly coloured species, subspecies and colour variants, which cannot all be considered here.)

No.	Scientific name	Popular name	Distribu-tion	Length cm	Characteristics	Sex differences
236	*Telmatochromis bifrenatus*		Lake Tan-ganyika	♂ 10 (3.9 in) ♀ 6 (2.4 in)	As No. 210	♂ considerably larger. No signifi-cant colour differ-ences

Maintenance	Breeding	Diet	Page/ Figure
As No. 228	As No. 228	Live and dried food, plant matter	
TS VI. Pg 9. 24–26 °C (75–78 °F) Keep with tall plants. Needs warmth	Z 12b. Sexes 1/1. Up to 30 °C (86 °F). Success depends upon having a compatible pair. Spawns on strong stems or leaves of water plants, but also tank glass or tubing. Unfortunately many pairs do not tend the brood, which must then be reared artificially. Normally brood protection is as captivating as in other non-mouthbrooding cichlids	Live and dried food, likes to eat other fish	XIII/2
TS V. 18–24 °C (64–75 °F). Only washed gravel and stones. Aeration and good filtration are essential. Provide hiding-places for ♀	Z 13. Sexes 1/1. 25 °C (77 °F). ♀ incubates about 12–14 days and tends the young for a few more days. Remove ♂ after spawning	Abundant live and dried food	XII/3
TS IV/V. Pg. 10. Gravel substrate and rocks arranged to form small caves. Likes to dig out cavities below the rocks. Inverted flowerpots are also very suitable	Z 12b. Sexes 1/1. Spawns in caves, both parents tending the brood. The young remain at first in the cave, where they are supplied with fresh water and food. Later they are taken out and brought back at night. Not difficult to rear	Live and dried food	260/5
TS VI. Pg. 9, with tall-growing plants. 25–27 °C (77–80 °F), MT 24 °C (75 °F). Must have plants and roots for hiding-places. Soft, slightly acid, peat-filtered water	Z 12b. 28–30 °C (82–86 °F). Soft water. At one time difficult to breed but no longer so. Spawns on leaves or other firm objects. Newly hatched fry hang from the leaves, later usually tended by both parents. At first they feed almost exclusively, later partly, on a skin secretion of the parents. On the whole not difficult to rear		
As No. 210	As No. 210	Live and dried food	

No.	Scientific name	Popular name	Distribu-tion	Length cm	Characteristics	Sex differences
237	*Thysia ansorgii* (formerly *Pelmatochromis annectens)*		West Africa, coastal areas	♂ 13 (5.1 in) ♀ 8 (3 in)	As No. 223	♀ with shiny scales in the anal region
238	*Tropheus moorii*		Lake Tan-ganyika, several lo-cal forms	12 (4.7 in)	Single fish are intol-erant. Keep 10–15 of each sex to ob-serve interesting group structure	Very uncertain. ♂ with longer ventral fins
239	*Tropheus duboisi*		Lake Tan-ganyika	10 (3.9 in)	The young are soli-tary and find their own mate	♂ with flatter belly and elongated ven-tral fins

Maintenance	Breeding	Diet	Page/Figure
As No. 223	Spawns in caves, as No. 223	Live and dried food	
TS VI/VII. 24–28 °C (75–82 °F). Otherwise as No. 217	Mouthbrooder laying few, very large eggs. Fry are released after about 30 days, when approx. 15 mm (0.6 in) long	Live and dried food	
TS V/VI. Otherwise as No. 217	As No. 238	Live and dried food	

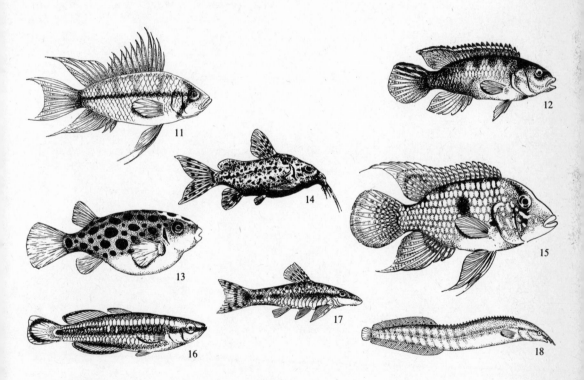

1 *Nothobranchius guentheri*, Guenther's nothobranchius (–) 2 *Rivulus milesi*, yellowtail panchax (131) 3 *Dermogenys pusillus*, half-beak (153) 4 *Betta taeniata*, striped fighting fish (–) 5 *Ophicephalus striatus*, striped snake-head (168) 6 *Trichopsis pumilus*, pygmy gourami (176) 7 *Luciocephalus pulcher*, pike-head (165) 8 *Aequidens portalegrensis*, port acara (181) 9 *Cichlasoma nigrofasciatum*, zebra cichlid (194) 10 *Hemichromis fasciatus*, banded jewelfish (207) 11 *Apistogramma cacatuoides*, cockatoo dwarf cichlid (–) 12 *Nanochromis nudiceps*, blue Congo dwarf cichlid (221) 13 *Tetraodon fluviatilis*, green pufferfish (249) 14 *Synodontis nigriventris*, upside-down catfish (275) 15 *Geophagus brasiliensis*, pearl cichlid (–) 16 *Bedotia geayi*, Madagascar rainbow fish (251) 17 *Otocinclus flexilis*, sucker catfish (272) 18 *Mastacembelus pancalus*, spotted spiny eel (286)

Other perch-like fishes

These are elongated to tall, more or less laterally compressed fish. The anal and dorsal fins have an anterior spiny and a posterior soft-rayed part. In some species there is a gap between the two parts of the dorsal fin. Many species are predatory or feed on invertebrates, but some are food specialists, for instance they are algae eaters.

Apart from the true perches of the family Percidae, only a few of which are suitable for a home tank, aquarists are primarily interested in sunfish (Centrarchidae), nandids (Nandidae), glassfish (Centropomidae), archerfish (Toxotidae) and argusfish (Scatophagidae). The pufferfish described in the table do not, in fact, belong among the perch-like fish, but are included here for the sake of convenience.

The true perches (Percidae), of which a few are included in the table of cold-water fish, are distributed throughout the northern hemisphere. The long, laterally compressed body is covered with ctenoid scales. The edges of the gill covers have spiny processes, and the dentition is well developed. The two dorsal fins are separated from one another, or almost so. These are essentially predatory fish which feed on other fish and on large aquatic insects.

The sunfish (Centrarchidae) are widely distributed in the fresh waters of North America. The body is moderately elongated or tall, with marked lateral compression. The numerous teeth are small and pointed. The two parts of the dorsal fin are not separated. Sunfish practise a superficial form of brood protection in that the eggs are guarded and fanned until they hatch. A few species of the genus *Elas-*

No.	Scientific name	Popular name	Distribution	Length cm	Characteristics	Sex differences
240	*Badis badis*	Badis	India, S.E. Asia	♂ 7 (2.7 in) ♀ 5 (1.9 in)	Very peaceful, retiring fish	♂ more colourful, ♀ brownish with rounded belly
241	*Carino-tetraodon somphongsi*	Thai pufferfish	Thailand (in fresh water)	6.5 (2.5 in)	Not very tolerant. Likes to remain near the bottom, with hiding-places which are defended	♂ dorsal fin red and when excited a red knife-like ridge develops on the belly
242	*Chanda ranga*	Indian glassfish	India, Bengal, Burma	5 (1.9 in)	Peaceful, sometimes active, but also rather timid fish	♂ intense golden, the dorsal and anal fins with a sky-blue border
243	*Elassoma evergladei*	Everglades pygmy sunfish	Florida	3 (1.1 in)	Peaceful, best kept in a species tank, otherwise becomes shy and colourless	♂ almost blue-black. ♀ brownish and stouter

soma live in the swampy part of Florida, where they lead a sheltered existence in quiet, shallow waters, seeking shelter in the dense vegetation.

The nandids (Nandidae) comprise only a few of the species found in the tropics of America, Africa and Asia. Most species are small, retiring fish with well-camouflaged bodies, which stalk or lie in wait for prey. In doing so they use the very transparent soft parts of the unpaired fins to move forward.

The glassfish (Centropomidae, formerly Ambassidae) are small, perch-like fish found in Australia and south-east Asia, where they live in fresh and brackish waters. Some species are very common in their home waters. The body is more or less glassy and transparent, and the two dorsal fins are joined together.

The archerfish (Toxotidae) comprise a few species from the coastal waters of the Indian Ocean and parts of the South Pacific. They are represented in the tables by a single species. They are essentially surface-living fish which in the wild usually live in brackish waters. Their most remarkable characteristic is the method of catching prey. They shoot down insects sitting on leaves by spitting well-aimed drops of water.

Of the argusfish (Scatophagidae) the species *Scatophagus argus* is occasionally kept in a freshwater aquarium, but it does not thrive there for very long. Like the preceding species, it belongs among those fish which are best kept in a separate brackish water tank to simulate their natural environment.

In the table the species are arranged alphabetically without reference to their family. The table ends with five species of the family Atherinidae.

Maintenance	Breeding	Diet	Page/Figure
TS I/II. Pg. 8, densely planted, floating plants. Peat substrate. Rocks, roots, flowerpots, coconut shells for shelter	Sexes 1/1. 24–28 °C (75–82 °F). Spawns in cover, the eggs attached to the cave roof as the fish encircle one another. Spawn protected by ♂. Fry easy to rear on brine shrimp. Remove ♂ after fry swim out	Small live food	XIV/8
TS IV/V. Pg. 10, densely planted. 24–28 °C (75–82 °F). Fresh water. Rocks and roots to provide hiding-places	So far not much success in breeding. Active mating with ♂ gripping ♀ with his jaws. Young free-swimming a few days after the spawning. Not yet reared successfully	Snails, worms, mosquito larvae, water insects, plants, dried food	
TS II/III. Pg. 8, densely planted. 18–25 °C (64–77 °F). Likes bright light, also half shade from floating plants. Rocks and roots for shelter. Some aquarists add a little salt to the water	Sexes 1/1. 24–26 °C (75–78 °F). Spawns especially on roots of floating fern. Eggs hatch in 24 hours. Very small fry difficult to rear as they need to be surrounded by tiny live food. Cyclops nauplii may attack fry	Fine live food	XIV/3
TS I/II. Pg. 11, with dense clumps of fine-leaved plants. Fine sand substrate, clear oxygen-rich water. 18–23 °C (64–73 °F), MT 10 °C (50 °F)	TS III. 20–22 °C (68–71 °F). Use several pairs. Spawns in plant thickets. Eggs hatch in 2–3 days. The parents can remain in the tank	Fine live food	XIV/2

No.	Scientific name	Popular name	Distribu-tion	Length cm	Characteristics	Sex differences
244	*Enneacanthus obesus*	Blue-spotted sunfish	Eastern U.S.A.	8 (3 in)	Peaceful, somewhat timid fish. The ♂ establishes a territory	♂ reddish with blue-green spots. ♀ more uniformly coloured
245	*Mesogonistius chaetodon*	Blue-banded sunfish	Eastern U.S.A.	10 (3.9 in)	Peaceful, rather active when young, less so when older	Scarcely distinguish-able externally. ♂ blanches during spawns. ♀ then more colourful
246	*Polycentropsis abbreviata*	African leaf-fish	Tropical West Africa	8 (3 in)	Peaceful, predatory fish	♂ somewhat smaller, ♀ consider-ably stouter
247	*Polycentrus schomburgki*	Schomburgk's leaf-fish	N.E. South America	8 (3 in)	Peaceful, nocturnal predatory fish	♂ more colourful, ♀ smaller, more rounded
248	*Scatophagus argus*	Argusfish	Coastal areas around In-dian Ocean	30 (7.8 in)	Harmless, active, very decorative	Unknown
249	*Tetraodon fluviatilis*	Green pufferfish	Coastal waters of India and S.E. Asia	15 (6 in)	Small specimens relatively peaceful. Later becomes in-creasingly intolerant and aggressive	Unknown
250	*Toxotes jaculatrix*	Archerfish	Coastal areas of the Indo-Pacific	15 (6 in)	Peaceful, rather shy fish which shoots water drops to bring down its insect prey	Unknown

Maintenance	Breeding	Diet	Page/Figure
TS II/III. Pg. 11. 18–22 °C (64–73 °F), MT 10 °C (50 °F). As for No. 245	Sexes 1/1. 20–22 °C (68–71 °F). Spawns in pits. ♂ fans the eggs in among the plants and tends them in dilatory fashion until they hatch. Not difficult to rear. From time to time the young should be sorted according to size	Live food	XV/2
TS II/IV. Pg. 11, with densely planted areas. 18–22 °C (64–71 °F), occasionally a little higher. Keep cool in winter; such individuals are healthier and stronger. Clear, clean water, pH 7 and over. Like all sunfish, can be kept in a garden pool in some areas	Sexes 1/1. 20–22 °C (68–71 °F), or even less. ♂ digs shallow pits in the sand. Eggs adhere to the sand and are guarded by ♂ until hatching, then remove ♂. The ♀ should be removed after spawning. Fry take very fine live food as soon as they are free-swimming	Live food	XV/3
TS III/IV. Pg. 6. 22–26 °C (71–78 °F), MT 22 °C (71 °F). Otherwise as No. 247	1/1. 28–30 °C (82–86 °F). So far only rarely bred. Spawns on the underside of water plant leaves. An earlier observation of air bubbles collecting under the leaf to increase buoyancy has not been confirmed. Remove ♀ after spawning, and ♂ after eggs hatch. Fry then sink to the bottom. Not difficult to rear	Abundant live food, including fish	
TS III/IV. Pg. 6. 22–26 °C (71–78 °F), MT 20 °C (68 °F). Subdued light. Rock, roots for shelter, and inverted flowerpot to form a cave	Sexes 1/1. Spawns in small caves, sometimes also attaches eggs to water plant leaves. Otherwise as No. 246. Easy to breed and very productive	Abundant live food, including fish	XV/1
TS IV/V. 20–28 °C (68–82 °F). Best kept in brackish water without plants. Decorate with rocks and roots. Filtration and aeration not necessary. Can be kept in fresh water, but life expectancy is then shorter	Not yet bred in the aquarium. Spawns in the wild on rocky areas or perhaps on coral reefs	Live and dried food, plant matter. An omnivorous, voracious feeder	XIV/6
TS IV/V. Pg. 9. 22–26 °C (71–78 °F). Rocks and roots for shelter. Frequent partial changes of water. Often occurs in brackish waters, so a little salt can be added	Not yet bred in the aquarium. Earlier reports say the eggs are laid on rocks and guarded by the ♂	Snails, worms, mosquito larvae, water insects, plants, dried food	253/13
TS IV/V. Pg. 9, densely planted. Floating plants. Jumps, so tank lid must fit closely. Very suitable for a tank with an area of land with marsh plants. 22–28 °C (71–82 °F)	Not yet bred in the aquarium	Shoots flies, also takes other food, e.g. mealworms, spiders from the surface	XV/7

No.	Scientific name	Popular name	Distribu-tion	Length cm	Characteristics	Sex differences
251	*Bedotia geayi*	Madagascar rainbow fish	Mada-gascar	9 (3.5 in)	Peaceful, active shoaling fish, good for a community tank	♂ somewhat larger, the 1st dorsal fin pointed
252	*Nematocentris maccullochi*	Dwarf rainbow fish	Australia	7 (2.7 in)	Peaceful, very active shoaling fish, good for a community tank	♂ more slender, more colourful, the 1st dorsal fin pointed
253	*Nematocentris fluviatilis* (formerly *Melanotaenia nigrans*)	Red-tailed rainbow fish	Australia	10 (3.9 in)	Peaceful, active shoaling fish, good for a community tank	♂ more colourful, all the fins pointed and with black borders
254	*Pseudomugil signifer*	Southern blue-eye	Eastern coast of Australia, in fresh and brackish waters	5 (1.9 in)	Peaceful, shoaling fish best kept with several pairs in a species tank	♂ lemon-yellow to orange on fins and body, ♀ yellow-brown
255	*Telmatherina ladigesi*	Celebes sailfish	Sulawesi (formerly Celebes)	5 (1.9 in)	Peaceful, very active shoaling fish	♂ more colourful, the dorsal and anal fins with much elongated rays

Maintenance	Breeding	Diet	Page/Figure
TS IV/V. Pg. 7. 21–24 °C (69–75 °F). Use an elongated tank with plenty of swimming space for this surface-living fish. Water not too soft	Sexes 1/1. 21–24 °C (69–75 °F). Preferably a large breeding tank with clumps of fine-leaved plants as a spawning site. Water hard, not below 10 °dH. Eggs laid among plants, hanging by fine filaments, hatch in about 1 week. Fry immediately take fine food, also brine shrimp if these are brought to the surface by brisk aeration. Parent fish scarcely attack eggs and young	Live and dried food, particularly mosquito larvae	253/16
TS III/IV. Pg. 7. As No. 251	As No. 251	Live and dried food	III/6
TS IV/V. Pg. 7. As No. 251	As No. 251	Live and dried food	
TS II/III. Pg. 7. As No. 251	As No. 255, but not so warm (22–25 °C or 71–77 °F)	Live and dried food	
As No. 251. Warmth-loving, 24–28 °C (75–82 °F). Likes clear, oxygen-rich, hard water	As No. 251. 28 °C (82 °F). Lower the water level. A spawning period may extend over a period of up to 3 weeks. At 28 °C (82 °F) the eggs hatch in 1–2 weeks. The fry should be caught at the surface and transferred to a rearing tank. They are very small, difficult to rear and slow-growing	Live and dried food	III/5

1 *Haplochromis burtoni*, Burton's mouthbrooder (205) 2 *Labeotropheus fuelleborni*, Fuelleborn's cichlid (214) 3 *Cichlasoma cyanoguttatum*, Rio Grande perch (190) 4 *Pelvicachromis taeniatus*, striped pelvicachromis (225) 5 *Steatocranus casuorius*, African blockhead (234) 6 *'Pelmatochromis' thomasi*, Thomasi cichlid (222) 7 *Pseudotropheus auratus*, Malawi golden cichlid (228) 8 *Carinotetraodon somphongsi*, Thai pufferfish (241) 9 *Tetraodon schoutedenii*, leopard pufferfish (–)

Catfishes (Siluriformes)

The catfish order contains a large number of species which characteristically have no normal fish scales. The skin is either naked and leathery or covered with bony plates, spines or other outgrowths. The mouth is surrounded by a varying number of barbels which serve to detect food. Without due care in handling, the sharp supporting spines of the pectoral fins and dorsal fin may cause painful wounds that are difficult to heal. Most catfish have an adipose fin between the dorsal and caudal fins, which is sometimes quite large, and often supported by a spine. Many catfish species have an accessory means of respiration involving the gut or other organs. This renders them largely independent of gill respiration so that they can survive in waters deficient in oxygen. Some are even able to move overland, which they do when their home waters dry out.

The order is divided into several families. The individual species described in the tables are arranged alphabetically without reference to families.

Apart from an introduced North American species there is only a single catfish species in central Europe. With a few exceptions the numerous species of catfish live exclusively in fresh waters. They particularly like standing or slow-flowing somewhat dark waters with a muddy bottom. Some species live in fast-flowing streams, where they either swim free against the current or are equipped with a sucking mouth which allows them to attach themselves to rocks and at the same time to browse on the algae growing there. Most catfish prefer the lower water layers. They live close to the bottom, often lying on it or sheltering in hiding-places, and a few even burrow into the substrate. However, there are also catfish that swim free in the middle water layers, or even lurk beneath the water surface.

Many catfish are predatory, and these are often large species, in fact, a few are among the largest of all freshwater fish. Others feed on invertebrates which they catch in the open water or dig out of the mud. Some species are specialized for feeding on plants, particularly algae, or they eat organic waste. In the aquarium they should be given a varied diet and they are not difficult to feed, taking all kinds of live and dried food.

Most catfish, in so far as they are crepuscular or nocturnal, require large, spacious tanks with subdued lighting. Many like hiding-places among rocks, or roots or reeds, in which they spend the day, sometimes in an upside-down position. The water must be clean and clear, and vigorous filtration is always an advantage. Temperature requirements vary according to the species, and further details are given in the tables. In general, it can be said that catfish are hardy and long-lasting. They are best kept in a separate catfish tank. The popular armoured catfish of the genus *Corydoras* are also suitable for a community tank, where they help to keep the tank clean, digging unconsumed food scraps out of the substrate. Although most catfish live in the wild in dim light they can be accustomed to the changed conditions of captivity and will show themselves during the day.

The reproduction of catfish is still largely unknown. A few species, such as armoured catfish, spawn readily in the aquarium. Brood protection is evidently not uncommon, and some information on this is given in the tables.

No.	Scientific name	Popular name	Distribution	Length cm	Characteristics	Sex differences
256	*Acanthodoras spinosissimus*	Spiny catfish	Amazon region	15 (6 in)	Peaceful crepuscular and nocturnal fish. Likes to burrow and emits growling sounds when taken from the water	None known
257	*Amblydoras hancocki*	Hancock's thorny catfish	Tropical South America	15 (6 in)	As No. 256	♂ smaller with dark spots on belly
258	*Bunocephalus bicolor*	Banjo catfish	Amazon region	20 (7.8 in)	Peaceful, nocturnal, burrows in the substrate by day	None known
259	*Callichthys callichthys*	Armoured catfish	Northern South America, Amazon and further south	18 (7 in)	Peaceful, sometimes lively crepuscular fish. Can move about on land, giving growling sounds	♂ more colourful, with larger pectoral fin spine
260	*Corydoras aeneus*	Bronze corydoras	Tropical and subtropical South America	7 (2.7 in)	Peaceful, sociable, good for community tank	♂ dorsal fin taller, more pointed. ♀ squat, stouter
261	*Corydoras maculatus*	Moon-spot corydoras	Tropical South America	6 (2.4 in)	As No. 260	♂ dorsal fin taller, more pointed, ♀ stouter
262	*Corydoras hastatus*	Pygmy corydoras	Amazon region	3.5 (1.3 in)	Peaceful, sociable, living in groups in the middle waters	♂ smaller, more colourful, dorsal fin more pointed
263	*Corydoras melanistius*	Black-spotted corydoras	Northern South America	6 (2.4 in)	As No. 260	Difficult to distinguish. ♀ stouter when seen from above
264	*Corydoras paleatus*	Peppered corydoras	S.E. Brazil, La Plata region	7 (2.7 in)	As No. 260	♂ smaller, more slender, dorsal fin taller, more pointed
265	*Corydoras punctatus julii*	Leopard corydoras	E. Brazil	6 (2.4 in)	As No. 260	♂ more slender, more colourful

Maintenance	Breeding	Diet	Page/Figure
TS VI. Pg. 10. 24 °C (75 °F). Rock, roots, plants to give hiding-places. Fine washed sand or peat substrate	Apparently not yet bred in the aquarium	*Tubifex,* insect larvae, plants, dried food	XVI/4
As No. 256	As No. 256	*Tubifex,* insect larvae, plants, dried food	
TS IV. Only plants requiring poor light. Sand or peat substrate with roots. Best kept alone. 20–24 °C (68–75 °F)	Not yet bred in the aquarium	Live and dried food	XVI/10
TS IV/V. Pg. 2. 18–24 °C (64–75 °F). Rocks, roots for shelter	Has bred several times. Eggs laid in bubble nest built on underside of floating leaves, guarded by male	Live and dried food taken from the bottom	XVI/5
TS II/III. Pg. 2. Peat substrate with roots. 18–24 °C (64–75 °F)	As No. 264. TS III/IV. 26 °C (78 °F). Up to 300 eggs hatch in 5 days	Omnivorous, bottom-feeding	266/2
As No. 260. 23–27 °C (73–80 °F), MT 18 °C (64 °F).	As No. 264. Up to 200 eggs hatch in 4–5 days	Omnivorous, bottom-feeding	266/3
TS II/III. Pg. 2. Corners and background densely planted. 24–26 °C (75–78 °F)	As No. 264. Few eggs hatch in 6–9 days. Fry keep near bottom. Feed at first on infusorians, powdered dried food	Fine live and dried food, on bottom or free-floating	266/5
TS II/III. Pg. 2. 22–26 °C (71–78 °F). As No. 260	As No. 264 but more difficult to breed	Omnivorous, bottom-feeding	266/4
TS II/III. Pg. 2. Peat substrate, with roots. 18–24 °C (64–75 °F), MT 15 °C (59 °F). Subdued light, clear clean water of any type	TS III/IV. 3/1. ♂ holds female's barbels with his pectoral fins. 50–200 eggs. At each mating only a few eggs released into a pouch made by ♀ ventral fins, where they are fertilized. Eggs attached to firm underlay. Remove parents when spawning ceases. Eggs hatch in 6–8 days. Relatively large fry not difficult to rear	Omnivorous, bottom-feeding	XVI/8
TS II/III, larger for breeding. Pg. 2. As for No. 260. 23–27 °C (73–80 °F)	As No. 264, but more difficult to breed	Omnivorous, bottom-feeding	XVI/9

No.	Scientific name	Popular name	Distribution	Length cm	Characteristics	Sex differences
266	*Corydoras reticulatus*	Reticulated corydoras	Amazon region	5 (1.9 in)	As No. 260	♂ more intensely coloured
267	*Corydoras schultzei*	Schultz's corydoras	Amazon region	6.5 (2.5 in)	As No. 260	♂ more colourful, pectoral fin spine longer. ♀ stouter, seen from above
268	*Dianema longibarbis*		Amazon region	9 (3.5 in)	Peaceful, rather shy. Keep in a shoal	♂ smaller, more colourful
269	*Hoplosternum thoracatum*		Guyana to Paraguay	18 (7 in)	Keep only with large fish	♂ with strikingly large red-brown 1st pectoral fin spine
270	*Kryptopterus bicirrhis*	Glass catfish	S.E. Asia, Indonesia	10 (3.9 in)	Harmless, active, freeswimming, transparent, shoaling fish	None known
271	*Loricaria parva* (?)	Dwarf whiptail	Paraguay, La Plata region	12 (4.7 in)	Peaceful, but not very active crepuscular and nocturnal fish	♂ with white bristles on mouth and pectoral fins
272	*Otocinclus flexilis*	Sucker catfish	S.E. Brazil	5.5 (2.1 in)	Good for removing algae in a community tank	Not known exactly, ♂ may be smaller, more slender
273	*Pimelodella gracilis*	Slender pimelodella	Venezuela to Argentina	17 (6.6 in)	Peaceful, sometimes very lively, crepuscular and nocturnal. Often hidden by day	None known
274	*Plecostomus commersoni*	Suckermouth catfish	Brazil, Argentina	40 (15.7 in)	Peaceful, but becomes too large for a normal aquarium, and then digs actively. Eats algae	None known
275	*Synodontis nigriventris*	Upside-down catfish	Congo region	7 (2.7 in)	Peaceful, sociable, nocturnal, shoaling fish which swims belly upwards	♂ more slender, with finer pattern
276	*Xenocara dolichoptera* (also sold as *Ancistrus* sp.)	Blue-chin xenocara	Nothern South America	13 (5.1 in)	Peaceful and very good consumer of algae	♂ with long, stout tentacles on forehead and snout, ♀ with short, thin tentacles on snout

Maintenance	Breeding	Diet	Page/Figure
TS II/III. Pg. 2. 24–27 °C (75–80 °F). As No. 260	As No. 264. 26–28 °C (78–82 °F). Not easy to breed. Fry are delicate	Omnivorous, bottom-feeding	266/6
TS II/III, larger for breeding. Pg. 2. As No. 260	As No. 264. Productive. Not difficult to breed	Omnivorous, bottom-feeding	266/7
TS IV/V, 20–25 °C (68–77 °F). Prefers to hide in dense vegetation	Builds bubble nest under broad floating plants. ♂ guards eggs which hatch in 5 days. Rear fry as No. 264	Omnivorous	
TS V. As No. 259	As No. 269. Very productive	Worms, insect larvae, small fish	
TS III/IV. Pg. 3. 24–30 °C (75–86 °F), MT 20 °C (68 °F). Leave sufficient space for swimming	Not yet bred in the aquarium	Small live and dried food	XVI/7
TS III. Pg. 3. Gravel substrate with rock caves or clay pipes. Clear, clean, oxygen-rich water. 20–24 °C (68–75 °F), MT 16 °C (60 °F)	Up to 200 eggs laid at night in a cavity, e.g. clay or plastic pipe. ♂ guards eggs until they hatch after 8–9 days. Rear mainly on plant matter	Algae, other plant matter, dried food, whiteworms	XVI/3
TS III. Pg. 3, with dense clumps. Gravel substrate with rocks, roots. 18–24 °C (64–75 °F). Bright light to encourage algae	Rarely bred in the aquarium. Details not known	Algae, other plant matter, dried food	253/17
TS III/IV. Pg. 3. Rocks and roots for shelter. 18–24 °C (64–75 °F). Subdued light	Not yet bred in the aquarium	Live and dried food, mainly from the bottom	266/8
TS V. Pg. 10. 20–26 °C (68–78 °F). Coarse gravel, rocks, roots	Not yet bred in the aquarium	Algae, other plant matter, dried food	XVI/2
TS III/IV. Pg. 3, dense planting, floating plants, subdued light. Roots for shelter. 24 °C (75 °F). Water not too hard	Occasionally bred. Eggs laid in dark places, hatch in about 1 week. Fry soon take brine shrimp. In first weeks they swim in normal position	Abundant live and dried food. Midge larvae for breeding	253/14
TS III/IV. 24–30 °C (75–86 °F). Numerous hiding-places under roots	Eggs laid under roots or in plastic tubes, guarded by ♂. Rearing may be difficult up to a length of 3 cm (1.1 in)	Algae, also dried food lying on the bottom	

265

1 *Brochis coeruleus*, emerald armoured catfish (–) 2 *Corydoras aeneus*, bronze corydoras (260) 3 *Corydoras caudimaculatus*, moon-spot corydoras (261) 4 *Corydoras melanistius*, black-spotted corydoras (263) 5 *Corydoras hastatus*, pygmy corydoras (262) 6 *Corydoras reticulatus*, reticulated corydoras (266) 7 *Corydoras schultzei*, Schultz's corydoras (267) 8 *Pimelodella gracilis*, slender pimelodella (273) 9 *Microglanis parahybae*, bumblebee catfish (–) 10 *Sperata vittata*, Indian striped catfish (–) 11 *Botia horae*, Hora's loach (278) 12 *Botia hymenophysa*, banded loach (279) 13 *Botia modesta*, orange-finned loach (281) 14 *Botia sidthimunki*, dwarf loach (282) 15 *Trinectes maculatus*, freshwater flounder (288)

Bottom-living fishes

Under this heading are a number of aquarium fish not all of which are related to one another, though some of them do have similar habits, including the fact that they live on or near the bottom.

The loaches of the family Cobitidae are very closely related to the barbs, which have already been discussed in some detail. They are now regarded as a separate family within the sub-order that includes the barbs. Loaches are elongated, worm-like to moderately tall fish with a small head and a ventral mouth which is surrounded by a few pairs of barbels. Most species have a one- or two-pointed erectile spine below each eye. Many have a form of accessory respiration in the alimentary tract which enables them to survive in waters deficient in oxygen. They live a more or less retiring life and some only become active at night. At certain times which may be associated with the natural spawning periods they may also become active by day and swim around the tank. The worm-like species of the genus *Acanthophthalmus* are attractive in a community tank where they swim about on the bottom. Members of the genus *Botia* are of quite a different type, but they also like to have hiding-places which serve as focal points in their territories. With a few exceptions they are intolerant of one another, so they are best kept singly in a large tank with other species. Loaches have only very rarely been bred in the aquarium, and then only by chance.

The gobies of the family Gobiidae are rather different in general appearance. They are mostly marine, but a few species are suitable for a freshwater or brackish water tank. All gobies have two dorsal fins, of which the front one has spiny rays, the rear one soft rays. The pectoral fins are broad and fan-like, and they often have a limb-like base. The ventral fins, positioned on the throat or breast, are usually fused to form a suction disc which enables the fish to attach itself to rocks in rough, stormy waters. Some species live in the tidal zone, or at ebb tide can remain out on the mud for a long time. In the aquarium the mudskippers (*Periophthalmus* and others) require a tank with a large area of land and humid air. Gobies are not particularly popular among aquarists. They may lie for hours on a rock or plant near the bottom or remain hidden during the day. They are essentially fish for the specialist who does not mind such habits. Most species have not yet been bred in the aquarium, the exceptions being the bumblebee fish *(Brachygobius)* and Australian species of *Mogurnda*.

Tropical or subtropical freshwater flounders are occasionally imported. These include the small *Trinectes maculatus* from the coastal regions south of New York which, like a few other flatfish, has found its way into fresh waters. They like to burrow in the sand and are able to change colour to match that of their surroundings.

The spiny eels of the family Mastacembelidae are also of some interest. They are elongated, eel-like fish in which the front part of the dorsal fin is divided up into several small spines. The head ends in a pointed snout. Spiny eels like to burrow in the substrate, and if it is soft enough they will even move through it. These fish can be kept in a sufficiently large community tank.

No.	Scientific name	Popular name	Distribution	Length cm	Characteristics	Sex differences
277	*Acantho-phthalmus semicinctus*	Coolie loach	Malaya, Sumatra	10 (3.9 in)	Attractive, worm-like, crepuscular loach, hiding by day, but sometimes very active. A few indi-viduals enliven the bottom of a commu-nity tank	♂ smaller, ♀ with stouter belly
278	*Botia horae*	Hora's loach	Thailand	8 (3 in)	Relatively peaceful, suitable for a com-munity tank	Unknown
279	*Botia hymenophysa*	Banded loach	S.E. Asia, Indonesia	15 (6 in)	Rather intolerant. Keep only as a single individual in a community tank	Unknown
280	*Botia macracantha*	Clown loach	Indonesia	15 (6 in)	Very active, not always absolutely peaceful	Unknown
281	*Botia modesta*	Orange-finned loach	S.E. Asia	15 (6 in)	Rather intolerant. Keep only as a single individual in a community tank	Unknown
282	*Botia sidtimunki*	Dwarf loach	Thailand	3.5 (1.3 in)	Small, tolerant, also active by day. Good for a community tank. Lives not only on the bottom	Unknown
283	*Brachygobius* sp.	Bumblebee fish	Malay, Indonesia	4 (1.5 in)	Peaceful, but scarcely suitable for a community tank. Attaches itself by suckers	♂ more intensely coloured. ♀ stouter
284	*Dormitator maculatus*	Sleeper goby	E. Brazil	20 (7.8 in)	Very peaceful, bottom-living fish	♂ more colourful
285	*Eleotris marmorata*	Marbled goby	Thailand, Malaya, Indonesia	40 (15.7 in)	Predatory, very vor-acious. Likes to bur-row in the sand	Unknown

Maintenance	Breeding	Diet	Page/Figure
TS II/III. Pg. 2 or 3, with plant clumps. Caves, roots, coconut shells for hiding. Fine sand or peat substrate. 22–28 °C (71–82 °F)	Not yet bred in the aquarium	Live and dried food, mostly taken from the bottom	XVI/6
TS III/IV. Pg. 2, with densely planted areas. Sand substrate not too coarse. Rocks and roots for hiding. Clear, clean water. 22–24 °C (71–75 °F)	Not yet bred in the aquarium	Live and dried food on the bottom	266/11
TS IV/V. 25–27 °C (77–80 °F). Needs plenty of swimming space, as very active. Otherwise as No. 278	Not yet bred in the aquarium	Live and dried food, can be floating in the water	266/12
TS IV/V. Pg. 2. 22–24 °C (71–75 °F). As No. 278	Not yet bred in the aquarium	Live and dried food, on the bottom or floating	XVI/1
TS IV/V. Pg. 2. Needs plenty of swimming space, as very active. Otherwise as No. 278	Not yet bred in the aquarium	Live food on the bottom, dried food	266/13
TS II/III. Pg. 2. 24–28 °C (75–82 °F). As No. 278	Not yet bred in the aquarium	Small live food, dried food	266/14
TS II/III. No plants. 26–28 °C (78–82 °F), sensitive to lower temperatures. Rocks, roots. Add heaped teaspoonful of salt to 10 litres (2.2 gals) water, as this is a brackish-water fish. Can plant with *Cryptocoryne ciliata* which tolerates brackish water	Not easy, but increasingly achieved. 29–30 °C (84–86 °F). Sexes 1/1 in a small all-glass tank, or several pairs in a larger tank. Up to 300 eggs laid in dark places on rocks etc. ♂ protects eggs until they hatch in 2–6 days. Fry remain near the surface and take very fine live food immediately	Live food	XV/5
TS III/IV. 22–30 °C (71–86 °F). Salt addition as No. 283. Sand not too coarse. Rocks for hiding	Occasionally achieved. Eggs attached to rocks	Live food	
TS V. 18–30 °C (64–86 °F). Add salt or sea water (including artificially prepared). Sand not too coarse. Rocks for hiding	Not yet bred in the aquarium	Abundant live food, including fish	XV/8

No.	Scientific name	Popular name	Distribu-tion	Length cm	Characteristics	Sex differences
286	*Mastacembelus pancalus*	Spotted spiny eel	India	20 (7.8 in)	Crepuscular and nocturnal, burying itself in the sand. Also seen by day when acclimatized	Unknown
287	*Periophthalmus barbarus*	Mudskipper	Mangrove swamps on the coasts of Africa, India and further east	12 (4.7 in)	Peculiar, amphib-ious fish with limb-like pectoral fins	Unknown
288	*Trinectes maculatus*	Freshwater flounder	Coastal areas of U.S.A., south of New York	10 (3.9 in)	Attractive small flat-fish, which likes to burrow or hangs on the glass panes	Unknown

Maintenance	Breeding	Diet	Page/Figure
TS IV/V. Pg. 10. 22–26 °C (71–78 °F). Plants in pots. Fine sand substrate, so that the fish can burrow. Clear, clean water. Sensitive to unhygienic conditions in the substrate	Only achieved occasionally, by chance	Live food on the bottom	253/18
Needs a large tank with water and an area of land, simulating a shoreline. Fresh/seawater 1:1. The water and air must be at the same temperature (26–30 °C or 78–86 °F)	Not yet bred in the aquarium	Abundant live food (insects, earthworms, mealworms)	XV/4
TS III. Pg. 10. Substrate of fine sand with several free areas. 16–22 °C (60–71 °F). The sand can be in patches of different colours, in order to demonstrate the ability to change colour	Not yet bred in the aquarium	Omnivorous, feeding on the bottom	266/15

European
cold-water fishes

In general, the cold-water fish of Europe are mainly of interest to the advanced aquarist. There are, however, a few species such as stickleback, bitterling, weatherfish and minnow which can be kept without much difficulty by the beginner. Sticklebacks and bitterling are of interest because of their methods of brood protection. The other species are not quite so easy to keep. Most of them have a high oxygen demand and are sensitive to high temperatures. They require large tanks and strong aeration, in some cases even a constant circulation of the water. Observations of their

No.	Scientific name	Popular name	Distribution	Length cm	Characteristics	Sex differences
289	*Acerina cernua*	Ruffe	Rivers and lakes, particularly in coastal areas	Up to 10 (3.9 in)	Predatory, very voracious. Eats fish spawn	Unknown
290	*Alburnus alburnus*	Bleak	Shoaling fish in open water	Up to 8 (3 in)	Peaceful, sociable shoaling fish	♂ more slender. The scales yield the pearly substance for artificial pearls
291	*Anguilla anguilla*	Eel	In all types of water	Up to 15 (6 in)	Crepuscular, likes to burrow	Unknown
292	*Barbus barbus*	Barbel	In flowing waters	Up to 10 (3.9 in)	Peaceful, bottom-living, sometimes very active	Unknown
293	*Carassius carassius*	Crucian carp	In all types of water	Up to 10 (3.9 in)	Peaceful, undemanding, likes to burrow	Unknown
294	*Cobitis taenia*	Spined loach	In all types of water, particularly those with a sandy bottom	10 (3.9 in)	Bottom-living, nocturnal, hidden by day. Accessory respiration in the gut	Unknown
295	*Cottus gobio*	Miller's thumb	Clear fast-flowing waters of the trout reaches, also lakes	Up to 10 (3.9 in)	Predatory, eats fish spawn. Likes to hide under stones	Unknown
296	*Cyprinus carpio*	Carp (scaled, mirror and leather)	In all types of warmer water	Up to 10 (3.9 in)	Peaceful, likes to dig	Unknown

habits do, however, provide information which may help in the acclimatization of valuable imported tropical fish, and some observations may also be of value to the fisheries biologist. The tables only contain general advice to help the aquarist to maintain and care for these cold-water fish; many of them, as will be seen from the tables, are regarded as unsuitable for breeding, but this should not prevent the experienced aquarist from making an attempt. It is possible that some of these species have already been bred in captivity without the fact being generally known. The information on length applies to the maximum size likely to be reached in a home aquarium, and does not usually apply to fish in the wild.

Maintenance	Breeding	Diet	Page/Figure
As No. 307	Not suitable for breeding in the aquarium	Abundant live food	278/1
TS III/IV. Pg. 11. Up to 18 °C (64 °F). Aeration. Otherwise as No. 301	Not suitable for breeding in the aquarium	Omnivorous	
Young specimens are suitable. TS II/III, fine sand, loose shoots of hornwort or Canadian pondweed	Not suitable for breeding in the aquarium	Large live food on the bottom	
TS III. Up to 18 °C (64 °F). Clean sand, brisk aeration Canadian pondweed, water moss, hornwort	Not suitable for breeding in the aquarium	Omnivorous	278/6
TS III. Up to 22 °C (71 °F). Well planted, sunny. Aeration. Washed sand	Not suitable for breeding in the aquarium	Omnivorous	
TS II. Up to 18 °C (64 °F). Fine sand, rocks for hiding. Aeration	Not suitable for breeding in the aquarium	Omnivorous	278/3
TS III/IV. Not over 15 °C (59 °F). Brisk aeration. Sand, gravel, large flat stones for hiding. Water moss. For the experienced aquarist	Not suitable for breeding in the aquarium	Abundant live food	278/2
As for No. 293	Not suitable for breeding in the aquarium	Omnivorous	278/7

No.	Scientific name	Popular name	Distribu-tion	Length cm	Characteristics	Sex differences
297	*Esox lucius*	Pike	In all types of water, in the reed zone	Up to 10 (3.9 in)	Large predator, somewhat lazy, lurks among the plants	Unknown
298	*Gasterosteus aculeatus*	Three-spined stickleback	In all types of water	8 (3 in)	Interesting, active, rather quarrelsome	♂ more slender, with bright red breast and throat at spawning time
299	*Gobio gobio*	Gudgeon	In flowing waters, also lakes with sandy bottom and rocks	15 (6 in)	Peaceful, bottom-living fish	Unknown
300	*Ictalurus nebulosus*	American catfish	Introduced from U.S.A.	Up to 10 (3.9 in)	Crepuscular, some-times very active. Likes to hide away	Unknown
301	*Leucaspius delineatus*	Moderlieschen	In ponds and ditches with dense vegetation. Not native to Britain	8 (3 in)	Active, peaceful shoaling fish	♂ more slender, with nuptial tuber-cles at spawning time
302	*Leuciscus idus*	Orfe or Ide	In all types of water, particularly near banks of rivers and lakes	Up to 10 (3.9 in)	Peaceful, surface-living fish	Unknown
303	*Leuciscus leuciscus*	Dace	Likes flow-ing waters	Up to 10 (3.9 in)	Peaceful, active shoaling fish	Unknown
304	*Lucioperca lucioperca*	Zander	In rivers and lakes. Likes warm, turbid water	Up to 10 (3.9 in)	Predatory, lying in wait for prey, like pike	Unknown
305	*Misgurnus fossilis*	Pond loach	In ponds and ditches with a muddy bot-tom	15 (6 in)	Becomes restless in unsettled weather, hence also called weatherfish. Acces-sory respiration in the gut. Buries itself in substrate	Unknown

Maintenance	Breeding	Diet	Page/Figure
TS IV/V. Only keep as a single specimen. Endemic plants. Roots and reeds for hiding-places	Not suitable for breeding in the aquarium	Abundant live food, particularly fish	
TS III/IV. Up to 22 °C (71 °F). Sufficient plants, sand substrate. Aeration not absolutely necessary, even with a number of individuals	Easy to breed. Sexes 1 ♂ to 3–5 ♀. ♂ builds nest of plant fragments on the bottom, into which he drives several ♀♀ to spawn. ♂ guards eggs and young. Remove ♀. Rear young on tiny live food	Live food	
TS III/IV. Clean sand and rocks. Brisk aeration. Water moss, hornwort, pondweed	Not suitable for breeding in the aquarium	Omnivorous. Food on the bottom	278/4
TS III/IV. Up to 22 °C (71 °F). No aeration. Sand substrate, rocks for shelter. Not to be kept with smaller fish	♂ protects the brood. Not usually suitable for breeding in the aquarium, but can be attempted in very large tanks	Abundant live food	
TS II/III. Up to 22 °C (71 °F). Sunlight. Aeration not necessary. Sufficient plants and space for swimming	♀ attaches eggs in spirals on plant stems. Eggs guarded by ♂ until they hatch	Omnivorous	278/5
TS III/IV. Up to 20 °C (68 °F). Plant with any endemic species. Aeration if possible. Easy to keep	Not suitable for breeding in the aquarium	Omnivorous	
As No. 302	Not suitable for breeding in the aquarium	Omnivorous	279/8
TS V. Up to 20 °C (68 °F). Water moss, pondweed, milfoil, pennywort. Sand substrate with stones	Not suitable for breeding in the aquarium	Abundant live food	279/14
TS III. Substrate of fine sand or boiled peat. No aeration necessary	Not suitable for breeding in the aquarium	Omnivorous	279/13

No.	Scientific name	Popular name	Distribution	Length cm	Characteristics	Sex differences
306	*Noemacheilus barbatulus*	Stone loach	In clear waters with gravel bottom, also in trout reaches	12 (4.7 in)	Bottom-living fish which likes to hide by day	♂ shows nuptial tubercles
307	*Perca fluviatilis*	Perch	In all types of water	Up to 10 (3.9 in)	Active predator	Unknown
308	*Phoxinus phoxinus*	Minnow	In flowing and standing waters, especially in trout reaches	12 (4.7 in)	Active shoaling fish	♂ coloured brighter reddish, pectoral fins brown
309	*Pungitius pungitius*	Nine-spined stickleback	In all types of small waters	6 (2.4 in)	Active, somewhat shoaling fish	♂ black at spawning time
310	*Rhodeus amarus sericeus*	Bitterling	Standing or slow-flowing waters, with fresh-water mussels	7 (2.7 in)	Harmless, peaceful	♂ more slender, more colourful at spawning time. ♀ with a long ovipositor
311	*Rutilus rutilus*	Roach	Particularly in lakes with dense vegetation	Up to 10 (3.9 in)	Peaceful, active shoaling fish	Unknown
312	*Scardinius erythrophthalmus*	Rudd	In all types of waters, especially among marginal vegetation	Up to 10 (3.9 in)	Peaceful, eats plants, likes to dig	Unknown
313	*Tinca tinca*	Tench	In all types of waters, particularly shallow lakes with dense vegetation	Up to 10 (3.9 in)	Peaceful	Unknown
314	*Umbra krameri*	Mud-minnow	Hungary, Lower Austria	10 (3.9 in)	Peaceful, undemanding	Unknown

276

Maintenance	Breeding	Diet	Page/Figure
TS III. Up to 20 °C (68 °F). Fine sand, rocks and roots for hiding-places. Aeration. Plant pennywort	Eggs can be hatched in the aquarium	Omnivorous	
TS IV or larger. Up to 20 °C (68 °F). Clear water, aeration. Sand substrate with gravel. Water moss, milfoil, pondweed	Not suitable for breeding in the aquarium	Abundant live food	279/9
TS III/IV. Clean sand, aeration, all kinds of vegetation. Space for swimming	Has been bred. Large tank with a shallow area. Rearing as for all Cyprinidae	Omnivorous	279/15
As for No. 298	Nest suspended among the plants. Otherwise as No. 298	Live food	
TS II/III, well planted. Up to 22 °C (71 °F). No aeration	♀ lays eggs with the ovipositor into the respiratory cavity of a freshwater mussel. The young, developing among the mussel's gills, swim out after 4–5 weeks	Omnivorous	279/12
As for No. 302	Not suitable for breeding in the aquarium	Omnivorous	279/10
As for No. 302	Not suitable for breeding in the aquarium	Omnivorous	
As for No. 293	Not suitable for breeding in the aquarium	Omnivorous	279/11
TS II/III, well planted, up to 22 °C (71 °F). Half shade. Aeration not necessary	Breeding has been achieved occasionally	Live food	279/16

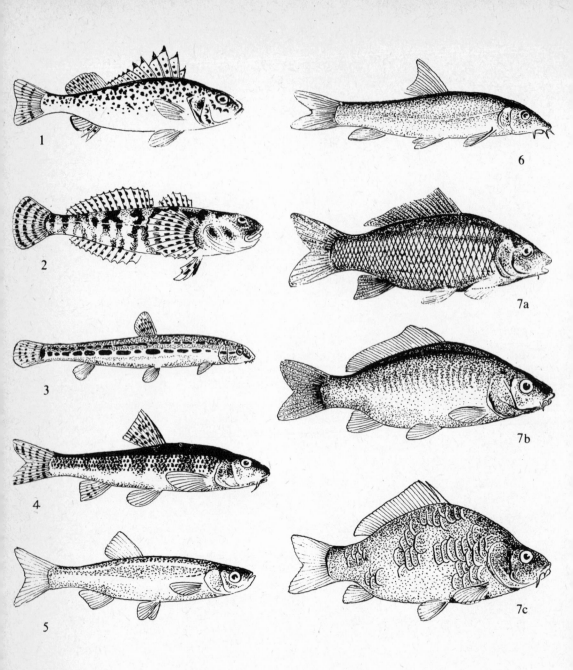

European cold-water fishes

1	*Acerina cernua*, ruffe	(289)
2	*Cottus gobio*, miller's thumb	(295)
3	*Cobitis taenia*, spined loach	(294)
4	*Gobio gobio*, gudgeon	(299)
5	*Leucaspius delineatus*, moderlieschen	(301)

6	*Barbus barbus*, barbel	(292)
7a	*Cyprinus carpio*, carp, scaled form	(296)
7b	leather carp	(296)
7c	mirror carp	(296)

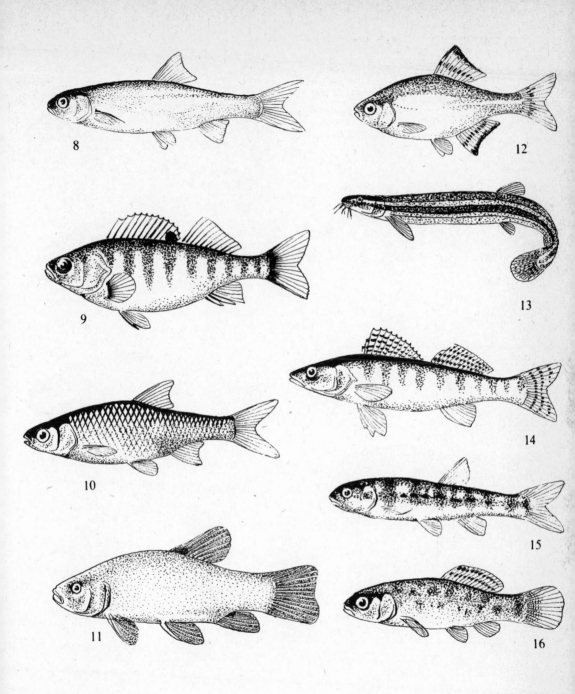

INDEX

Numbers in italics indicate illustrations. All numbers refer to page numbers apart from the Roman numerals which indicate plate numbers for the illustrations between pages 153 and 168.